NATURE'S MASTERPIECE
A Family Survival Book

NATURE'S MASTERPIECE

A FAMILY SURVIVAL BOOK

LIBBY PURVES

Hodder & Stoughton

First published in 2000 by Hodder & Stoughton
A division of Hodder Headline

10 9 8 7 6 5 4 3 2 1

A CIP catalogue record for this title is
available from the British Library

ISBN 0 340 75135 5

Typeset by Hewer Text Ltd, Edinburgh
Printed and bound in Great Britain by Clays Ltd, St Ives plc

Hodder & Stoughton
A division of Hodder Headline
338 Euston Road
London NW1 3BH

To the teachers of Coldfair Green First School,
who made me a better mother

Acknowledgement:

Chicago
Words and Music by Fred Ebb and John Kander
© (1992) Kander-Ebb Inc and Unichappell Music Inc
Warner/Chappell Music Limited, London W6 8BS
Reproduced by permission of International Music Publications Ltd

Contents

Contents

False Teeth By Post?
How to Read This Book

My good friend Christina Hardyment, a rigorous historian of baby-management books and domesticity in general, once remarked that writing how-to books on childcare and family life is a bit like selling false teeth by post. The craftsmanship may be irreproachable, the intentions excellent, but the damn things never will *quite* fit.

Once you accept that, everything becomes easier. Nobody else's image of family life is going to ring precisely true; any blueprint for the perfect home is to be treated with the greatest suspicion. If you take it too earnestly, then at worst it will make you feel guilty about your life, and at best it will enrage you.

So take this, and all such books, as an aid to confidence rather than a sapper of it. There will be areas in which you are doing rather better than I – or any of my research sources and advisers – ever have. There will be areas where we can help you focus more clearly on what is going on beneath the turbulent surface of daily life. Take what is useful, and use the rest to line the rabbit hutch.

The format needs explaining. In the beginning, there were three short books which I wrote while my own children were small. *How Not to Be a Perfect Mother* covered the first positive pregnancy test to the baby's arrival and ended at the age of three. It is still on sale, but is not incorporated in this book; it stands best alone because that initial bewildering period of change and mutual adaptation between parents and new babies is a subject in its own right (also because there are limits to the weight of paperback you can conveniently carry in a nappy bag).

There were two sequels – *How Not to Raise a Perfect Child* (which goes from three to eight years old) and *How Not to Be a Perfect Family*, which considers the wider implications of being no longer a free individual or companionable couple, but a small ramshackle miniature nation with its own democracy and economy and makeshift legal system to run.

These are both mainly subsumed into this new book, but altered and amplified with a lot of new thoughts and experiences about teenage years, the pressures of modernity on the ancient structure of the family, and the changing marital balance. Revising material I wrote before, I have sometimes changed my mind and sometimes adapted my view to the rapid evolution of society. Sometimes, however, I have resisted on principle the temptation to change anything at all. There is a real risk that as your own children grow up into near-adults you forget the day-to-day practical frustrations of living with far smaller ones. Any merit the original books had depended largely on the fact that they were genuine dispatches from the battle front, covered in small grimy fingerprints and Plasticine. I would hate to dilute that with the sort of dignified hindsight which comes over you when your youngest child is herself big enough to go out babysitting. So some of the old surreal madness, the daily frustration and glory, of the early years is still reflected here.

After the first essay – which is about why I still believe in the family at all – the book divides into two parts. The first is about children, the second about family life.

It seemed a distinction worth keeping, because although there would be no family life without children, they are not the whole story. There are times when you have to concentrate utterly on children's needs; but other times, too, when if the family is to survive intact you have to look beyond the fume and fret of mere childrearing and consider the wider net of relationships, duties, rights and precautions which hold the tribe together. So there are times for Part I, and times for Part II; the degree of overlap will vary. Some sections – like much of the discussion on sibling rivalries (in Part II) or the reflections on sex education (in Part I), could equally well have been in either half. The index should help.

As for the variations in tone and pace, that's family life for you. One moment you're confronting a central philosophical crux of human existence, the next you're trying to fish the car keys out of the S-bend (straightened coathangers are best. I see I forgot to mention this in the main text). The tone varies because you cannot muse on the implications of human relations with cyberspace in the same brisk tone that you pass on stuff about guinea pigs needing Vitamin C. The matter of gender may raise a few eyebrows too; I am unwilling to keep on doubling up, forever saying 'mother/father', 'son/daughter' or 'he/she', simply because it is a graceless form and makes the reader stumble. So at times I have made the choice that seems most natural. Take it as read that everything a mother does – short of breastfeeding – can be achieved by a father, and vice versa; and that the same applies to sons and daughters, uncles and aunts, grandmothers and grandfathers.

One more word: if at the moment you have a small baby, or a pre-school child, skip like mad. Avoid the sections about secondary schools, teenagers, etc., like the plague. In a time of small families and scattered tribes, parents of very young children may be thrown into a state of alarmed incomprehension by the sight of older ones. What connection can there possibly be between the small, laughing, sociable, affectionate, curious, graceful little creature at your feet and these huge, scowling, stroppy, spotty louts with their Walkman headphones clamped to their ears, their trollopy clothes and cruel music? When you expect a baby, you do not expect a teenager. Nobody even *really* expects a ten-year-old. They just sort of creep up on you. You evolve, together, towards a new kind of relationship. So if you reach a chapter which feels utterly irrelevant to your own life, ignore it. One day you may just see the point.

Or, of course, you may not. Again I say it: there is no such thing as a perfect handbook on family life and children. There are many good and healthy ways to grow up and run a home, and mine may not be yours. There are a few immutable principles in this family business, but very few.

So think of the author as a dippy old aunt in the chimney corner, who dozes and rambles and occasionally says something wise or shows you a good short cut. That is good enough for any childcare writer. Those who claim to know it all, or offer easy formulae, are lying.

3

The Enduring Family

'The family,' wrote George Santayana, 'is one of Nature's Masterpieces.' I like that line. It pays tribute to something which many of us still strongly and instinctively feel: that however much we talk it down, spread alarm about it and generally beset it round with dismal stories, the family somehow marches on.

More importantly, it asserts that the family deserves to march on. It is a good thing, a useful structure, our best hope of sanity and security as individuals. This, too, I believe. No personal horror stories or unhappy mutations can disprove the essential strength and usefulness of an arrangement in which, bound by instinctive love and dependence and sparks of genetic likeness, old and young human beings support and amuse one another. The strong live alongside the weak, the male and the female modify one another's extremes, the old and feeble have a claim on the young and vigorous, and children can explore the world from a base of absolute certainty that there is one place – however damn dull it looks at the moment – where they can always return.

The family is the smallest kind of community, and an essential knot in the wider net of human society. Because of the diversity of its members it is able to reach out and make connections in many directions. This happens every time two grandmothers gossip, or a child makes a new friend in the park and the mothers desultorily chat. When teenagers fall in love, or two office workers compare notes in the lift on their babies' progress, another vital link is made and the social net is strengthened. Every wedding photograph proves it. The family is a force for inclusiveness. However nervously some members may try to protect their own social turf, the diversity of ages and the natural rebelliousness that arises in a family means that it must, willy-nilly, find itself from time to time connected with those who live in other ways, on other levels. This – to all but the most fearful or insanely exclusive social tribes – is patently a very good thing indeed.

Like every human gift, the family has a history of being abused, exploited, twisted, turned into a prison cell and used as a power base for the wicked and an engine of oppression. Nobody in their right mind would deny that these perversions of family life exist, or that they matter. At times, regrettably, it is necessary for the wider family – the state – to intervene and save the weak from the cruelty of the strong.

But that does not make any difference to the central truth: that the family itself is worth having, and is not about to die out for lack of support. In Britain we hear a great deal about cycles of deprivation and the 'parenting deficit' producing a generation of bewildered, damaged young people who were never properly looked after themselves and therefore cannot look after their own children without intense help and training. I would be the last to deny anybody such help if they do need and want it; in a high-speed, high-spending, complicated society there are plenty of problems facing the modern family, and the following pages go into quite a few of them.

But I am constantly encouraged in my wilfully pro-family beliefs by meeting people who have come out of lousy childhoods with a resolution to do better, to found strong families themselves, and to achieve as adults – and pass on – the solidity and emotional safety they were denied as children. Even though many families fail, the idea of the good family exists independently of all individual disasters. It is one of the eternal archetypes, like fitness, or happiness, or democracy. That does not mean that we should all yearn towards an impossibly rosy, perfectionist, sickly-sweet and impossible ideal. It just means that it is always worth trying to hold together a good-enough family; a ramshackle, familiar, well-meaning structure in which the weak are protected, the strong learn to curb their worst instincts, and a web of scruffy traditions and timeworn jokes creates a common background to diverse lives.

I am also encouraged by the visible flexibility of the family. In my own lifetime, within the British family, all kinds of things have changed. Paternal authority is not what it was, nor is motherhood any longer widely accepted as a full-time and permanent job. We have entirely lost the assumption – current well into the 1970s in some circles – that marriage automatically marks the end of a young woman's working career. The roles of the sexes are no longer predictable, so men have (with some pain) often needed to accept that a woman can be the main breadwinner, and women have had to learn to take that part with grace.

Expectations, if not always practice, have changed radically within the home. As recently as the late 1960s a book on marriage by a go-ahead young newspaper columnist called Jilly Cooper recommended that a young wife – if she did have to work – should make certain to get home before her husband so that she could do the housework and change into a pretty dress for him because men hate seeing women fiddling around with Hoovers and dusters (I can reassure readers that Cooper herself – now in her sixties, a millionaire novelist who usually has her supper made by the said husband – roars with laughter when confronted with that passage).

Attitudes to children have changed; if there ever was a time when they were seen (neat and tidy in sailor suits) but not heard, it has long gone. Middle-class parents today occasionally glance back, in bitter wonderment at the change of emphasis, to question how it is that our generation, who spent long dull Sunday afternoons of childhood boredom sitting on hard chairs being polite to Granny because children had to fit in with parents' wishes, now spend long dull Sunday afternoons drinking coffee out of polystyrene cups while waiting for their offspring to be finished with judo, or swimming club, or football – because these days it seems that parents have to fit in with children, not vice versa.

Apart from large and formal changes like the UN declaration on the rights of the child, there have been a thousand smaller ones in education and understanding and general child management which have filtered into family life and changed it. I think that today's parents talk more frankly with their children than ours did. Dual career families have risen until they are seen as a norm; attitudes to hired household help, to mealtimes, schooling, transport, to every building block of life have adapted through eras of rapid change, with varying degrees of conviction and success. The era of the stepfamily, the serial marriage, and the child with two homes has required the ancient institution to take on the flexibility of a circus tumblers' pyramid; but everyone knows cases where, miraculously, the good old Family has managed the trick with considerable grace.

You could argue that many of the recent changes have been for the worse, and endangered the best aspects of family life. You could – as some families do – resist them. We, for instance, have generally tried to resist the habit of serial and separate 'grazing' for food, and to ensure that if we are all home, once a day we all sit down together if only for twenty minutes so as to observe the immemorial ritual of eating and talking in company.

You could argue that the rise of the stepfamily, and the number of children who have two alternative homes, poses a grave threat to the very idea of family life. You could say that the easiness of divorce has undermined the essential feature of family life, which is that everyone concerned is committed to it, for better or worse. But if you discount the most chaotic and unhappy situations (which always have existed) the evidence is rather that people are building new kinds of family life, new kinds of tolerance and loyalty. Lately I got talking to a young man who was expertly assisting a four-year-old into roller skates at my local leisure centre. I assumed that he was the father, and that since it was a weekday, he was either a shift worker who took turns at childcare with his wife, or else unemployed.

I was wrong on both counts. He was a mature student, taking the day off to amuse his stepsister's boyfriend's little half-brother while the mother was having hospital tests. The families had been neighbours for years, he explained, and the child's father used to run this lad's school football team. A brother whose nephew had lent the roller skates came into it

7

somewhere too. I found it hard to follow, but every word was evidence of the way that casual familial links spread out and become a network of community. This ordinary, unofficial bonding and mutual help is a better guarantee of general safety and good lives than anything which any government could ever provide. And it goes on, every day, all around us.

The ordinary family rules make it work: rules of tolerance, of trust, of sensible taboos and the kind of well-accustomed mutual knowledge that foresees and forestalls behavioural breakdown and disaster. Some of this is on an ordinary humdrum level: 'John's very edgy again . . . perhaps if we took the children and he had a quiet night out with Sarah on their own . . .' Some families handle and contain the most extreme horrors. 'Nat's been drinking. Better get the children away for the night to Mary's' or 'When Grandad's mind wanders, he says some pretty awful things to little girls. We've learnt not to wheel him past the junior school at playtime. Terrible, but you have to laugh, don't you? He *is* ninety.'

Without training, without psychological consultants to hand, every week tens of thousands of families ward off disaster with astonishing efficiency. Sometimes they need outside help; but the family members are the experts, because they alone have the long, loving perspective of old habit. They knew Grandad before he lost his marbles, Nat before he drank, John before he lost his job. They love them; not sentimentally, but because they are used to it. It is fashionable to talk about 'families of friends' as a future substitute for the washed-out, frustrating old biological unit; certainly friends can grow almost as close, and some friends either virtually join a family circle or supplement it wonderfully. But with friendship there is always an element of choice, and a possibility of rejection. The closest of circles may break up without the slightest legal or formal recognition that this is an aberration or a disaster. But your father or brother – blast him! – is yours for life.

Beyond the doomsayers who lament the death of the family every few months in the public prints, there is an even more extreme layer of opinion which genuinely *hopes* that the biological family will become extinct. Their prophet – who is worth mentioning here, because the inspired battiness of his beliefs serves to focus the mind on what we want to keep – is one Dr Robin Baker, who marked the last creaking year of the old millennium by publishing a book called *Sex in the Future* about his vision of how reproductive technology would change society. In his world everybody would bank their eggs and sperm at puberty, get sterilized, and thereafter reproduce only by conscious, organized choice.

'As we approach the new millennium, basic biological factors that have shaped our reproductive behaviour for millions of years are suddenly changing in major ways. The combination of in-vitro fertilization and surrogate motherhood could mark the end not only of infertility, but also the need for men and women to form relationships, or for busy women to take time out of their careers for pregnancy.'

He sees sex as divorced entirely from conception, young people banking their eggs or sperm for future convenient use, the rise of cloning, and the ending of the incest taboo. With DNA testing of babies forcing fathers to support their child financially, he reckons that couples will soon have little practical reason to stay together once the early spark of excitement has disappeared. Lone parent families will be 'the social norm'. Our descendants will 'give their emotions free rein in a way that we never could. The beast within could be released on a longer lead than for centuries . . . freed from financial anxieties, someone might choose to live with one person, have sex with another and have a baby by a third.'

Ah well, the man's a zoologist. They can't help it. But his book – which however hard you scan it does not appear to be a leg-pull – is oddly useful, and worth looking at because by totally ignoring the old mysteries of love, affinity, kinship and loyalty it throws them into sharp relief. After ten minutes with his dreary vision of clinical reproduction, meaningless sex and endless, restless lifestyle realignments, the vision of something else, something ancient and natural and habitually comforting, begins to arise with a new solidity and hope. There are, of course, sacrifices in family life – but as long as the same person is not always cast as the sacrificial victim, that is no bad thing.

There are constraints: most of them are useful. The Baker vision of a world without incest taboos is terrifying because the incest taboo does not, as he avers, only exist for biological reasons. It also acts as a powerful protection to ensure that the developing child is not preyed upon by those who have power and responsibility for him, or her. Why else do we set up an artificial, non-biological incest taboo against teachers sleeping with pupils, or doctors with patients?

He also discounts the value of sheer familiarity; but we all know how calming and reassuring it is, when you leave home as a college student and plunge into new kinds of identity and relationship, to be able to come back to your mangy old bedroom and faded teddy for a few days to recuperate. As for ending the tie of domestic kinship, that is downright risky. While stepfamilies can work very well, they also have inherent dangers. It is regrettably true that most child-battering involves a 'parent' who is not a blood relation. Many parents will tell how, staring into the furious contorted face of an impossible toddler, they have suddenly seen a partner's, father's, or mother's or sibling's features, and been turned aside from wrath by the sheer miracle, the cosmic joke, of kinship.

I do not think that humankind will lightly give up these ancient things. The family will go on changing and evolving to meet new needs; sometimes it will take a step back into older patterns, sometimes invent genuinely new ones. The tapestry will be patched and changed, but never, I think, entirely unravelled.

I THE CHILD

Not a Baby Any More:
Farewell, fat legs . . .

After the tornado years of toddlerhood, there comes a different stage. It is not as obvious or dramatic as the beginnings of speech, or the leaving-off of nappies, or walking; but all the same it is a big change and it needs to be responded to. If you go on treating a big pre-school child in the same way as you dealt with a toddler, you will waste as much effort and cause as much annoyance as if you tried to strap nappies onto a ten-year-old or carry a teenager around in a backpack. Children grow and change fast; if you are tired, or overworked, or agitated about something else entirely, you can miss a whole set of signals. Other things which blur the picture are doctrinaire theories in baby books, scare stories in newspapers, and problematic childhood memories of your own. It can be hard to shut these out and concentrate on the real, personal changes happening in your own real child, now.

You can miss changes that are happening right in front of your eyes, even though many of them are things which, taken the right way, would actually make everyone's life a lot easier. You can find you are wasting half an hour chivvying your baby off to bed so you can see the early evening TV news – when in fact what you have there is no baby but a young child of five, who would be quite interested to watch the news with you and have a solemn discussion about helping Kosovan refugees, before going off to bed at about the same time he would have done anyway. You can spend ages on the phone trying to organize someone to mind the baby while you go for some essential clothes shopping, because it was such a nightmare last time in the changing room; and not quite realize that your bright four-year-old would rather enjoy the outing now, feel grown-up if consulted about colours and, far from lying on the ground drumming her heels, would charm the socks off the

13

sales ladies and come home to play dressing-up shops with her friends for days.

The border between toddlerhood and childhood is a real one. I have often thought that there must be a magical protective quality in fat legs: a baby or toddler has a cheerful, roundish, solid, uncompromising sort of shape. Solid chubby legs seem to go well with an opinionated, Rabelaisian, highly practical outlook on life. A toddler's jokes are uproarious, his wishes imperious, his temper uncontrollable and his actions – as far as he is concerned – totally without consequences. Someone will mop it up. Someone will mend it. We shall buy anuzzer one, Mummy, at the Big Shop. There is no problem so pressing that a hug and a warm drink can't solve it.

Then the child changes shape: everything grows lengthways and slims down. Fat legs turn into long spindly ones, the protruding tummy develops graceful hollows, and suddenly your ex-baby has begun to turn large, worried, wondering eyes on the rest of the universe. Why is it raining? Will the mouse never come alive again if Tibby bites it dead? Will I go to prison if I say a rude word to a policeman? Modesty begins to surface; the hilarity of farts and belches starts to fade, and it begins to matter who sees your bottom. Suddenly, getting a word wrong and being laughed at for it is no longer fun: the concept of ignorance and ridicule becomes very real, and for the first time, a child knows what it is to blush and feel small.

The outer world becomes more menacing. The difference between toddler and child came home to me when my own two – who are twenty months apart – were on either side of it. An item came up on a children's news programme about the hole in the ozone layer. The elder child took days to calm down from the swirling black fears stirred up by this: a hole in the sky, letting in bad rays and making the sea flood us and the sun burn us up! There was real horror in his eyes. The three-year-old, on the other hand, merely said, 'Aahhaaa! We shall all fry up, frizzle frizzle, I shall be a sausage!' without really believing a word of it. At first, I thought that it was a mere difference of temperament, but then I remembered that a year earlier, the elder child had had the same gung-ho, sanguine attitude to

14

disaster. So I suspected – correctly, as it turned out – that in a year or so the younger one too would fall prey to cosmic fears. And the memory came back from many decades ago, of how at six years old I would lie in my bed shuddering with terror at the thought of the new Sizewell A nuclear reactor up the road, because I had just heard about radioactivity; and of how blighted was a 1950s childhood by the shadow of the 'H-bomb', as we called it. Yet even then I can remember my much younger brother being rather pleased at the idea of going radioactive. He wanted to glow all over, 'like a gloominous watch'.

It is easy to misjudge the borderline, in the general muck and muddle of rearing a family. It can happen any time between nearly four and around six; if you are busy, and especially if you are marshalling younger children all day, you can miss it. You can also risk missing it if you are a natural mother: someone who has become so good at the physical, reassuring, singing, playing, cuddly side of motherhood that you find it hard to let go of the tried and tested responses. Actually, fathers are sometimes better at spotting the mental development of young children. I found myself going on too long with the cheery, protective, prattling nonsense which keeps a toddler happy, while my child was really asking for some more con- centrating listening and serious talk. One day he sternly told me, 'Don't make a joke about everything,' and he was quite right to do so. But it is an easy mistake. Sometimes it helps if you are away from your child for a day or two, so that you can come back and look with a rather more detached eye at what is being asked of you. And if you have a regular babysitter, nanny or au pair, it is worth watching what kind of conversations she (or he) is having with the child these days, and whether they still seem to get on as well as they did in uproarious baby days.

Somehow or another, you have to meet and acknowledge this change when it comes. This is as serious a demand as the baby's cries for milk ever were. Growing up is tough, and this four-year-old stage is almost like a rehearsal for adolescence. That child may seem, most of the time, to be an active, cheerful, destructive bundle of animal spirits, riding a bike and building Lego models, but is also going through great bewilderments

15

and revelations. Emerging from toddlerhood, you grasp all sorts of concepts and adult truths which rock the foundations of your small world. It is like discovering a new planet, or a new scientific law, or a new religion every week.

Take death, for instance. Tell a two-year-old that Grandad has gone to heaven, and that is that (apart from a number of questions about when the next bus goes, and whether there are harps). A couple of years later, the same event strikes home with a new and awful significance. Even if you use the idea of heaven to soften the blow, you have to admit that it is a one-way trip into invisibility: people (and pet rabbits) don't come back from death, not ever. Some adults spend most of their lives trying to come to terms with this unnerving fact, and the clear troubled eyes of children perceive it without any of the flummery consolations that the rest of us pull round the event ('had a good life, would have wanted to go doing something he liked, didn't suffer, lives on in memory' etc.). The concept of death so appals young children that some of them even modify the bang-bang-you're-dead games. I have heard one say, 'I'll shoot yer dead. But not dead to heaven dead, just *bang* dead.'

Smaller matters cause upsets too. For months we were driven crazy by the droning repetition of 'I want one of my own'. We could no longer go, as we had six months earlier, to a steam fair or a railway museum, share the uncomplicated joys of looking at the machines, and come home to draw and remember them with equal pleasure. The child who had once said goodbye happily at the end of a day's treat turned into an anxious monster who nagged all the way home for a real steam locomotive 'of my own', a private cinema, or a real traction engine to keep in the bedroom. He sometimes got quite aggressive about it. It would have been easy to get cross, and assume that we had accidentally bred a spoilt materialist, but we held our irritation in check for much of the time. We had a theory, and I still believe it is true, that he was actually expressing not greed but a sort of shock and fear at having realized the temporariness of things. He had suddenly realized that treats and visits come to an end, earth's comforts flee and pleasures pass away. I know children who have cried bitterly

16

on their birthdays, or on Christmas evening, because they realize that the day is ending and will take a long uncertain year to come round again. A grown man once admitted to me that when he was four years old he threw his best teddy bear on the fire, not because he was angry with it but because he had been read a story about a lost teddy, realized that the same might happen to his, and consciously decided to get the awful moment over with quickly.

You cannot do much to help with such feelings, but you can be ready to understand. The baby lived blithely for the moment, but the child bears a burden of unfulfilled and delayed longings. Time is long, the world is wide; on a good day the four-year-old is delighted with the idea. Stories about when Mummy was little, or of countries far away, or of what she can do when she grows up all get a raptly attentive audience. On a bad day, the child suddenly wants the world to be small and cosy again. So suddenly he – or she – will cling. All parents seem to get patches when their child wants to stay at home and refuses point-blank to go to the nursery where he has been perfectly happy for nearly a year. He prefers the boredom of sitting on the floor beside a furiously busy and grumpy Mummy or Granny. He doesn't want to do big brave grown-up things or see his friends or have new books to read or watch the Punch and Judy. He wants to sit on a knee and have the ten thousandth reading of *Polly Pig and the Bee* (my least favourite children's book of all time). All the childcare books stress the importance of regular 'socialization', and all government policies work on the assumption that once a woman has got 'daycare', that is that, and she can be freed to bolster a dynamic modern economy by working down the burger bar. But I have yet to meet a parent who didn't admit that between three years old and schooldays (and sometimes well into schooldays too) there are unaccountable periods – days, weeks, or months long – when their child has appeared to hate all other children and refuse outings.

It can be difficult, frustrating, boring and embarrassing for the parents. Being clung to, once so sweet and warm a feeling, can sometimes make you feel helpless and inadequate, espe-

17

cially when all the other children in the park or at the party are happily running around together. But it makes it easier if you consider that fear of the outside world is a perfectly understandable part of discovering it. When my children were tiny and played on the beach on their chubby legs, I often thought sentimentally of Isaac Newton's words at the end of his life: 'To myself I seem to have been only a child playing on the seashore . . . whilst the great ocean of truth lay undiscovered before me.'

In those days of fat legs they were indeed looking at each shiny stone, concentrating on what was close and touchable and throwable and made satisfying small pings in a tin bucket. It is as they grow older that their eyes become raised in half-troubled wonderment, and they notice that great ocean of undiscovered truth stretching away from their feet. It is no wonder that they sometimes hesitate to confront it.

But time wears on, and children learn fast, and familiarity breeds confidence. By six or seven years old a child will have worked out, with your help, a basic philosophy for dealing with the vastness and the risk of life. A growing child becomes more competent in action, and less dependent: instead of demanding a traction engine of his own, he can go outside with a heap of junk and convince himself that he is building one. Instead of merely quailing with horror at the thought of a world full of homeless or hungry children, primary school children will busy themselves collecting aluminium cans or used stamps to send up to programmes like *Blue Peter*, so that they can be part of the practical help the world's poorest people need. Instead of having nightmares about being put in prison, they develop a hearty appreciation of rules and laws: reading out speed limit signs in the car in an accusing tone, and clucking disgustedly if you omit to fasten your seat belt before you move down the drive. They start to like winning badges at Cubs or Brownies, getting swimming grades, fitting themselves in to a system of social orderliness. This is the point when some parents (like teachers) start using sticky gold stars to encourage tidying-up and helpfulness. A year or so back, the carefree toddler – a free-spirited Rhett Butler sort of creature – would not have given a damn for your gold stars. But the child thinks harder, grows more anxious, and likes the reassurance of a moral structure.

These are vital thinking years, the years when you pass on your personal philosophy, and the beginnings of your religion or culture, to your child. Social, emotional and spiritual values are on their way to the next generation. This may be a distinctly alarming prospect. Most of us manage to scramble through adulthood for months or years on end without being aware of having a personal philosophy at all. Teenagers think about morality and ethics, and old people consider eternity, but unless you are a fervently committed believer of one kind or another, the years you pass in getting and spending and scrabbling around in the everyday world of work and mortgages do tend to blur the eternal verities. We may know which political party we support and whether we condone adultery, but we start to flounder a bit when a questing four-year-old starts coming up with questions about why God lets people die in earthquakes, why Mr Rushdie had to go into hiding, or why Daddy shouts bad things at the Prime Minister on television when everybody knows that the government is 'demmercratically' elected by everybody.

It is a healthy sign when we do flounder at such questions. It indicates that we are trying to find the truth, and willing to share our uncertainties with our children and teach them, too, to think honestly. There is something alarming about people whose beliefs make them think they know it all, and a real risk for them of raising little bigots. Liberal parents share questions, as well as answers, with their children but manage to avoid confusing them in the process. To take a fashionable issue as an example, they don't offer simplifications like, 'Wicked people are cutting down the rainforests because they are greedy and bad.' They haver about, more or less creatively, explaining about poor farmers, international loans, beleaguered government, short-term thinking and ignorance. With luck, they arrive at a few simple facts, such as the fact that yes, cutting down rainforests without replenishing them is bad for the planet, and that all people of goodwill must try to find ways of helping the South Americans, Indonesians, etc. not to do it.

Such parents may tie themselves in knots occasionally and bring down ridicule from others – there are few spectacles so richly comic as a concerned Mummy trying to explain her environmental and economic philosophy in a supermarket queue – but they are still doing a more intelligent job than those who snap, 'Never mind the rainforests, get on with your tea.'

Mind you, there are some impossible questions. It is no fun to be confronted by such queries as, 'Why doesn't Father Christmas make leukaemia children better?' or 'If Daddy loved me, why did he go away?' And there will be moments when policies of open, questing discussions on big issues will come unstuck. Years ago we had a child of seven or eight to stay whose parents were dynamically and utterly open in their discussions. In one afternoon we heard them talking rationally and helpfully to him about nuclear war, lesbianism, terrorist bombs, child molesters and the death penalty, as well as explaining the roots of the Irish Question. He knew about sex, he knew about napalm, he watched films with pathology labs in them. We were lost in wondering admiration of the whole family's cool (at the time, our baby was too small to be interested in much disclosure beyond raucous cries of 'Poo-poo!').

But then at supper Paul and I started telling the assembled company about how we had just dealt with a plague of big rats in our creaking farmhouse larder. As we reached the bit where Paul blocked up their hole in the wall with cement, and the next morning they had kicked the plug out and were calmly sitting in the middle of the floor guzzling pork pies and giving us cold ratty stares, we noticed the little boy's eyes growing wider and wider. He went white. It took his mother hours to get him to sleep, and she was pretty cross (well, ratty) with us for mentioning something so alarming. The lad had come to terms with a potential nuclear holocaust and any number of psychopathic perversions, but he drew the line at rats. Even dead rats. Not being his parents, we simply got it wrong: we were not close enough to understand and predict his areas of terror.

The point is – throughout these years of early childhood – to stay close, intellectually and emotionally. Not smotheringly close, for this is the age of the playroom, of vanishing upstairs with friends for hours of private games; but close enough to pick up the signals. Be around, be available, and listen when you are being talked to.

It is hard, especially hard if you have gone back to work and would prefer nice mindless cuddles and romps of an evening; but listening to young children's preoccupations and questions, and talking sense in return, is as important as cleaning their teeth or reading them stories. And a lot more important than combing their hair or nagging them to use the fork the right way up. It counts for more than fashionable violin lessons and expensive educational toys. This listening, and explaining of the world, may at times also be something you have to delegate to someone else: a babysitter, partner, grandparent or whoever. If so, it is important to make sure that she or he understands that listening is part of the job and, what is more, has a set of basic values and an understanding of life that echoes your own.

Whoever does it, the listening and interpreting is vital. It is the one corner you can't cut with impunity. Coming from a confirmed corner-cutter like myself, that is quite an admission.

First Friends:
Other people's children

For the first four years, your children have to put up with your friends' children as company. For the next fourteen, you are stuck with their friends' parents. Crawling babies will crawl round the room together while their mothers gossip, toddlers will adapt – albeit grudgingly – to the company of whatever peers you plonk down in front of them. But once a healthy child gets to kindergarten age and meets what psychologists call 'a pool of eligibles', the choice is taken from you.

'Gillie is my best friend,' they will say firmly, and however bored you are by Gillie's vapid gossip of a mother, you must smile and make friends and have them both to tea. It is only fair. Actually, you might get to like Gillie's mother. Some of my best friends were originally adopted by my children. But even if you don't, you are stuck with it. You may even have to listen to Duane's father's golfing anecdotes while you both wait beside the swimming pool. This is a drawback of parenthood which is not pointed out sufficiently often.

You daren't impede friendship, of any kind, because the worst dread of all is that your child won't make friends. Suppose he stands alone in the playgroup, alone in the playground? Break, heart! I can think of nothing in routine parenthood which wrings your withers more painfully than the sight of your own child standing sadly on the borderline. I am a confident enough type myself, yet I have never given a children's birthday party without a crazy secret dread that nobody would turn up. This resulted, of course, in my inviting too many and spending half the night filling twenty party bags and willing half an acre of red jelly to set; whereon they all turned up and we ran out of chairs. But it is the worst, coldest fear to have for your child: that he or she will grow up without the gift of friendship.

Because, after all, what else is there? There is no point being rich or beautiful or brilliant if you're lonely. And of all human relationships, the most reliable and least painful is real friendship. Even the best marriages are founded largely upon it. I remember watching a group romping on the lawn once, and thinking that whatever happens to my children in the next seventy years, if I were granted one wish for them I would ask the fairy godmother to guarantee that at the end of each fraught day there would always be a few numbers they can ring, and a welcoming sofa they can sleep on when they're down. Then, and only then, can parents be reconciled to their own eventual disappearance. Not to mention the fact that there will be times, in adolescence, when their children do not seem to tell them anything at all; and when the greatest hope is that there will be someone they can tell.

The moment when your own child first thrusts a toy train under another toddler's nose, willing him to take it or look at it, is the beginning of all this. Try to note the moment. It may not last long, since the next stage is, with regrettable frequency, a sudden change of mind and a sharp blow on the head with the same train. But it is a start, and to be encouraged.

From experience, mistakes, and a straw poll of the saner class of psychologists, here are some ways to encourage a gift for friendship:

Don't try too hard If your belovedest, oldest friend is coming for the weekend with her five-year-old, who hasn't encountered yours since both were *in utero*, it is a pretty safe bet that they will start by hating each other. The tension is just too much. Enforce common courtesy, getting your child to show the visitor round the house and so forth, then ignore them. Don't automatically assume your own child wants to share a bedroom with some total stranger. Suppose someone said to you, 'There's another girl of thirty-two coming, that'll be fun, you can sleep in the bunks together and be together all day long.' You'd think they were mad, or that you were on a really cheap package holiday.

23

Demonstrate the art of friendship When you are going to see your own friends, show obvious pleasure: talk about them eagerly, refer to them, explain if you're doing shopping as a favour for them, or they for you. Make a heroic effort not to be heard referring to 'Daddy's friend in the golf club/darts team' as if they were an unpleasant affliction. Even if they are.

Provide the raw material The sooner a child gets the idea of making a free and joyful choice of friend, the better. Grit your teeth. Provide your child with that 'pool of eligibles' – children the same age or thereabouts – seen fairly regularly. Before school, this entails either a playgroup or a pretty intensive round of coffee-drinking in various kitchens. This is a lot harder if both parents go out to work, but it is still worth trying. Make acquaintances among other parents at the nursery or childminder's, and see them off-duty sometimes, with your children. Persuade your nanny or babysitter to see the child's friends rather than just her own. See other families at weekends. Yes, it is tough. But truly, it pays off in terms of your convenience as well as your child's good. You will always have an emergency family to fall back on, where the child is actually happy to go.

Unless you live ten miles up a farm track or have accidentally settled in the middle of a block of sheltered housing for the elderly, there will be children around somewhere. Find them.

If you consider the other children in your street 'rough' or 'unsuitable', that is a problem. It is not for me to write you off as a snob. It is indeed very annoying to have your carefully nurtured, childlike, innocent offspring coming home raving about repulsive teen idols and demanding luminous sweets, still worse if they suddenly show a distressing familiarity with the etiquette of 'nicking wheels' passed down from their friend's big brother who is doing two years' probation. All you can do is reiterate your own values in a quiet, holy way and make damn sure that when the minxy miniature Spice Girl in the pelmet skirt comes round to your house, you make her play Animal Snap, however loudly she demands a rock video.

Don't interfere If a friendship is going well, let them get on with it. Between three and eight, children play a lot of really, really silly games. It is not your business to improve them unless bloodshed threatens.

Don't accidentally discourage companionship If your child is shy with other children, don't reward it by saying, 'Oh, he's Mummy's boy, always on my knee, aren't you, sweetie?' Don't make remarks to other adults which suggest that social contact is something undesirable ('Aren't they noisy when you get two of them together?'). Yes, of course it's true. But say it privately.

Help your child to be nice not nasty To be a friend requires a degree of social sensitivity. Babies are not born with this. They don't know what being nice, or nasty, is. Gradually you teach them.

How? 'If the immediate circle is happy, relaxed and out-going', says the psychologist Martin Herbert, 'with plenty of love and admiration for the baby, he will have a good self-image and get on well with others.' If you are cold and formal and forever judging and disapproving, your child will become anxious and defensive, and find it hard to relax into happy-go-lucky tolerant friendships.

Teach sharing Aggressive children, your own or others', are sometimes merely in need of advice on other ways to cope. They may actually not know about 'taking turns' or 'sharing' because nobody ever told them. Tell them, gently. Then tell them again. And again. And show them. Keep sharing things. Let the cat have a turn with your knitting wool, and your daughter have a turn with your lipstick. One day it will sink in.

Don't let doors slam When school starts, try to make sure there are still contacts with some friends at other schools, or visits from scattered relations. It can be a blessed relief – for all concerned – to get out of the hothouse world of classroom friendships into something calmer and more enduring. A child who is feeling at odds with the world because George at school

25

has deserted him will be immeasurably soothed by remembering that Jeremy – who is back from boarding school this very weekend – is keen to see him, and pick up where they left off.

Accept children's choices Just in case you are George's mummy in the above case, don't be shocked by his fickleness. Children's friendships can be brief as a bubble, but short does not mean shallow. Don't force it. Unkindness is taboo, but fickleness isn't. If Laura has gone off Becky, she has to be nice to Becky if she meets her, but she does not have to ask her to tea. You, on the other hand, have to smooth things over with Becky's mother. Especially since the little madams will be inseparable again in a week or so. Girls, I fear, are rather more prone to this sort of Burton-Taylor relationship than boys. Boys either fight or ignore each other or get on fine. Girls seem to practise all the nuances of relationships just for the fun of it. 'I hate you, Zoe. Mummy, I hate Zoe. She's my best friend, I hate her. I'm going to make her only my second-best friend after Sarah. Sarah, hate you!' Having a gang of little girls round for the afternoon is like living in the Miss World dressing room. I am sorry to be sexist, but it is. They – we! – grow out of it. Mostly.

On this subject, what about your own relationship with other people's children? All new mothers know the feeling so beautifully expressed by Pam Ayres – 'It's hard to explain/When I look at your Wayne/Why you bothered to have one at all.' And which of us can say, hand on heart, that she has never looked at the pudgy, whining little brat next door and thought, ever so quietly to herself, 'Eeugh!'?

Yet there is something nice about a gang of children in the house, a basketful of rowdy puppies, growing up together in a close neighbourhood. We have lost the extended family, in the West, and I rather regret it. Other people's children are fun, because you aren't deeply responsible for them and they can't wind you up into a rage the way your own can. If they are round to play, you keep them safe and prevent any real crimes but don't particularly care if they wipe their mouth on their sleeve. On the other hand, if you fall into a cross panic trying to find everyone's wellies, your own children will resent it but the outsiders will look on fairly placidly. It is fun to give presents to other children, guessing what they want with fresh, outsiders' eyes. And if they do misbehave badly, you find it surprisingly easy to pull them up sharp: they are warier of non-parents. You get a glimmering of the answer to that great mystery of all mysteries, which is how on earth primary school teachers manage to get twenty-five children under five to sit in a row singing 'The Wheels on the Bus', when you can't seem to control your one or two.

There is, however, a double standard about disciplining other people's children. Every mother I speak to says that she hopes very much that other parents do occasionally bawl her child out for violence or destructiveness, or even bad manners, but that she feels awkward doing it herself to other children. I used to coo and pussyfoot around other people's offspring in my uncertain days, and would go to great lengths rather than bark severely at them or withhold their pudding course. I have gradually got tougher. Once, three families together, we went on a wild windy holiday on the Norfolk Broads with nine children aged between two and ten. On the first evening the three mothers drank a ceremonial gin and solemnly gave one another full permission to shout at or in extremis even slap one another's offspring. It worked fine. Except that I did observe the rather curious law of nature which decrees that when four little boys are having social difficulties and one of them gets excluded from the gang, the mothers who keep saying 'Let them sort it out for themselves' are invariably the mothers of the three who are winning. The mother of the outcast is not so sure. Thereafter, their alliances were drawn up in no fewer than three permutations. We, and our sons, remain friends to this day. It can be done.

So if you are not a natural earth mother, if you are currently rather shy and awkward with your children's peers, persevere. Anyone can get the hang of it. Occasionally, the mingling of families gives you a sense of the vast closeness of the whole human family: all children belonging to all parents. One night when her father was away on a long trip, my daughter narrowly watched a visiting Daddy giving his little girl a hug. 'May I join that hug?' she asked, and did so. He didn't replace her own father and had no ambition to, but the hug, on both sides, was very welcome. Tears sprang to my eyes. Later on, I saw the chaos they had all made of the newly tidied playroom. But I minded less than usual.

Mum-upmanship:
Other children's parents

I have said it before, and I shall say it again: the best present you can give a pregnant woman is to introduce her to another pregnant woman who lives in the same street. We need each other. It is not a glamorous relationship: so baby gurus confine themselves as a rule to droning on about bonding and the role of the father and how to find a good GP. They discuss siblings, and grandparents, the childminders; they worry about our children's need to 'interact' with other children. Feminists write about the relationship of mothers to the hard outer world of work and careers. Nobody thinks about the need for a mother who inhabits a home (full or part time) to interact occasionally with someone who is in that world yet is over seven years old.

You need friends. No, more than friends – childless people at the office can be friends. You need fellow enthusiasts, comrades-in-arms, people who really understand. Mothers need other mothers. (I suppose that role-reversed fathers also need others, but let's not complicate things right now.)

Some women pretend they can do without other mothers. I was like this. When I first stared at that miraculous brown ring on the home predictor test tube, I looked forward to the baby but dreaded the rest. I had a nasty suspicion that motherhood would involve sitting a round in kitchens littered with hideous plastic toys, discussing potty training while other people's toddlers wiped their noses on my knee. I wanted none of it. My baby and I would mix, I swore, with the same sort of friends as before: single men, working girls, old mates, and colleagues. I would refuse to join a coffee circle. I didn't like mumsy women, and I didn't even like coffee much.

As in so many other prenatal theories, I was comically

wrong. Society belittles mothers and babies, and it would be folly not to stick together.

It often begins with extraordinary, instant intimacy: reserved types begin discussing nipple-shields and nappies, and if you are not careful you progress rapidly to shaming admissions about your married life, which in a less uproarious hormonal state you would not risk sharing with someone you had only just met at the clinic.

But as the years roll by, the picture changes. Mother-and-toddler groups and playgroups widen the trawl of your net, and you have more of a choice. You also start to discover the pitfalls of inter-mother comradeship. The instant intimacy which springs up between two women whose babies are sweetly hugging one another under a kitchen table can mask a lot of basic incompatibility. This temporary blindness has its advantages: frankly, if you are at home with a baby it is probably better to mix with the odd bore or bigot than with nobody at all. Everyone has their good points and there's no sense in picking fights. Soldiers in isolated barracks know that, and so do women sitting on the floor of Methodist church halls watching their babies stagger round in circles while the rain drums on the tin roof.

But as babies grow into schoolchildren, the expedient friend-ships wither away – gently, one hopes – and the real ones develop into something else. But we still retain the instinct to put out a glad hand to another woman – any woman – with a child the same age as ours. It is an instinct that can lead us somewhat astray.

Here are six sisters to be wary of. Some of them may be you, at times. Some have been me. Some can be converted into proper friends for life; it all depends on the degree of intensity with which they match the stereotype. Spot the ones you recognize:

Dreary Deirdre She is a wonderful friend to those in trouble. She looks after their children, helps change the lock against your drunken estranged husband, cooks you meals, and listens sympathetically for hours to the chronicle of disasters. The curious thing is that she gets quite annoyed when your troubles are over, and you realize that she has been treating you as a sort of soap opera all along.

Sloppy Sal You love her for being untidier than you are, for letting the dog lick the plates, never combing her children's hair, carrying around three stone of postnatal flab and forgetting which night is parents' evening at school. Encouraged by her example, you become even worse, until you suddenly realize that she is, in fact, not happy-go-lucky at all but more than a little depressed. You react against her and make friends with:

Perfect Pru whose house is immaculate, her curtains and carpet white, and who keeps toys perfectly arranged in designer boxes. Her children never touch sweets, crisps, or anything with an E number on the packet. So far so good. The trouble is that whenever she comes to your house she manages – (in a casual way – to fire off some small but deadly request to underline your deficiencies. Like, 'Have you a needle and white thread handy?' or, 'Is there a clean hanky I could borrow?' If you have the nerve, lend her all the greyish hankies in the drawer. They will come back whiter than white, and ironed. However, by this time you may have figured out that she, too, is a shade depressed, and decided to liven her up with the aid of Sloppy Sal, a Kevin Kline video and a large bottle of gin.

Defensive Dora is hard to handle. Fun, lively and uncritical most of the time, she has a blind spot about her own child. Whenever there is fighting, biting, or a splintering crash of china, it is not her darling baby's fault. It is not even neutral: it is your child's fault, so there.

Moaning Min on the other hand blames her children for everything, from her figure to her premenstrual tension. She comes on like a trapped bird, fluttering desperately against the bars of motherhood. She seems to get no kick from the brief anarchic fun of nursery days, and can't wait till they grow up. She radiates unhappiness, and you worry about her children. No need: amazingly enough, she is not depressed at all really. Having used up her misery on you, Min is a ray of sunshine at home.

Penny the Parasite You never grow tired of her company because you never see her for very long. She will pop round ostensibly to visit you, remember a bit of shopping, leave little Tarquin playing 'so sweetly, bless them' with your child, and vanish for three and a half hours. When you try to retaliate by dropping off your little Germaine for twenty minutes, she will claim that her mother is staying and has a nervous dread of non-grandchildren. However, if your child has a real friendship with hers, she might actually be the best of the bunch: you get hours of peace at home to read or write while the children amuse one another, and you don't have to drink any coffee.

Nice women, all of them, really. Enjoy them now. Another few months and you'll be dragooned back to work. Listening to your colleagues bragging about their big deals or moaning about corporate restructuring, listening to the MD going on about golf and cash flow, you will think nostalgically of Min and Dora. Not so, however, with the last and most dangerous type: a specimen who, – unlike the others, – is even more dangerous to the full-time working mother. She is:

Competitive Clara Her baby rolled, sat, teethed, crawled, walked, talked and aimed accurately at the potty before anyone else's. So she says. He is also amazingly sensitive, musical, athletic and socially well-adjusted. The entire neighbourhood hopes, with a distressing lack of charity, that one day young Victor will wet his pants and bite the class teacher to the bone. A cheer will go up from the whole street.

This business of Mum-upmanship is worth going into, if only because it blights so many happy moments and clouds so many relationships. There are two great vices which mar the fair face of motherhood. One is guilt, and the other is competitiveness. Both are rampant from the very start: maternity wards are full of women weeping guiltily because they aren't good enough at breastfeeding, while at the same time noting that none of the other babies in the ward is as good-looking and alert as their own. The fact that most of us see no contradiction in indulging these two emotions simultaneously is a great tribute to the blurring power of hormones.

Maternal guilt tends to wither away after the first few years. This is probably because as soon as your children can talk clearly, they start periodically accusing you of being a hateful Mummy, thus saving you the bother of accusing yourself. But competitiveness does not wither.

Maybe it is because Western society so worships careers, and gives mothers so little sense of personal value, that the non-earning mother is almost forced to turn her child into an award-winning, business-expansion product just in order to feel part of society. Career mothers are oddly less competitive, in my experience. They get their urge to win over with at the office. Among most of us, competitiveness flourishes horribly.

And whereas it didn't matter too much in the early stages – babies frankly do not give a damn whether Jason down the road has got more teeth than they have – as children grow older the terrible sport of Mum-upmanship does ever more harm. Normally sane, kindly women become cruel. 'Oh, Jamie's at the local playgroup, is he? Well, we did look, of course, but it wasn't quite Victor's cup of tea. Driving twelve miles every morning is an awful bore, of course, but having him in the pre-pre-prep at St Bastard's has really done wonders. Their early reading scheme is marvellous, he just adores his books.' You gasp, and rally your own forces. 'Well, that's nice . . . such a comfort, especially with a child who's not too happy socially.' Victor's mother recognizes her tactical error and changes ground. 'Oh, the books are just for his quiet time indoors. He's completely fanatical about his tennis, though. It's been well worth the coaching.'

And you slink off resentfully, plotting a comeback as if you were some paranoid press tycoon who has had his circulation dented. The actual children, needless to say, are pleasant little boys of five with average brains, and interests which change completely once a fortnight. If they feel competitive, they push one another over in a nice straightforward way. They do not have a problem. Their mothers do.

A primary school head once told me that he had given up using only one reading scheme, but mixes up the books from different schemes. Not for any particular educational reason, but because he was getting so many tight-lipped mothers coming to ask him, 'Why is Rowanne only on Blue Book Two when Jackie, who's got the same birthday, is on Red Book One already?' The head would do his best to reassure her, knowing guiltily all the time that her lips would tighten even further when she discovered that Jackie is playing the Virgin Mary in the Christmas play, and Rowanne is only a minor chorus angel. Back home, you may be sure that Rowanne's mother keeps as close an eye on the goings-on at Jackie's house as any industrial spy does on his rival. Jackie's taken the stabilizers off her bike? Right, out comes the spanner and poor old wobbly Rowanne is in for a week of grazed elbows and tears. Jackie's going to ballet class in trendy legwarmers? Rowanne, get your coat. We are off to be measured for a tutu. Suck in your tummy, dear.

The two mothers pretend to be great friends; when they meet in the supermarket you can see their teeth glittering from the other end of the aisle.

Fathers are not exempt, either. A really keen New Man can impersonate any of the above categories of women, and becomes Competitive Keith whenever a) size of willies is the issue or b) it is school sports day. Woe betide the confused five-year-old who runs the wrong way, the unathletic six who can't get into his sack fast enough, the poet and dreamer who is so surprised to see the tape that he stops dead within a metre of it while the field thunders by. Daddy will be out and on to his car phone within seconds, trying to book him a personal athletics coach.

All right, I exaggerate. A little. But there are thousands of us who – in short bursts of insecurity, or anxiety – willingly lock ourselves into one of the saddest, least profitable competitions in the world. Nobody will ever win. Exaggerated pride in one's own child's achievements is not a sign of love, but a lack of love. Instead of vainly hunting for reasonable explanations as to why we love our child best (because he is musical, reads faster, got more teeth sooner, is brighter and stronger) we should accept that we rate him more highly because he is our own, and that is the end of the matter. Look at the parents of severely handicapped children: theirs will never compete on any obvious level, and do they keep apologizing for them, or nervously bragging about how many steps theirs took compared to the other cerebral palsy child down the road? They do not. They just love them and help them as far as they can go. The central lesson they have learned, with some pain, is about individuality. It would do the rest of us no harm to learn it too.

Nursery Tales

This is tough territory, bandit country: political, contentious, uncomfortable stuff. It makes people start shouting at one another, mothers grow tearful and fathers competitive. It causes rows to break out in both tabloid newspapers and learned societies. It sparks off generation and class warfare, and sets MPs blustering across the dispatch boxes.

Who would ever think that it is all about small, smiling children clustered round tables of play-dough and finger paints? How did the question of how pre-school children spend their day – and with whom – turn into such a snake pit of controversy? How on earth did we become so unsure of ourselves, so far out of touch with the most basic simplicities of human life, that nursery education should become the hot potato that it is? Surely, one wails sentimentally, there must have been other times, simpler times, when everyone more or less knew how to raise small children, and got on with it in a matter-of-fact way, going about their daily tasks with small figures trotting behind them, messing about with the clay from the furrow or playing with the workshop cat?

There never was a perfect time. All we can look back to are harder, less flexible and ambitious times, when small children just scrambled up somehow because their parents were pre-occupied with scratching a living and keeping a labour-intensive home in some kind of order. When women peeled vegetables and laboured over a washtub, there were plenty of simple and quite educational things for infants to do along-side them, messing about with soap shavings or making patterns with discarded potato peelings. When elderly parents lived perforce under the same roof as their grown children, there would always be a granny in the chimney corner to tell stories and tie handkerchiefs into dollies. In the days of 'surplus women' and indigent spinster aunts, even if Mother was busy there was always another pair of ears and hands around the home to keep young children out of the fireplace and run through the ABC with them when the moment arose. Let us not make rosy and idealized pictures of the past – there were undoubtedly lots of senile grannies, deeply unpleasant aunts and frightened neglected children – but it is a fact that well into the 20th century there existed a more tribal, extended sort of household than most of us inherit in the 21st.

Today, several changes have made their mark. Academics and psychologists have studied early childhood and been drawn into the fascination of these astonishingly fast, and rather alien, minds. Being close to a small child, and immersed in its strange perceptions, is the nearest thing to regression therapy that most of us ever get; so it is no wonder that some of the experts have turned out some rather strange theories, and held to them so emotionally. Seventeenth-century Puritans earnestly believed that 'iniquity is co-natural to infants' and must be whipped out of them. Listen to the New England minister, John Hersey:

'Break their will betimes . . . let a child from a year old be taught to fear the rod and cry softly. Make him do as he is bid if you whip him ten times running to do it . . .' Many believed that only holy learning could protect the child from its own wicked nature. Hester Thrale in 1764 boasted that her Queenie, at two, 'repeats the Pater Noster, the three Christian Virtues and the signs of the Zodiac . . . knows all the Heathen deities and their attributes'. Rousseau, rather later, pleaded for 'natural, free and innocent' neglect. In this century theories range from A.S.Neill's rejection of compulsory literacy to the 1980s fad for waving lettered 'flashcards' at bewildered neonates.

The question of what under-fives should learn, and how, has never been settled. Throughout history, it is probable that most infants merely scrambled up their own way, learning by helping at home, enjoying stories, peering at hornbooks if they were lucky and messing with mud. There have always been theorists, but the odds are that few families had the inclination to follow, for instance, Locke's advice to make a child sleep on a different surface every night, or the unkindness to 'harden' infants by dipping them in icy water and firing off pistols near their heads. Indeed, the whole history of experts on infancy suggests that it is, frankly, often a mercy when parents ignore them entirely.

But today we live in a regulated society, and once a new orthodoxy catches government enthusiasm, it is rapidly imposed on all. Yet we cannot be certain that we are right, any more than the whipping Puritans or the loony 1920s behaviourist John B. Watson who thought cuddling infants was dangerous and advocated a manly handshake once a day, and supervision of play via a periscope lest the child guess that you care. Modern theorists on early learning are not necessarily one hundred per cent right; they disagree amongst themselves. But in any nation at any moment, one lot will have the ascendancy, and the ability to influence a far greater number of families than ever before.

Several changes have made it easier for us in the West to embrace the idea of nursery education. One is the shrinking of the family circle in the age of easy contraception; another is the emancipation of women. In half a century most of the world's developed countries have come from a situation where it was still surprising if a wife worked, let alone a mother, to one where it is becoming surprising if she doesn't. We now have the choice of returning to work well before our children are five, and leaving them for long periods in the care of a childminder, nursery, au pair or nanny.

And once the bond of constant daily closeness is broken, however rational and necessary a decision this is for the individual, it is a short step to convincing ourselves that this move is all for the best, and to make the most of the separation by persuading ourself it 'adds value' – horrid mercenary phrase – to the child's day by including an element of deliberate, rather than incidental, education. I am not saying that any of us are actually hypocrites; but it is a great deal easier on the mind to leave a child who you believe to be 'learning' than one who is just messing around, as he or she might just as well have done in your own kitchen.

38

All this increases the sense that pre-school children – even three-year-olds – should be the subject of constant education, and constant assessment. An economic and social need for mothers to work feeds a restless search for improvement and measurable, reassuring, almost "marketable" progress in their children. It is easier to nod agreement with the general view that formal nursery education is an unqualified good than to challenge it and declare that the emperor has not many clothes, and that a small child kept at home until five, with friends and toys and plenty of chat, will do every bit as well as his nursery cousin.

The waters are further muddied by the fact that there are certain very underprivileged and vulnerable children around, born to less capable or too young mothers, the unsupported and confused, the drug-dependent or mentally limited or despairing women at the bottom of the heap. These children really do need extra care, extra help from the public services, just to get them up to a reasonable level of confidence and competence before they start proper school. Meanwhile the children of their far more affluent and capable sisters also need a nursery, for the purely practical reason that their mothers have to, or want to, go out to work.

Thus childminding, education, and the rescue of the neediest children all get uncomfortably lumped together under the umbrella title of 'childcare', which then becomes something seen as a necessity and therefore as a right. 'Childcare provision' for working mothers has long been a rallying cry of feminist campaigners; right back in the late sixties there were highly confusing banners demanding 'women's right to contraception, abortion, creches' as if children were some kind of disease to be kept at a distance. Today, some governments boast of proffering 'childcare' as a component of employment provision, urging single mothers in particular to get out into the workplace on a promise of 'childcare entitlement' to be fulfilled by some patchwork of vouchers and tied allowances. Employers preen themselves on providing workplace creches and never think too hard about the daily reality of commuting to work with an unwilling, weary or feverish small child.

The assumption behind all of this is mechanistic and

businesslike: once this mother, this worker bee, is slotted into a job and her infant is slotted into a nursery during her hours of work, the job is done. Everything can progress smoothly from there.

But it doesn't, not necessarily. This brisk approach is at odds with the messy, warm, idiosyncratic reality of any real child under five. Families cope, of course they do: they have to. Sometimes a lucky working couple find that there is a local nursery with an affordable place open for the right hours, careful loving staff and an easygoing attitude; if that family also happens to have bred a sociable, outgoing, consistent little person who thoroughly enjoys nursery life, than bingo! It all works. Sometimes a family finds a nanny or au pair they can afford, and who becomes more of a beloved surrogate aunt or elder daughter than an employee, stays for years and keeps in touch forever. Sometimes one parent simply decides to stay at home and build a sociable circle and a set of activities which are educational in the broadest sense.

More often, these pre-school years become a confused, tense pattern of compromise and worry. There are days of Calpol and clinginess, sadness and snivelling, when you wish with all your heart that you didn't have to leave home but could trail around the house and the park, secure and familiar, easing your child's heart by your presence. There will be stages of firework brilliance, when it tears your heart to leave a child whose every day brings new discoveries and jokes you can hardly bear to miss. And, of course, there will be other days when you dash down the road with a song on your lips, rejoicing at the prospect of a whole day among people who can wipe their own noses.

It all has to be got through. It is, however, worth standing back occasionally from the whole situation and weighing up what really is best both for the adults in the family and the child. It could be a mother staying mainly at home, supported by a playground and part-time babysitting; perhaps teleworking to support the budget. It could be a father doing the same. It could be a nursery and a part-time job, or a nanny supported by a full-time one. It could be all those things, in succession, as a shy child develops into a confident one. Hence the cynical tone of the beginning of this chapter. But always, it is useful to question the sacred cow of 'childcare' and make up your own mind what you want from it most, and which of the three central elements – convenience, homeliness and education – matters most. It is also useful to question how far you actually need professionals to teach your child in the early years, and how much awareness of child development and educational needs you require in whatever childminder, nanny, nursery or indeed granny looks after your child when you don't.

This is an important question, lately highlighted in Britain where government has brought in a 'nursery curriculum' of desirable attainments for four-year-olds, to match the rest of its key stage educational targets. Our masters seem strangely unaware that we the developed world are almost alone in our obsession with very early literacy and numerary. Indeed curiously, New Zealand is the other country which has a similar keenness on reading before five or six, and also happens to have many of the same problems later – a gender gap between boys and girls, and low literacy among less able pupils.

Here are some basic thoughts.

What does a small child need to learn?

The official 'early learning goals' lately laid down by the British government for under-fives are the letters of the alphabet, an ability to count, to write their names and spell simple words. Other nursery goals are things like the names of colours, how to dress yourself, and how to talk in sentences.

But you can't timetable a small child, or not without causing undue anxiety or open rebellion. Playing, remember, is serious work at this age. An infant in a sandpit with a bucket and paddling pool to hand is doing physics, maths, resistant materials technology, art and design, hydraulics, earth science and (if babbling to himself) language. A child burying Teddy in the sand is doing ethics and drama; up-ending a bucket of water on his head is a fine training in comedy which may eventually lead

41

to a lucrative film contract. What is served by interfering with this personal curriculum in order to chant ABC, or learn the names of geometric shapes? Adult convenience, certainly; parental neurosis about education, undoubtedly; government statistics improved by measurable results, definitely. But two things are worth keeping in sight: firstly, that early development does not follow an even pattern, because not every child learns things in the same order; and secondly, that all the above achievements are things which any parent can teach. Certainly any parent who reads well enough to have got this far down the page.

Does it do any harm if a child has no early education at all?

Well, it certainly does harm if a child has no stimulus, no conversation, no company and nothing to play with, and never gets the chance to be in a group of other children. But if you mean 'Is it a disaster to turn up at school not knowing the alphabet', the answer is no. It is a great bore for the reception teacher, certainly, and can cause frustration if the class is too big for individual attention; but a child who has played and chatted and been read to for five years will pick up the symbols and codes of adult life remarkably fast once offered them.

Can you overload a child with education?

Yes, unfortunately. One of the great irritations of modern life is that while hundreds of seriously underprivileged children go short of even bricks to play with, overprivileged children are pushed, and hothoused, and harried, and urged into so many formal activities that they never have time to play with the bricks at all. The mystery and the sense of discovery goes out of that child's world, replaced by an arbitrary adult pattern.

This is not a rejection of all nursery education; just a counter-weight, something to help new parents think clearly, and a bit cynically, before rushing lemming-like into the burgeoning world of educational childcare before they actually need to.

Once a child starts in a nursery group, is that it?

Er . . . no. Some storm ahead and never look back, others progress on the 'two steps forward, one step back' principle. Our own children's lives were immeasurably enhanced by the late Margaret, a wonderful woman who ran a series of little low-budget private nursery groups in our patch of Suffolk. But even so, and even though neither ever did more than half a day at a time, there was one instance when a three-and-a-half year old, who had been delighted with her time there for a whole term, suddenly became withdrawn and morose, not complaining but downbeat every time I dropped her off and silent for hours afterwards. I rang Margaret to discuss this and with a gasp of thankfulness she said, 'Oh, I am so pleased. I was wondering how to put it to you. It isn't going well, is it? She's no trouble, but where she used to be the motor of the whole group, full of life, she's gone quiet.'

What, I asked, did she think ought to happen?

'Well . . . you work,' she began. 'I know it's hard but ideally, I'd just say take her back under your wing for a term. Then try again.' Well, I was lucky; I worked at home a lot and could claw back some of my nanny time. So the child stayed home, mainly under the kitchen table making unintellectual conversation with the cat, and after a term gladly went back into the system and loved it again, cutting and sticking with fierce intensity.

But that experience taught me that 'childcare' is not a business arrangement or a contract, but a relationship. And if, for your small child, that relationship is not going well, your instinct may tell you quite correctly to get the hell out of it. This may be hideously awkward if you were also using it as babysitting while you earned a crust. All I am saying is, keep your options open.

Do proper nurseries give better educational opportunities than playgroups or childminders?

Not necessarily. Some childminders are fantastic, just like the perfect mother that you wish you were – singing, reading, cuddling, laughing, teaching marvels. Some childminders are so good that you don't need anything else. Others are dreary unstimulating baby farms. You have to judge.

Playgroups are run by communities, not for profit, and are the least formal, most homelike form of sociable-educational structure. Mothers help, but the playleaders have training and experience and, above all, ideas. Give them a pile of paper plates and some wool and felt pens, and they will have the children turning out clown faces, dazzled by their own proficiency. They will also – in a decent playgroup – introduce the dread numbers-and-letters in a playful context.

A nursery class may be very similar but will have more trained staff and usually no mother helpers. This is not necessarily an unqualified advantage. You have to judge.

How?

Look around. Is the equipment good and varied (building sets, play-dough, paints, suitable tables and chairs, musical instruments)? It doesn't matter if it is battered and well-used, but it does matter whether it is reasonably attractive looking, safe (not jagged or crusted with old spit) and kept in logical order. If your child wants a chaotic, jumbled-up toy cupboard, the odds are there is one at home.

Find out about the staff. Are enough of them qualified, and how much experience have they? Have they all been cleared with police and social services? Do they look happy to see the children in the morning? Do they, in any way, give you or your child the creeps?

Find out about the day: how structured is it, and how much scope is there for children to depart from the planned time-table? If a child does not want to come to the Story Corner because the sandpit game has reached a crucial stage, how much pressure is put on him to conform? The desirable answer depends rather on the age: when you are nearly five and will shortly be in school, it is a good idea to learn about rules and timetables. When you are three and a bit, it is an unwarrantable imposition.

Ideally, a prospective parent should be allowed to spend a session in the group, taking in the atmosphere. It is surprising how many of us never quite spare the time. Heigh-ho.

Watch the children at home time. Do they seem relaxed, pleased to see their parents but full of news of the day? Finally, ask other parents. As with schools, there is a certain risk in this, because nobody likes to admit that they send their child somewhere which is less than perfect. But with careful attention to what they say, you can usually pick up hints.

This may all sound a bit labour-intensive, especially if you have a younger baby or a demanding schoolchild or job. But making the right decision about a nursery (or indeed childminder, or both) is, to put it crassly, money in the bank. Nothing – *absolutely nothing* – rots up your own life worse than the constant anxiety about an unhappy child. You miss trains, walk into lampposts, and burst into tears during business meetings. Well, I do, anyway.

What makes starting easier, for a child?

Common-sense stuff. Ask one or two of the established children at that nursery round to play beforehand. Go on a couple of visits and get to know the playleader, and chat about her to your child in the days beforehand (even knowing the name of her cat at home can somehow help). Run through the drill about asking for the lavatory, getting your own coat on and off, etc. Send along Teddy for company (only tell the staff how precious Teddy is, so he gets put on a high commanding shelf away from rival children once your own child drops him).

And if I get it wrong?

If a child is seriously unhappy or afraid in a pre-school group, it affects his or her view of the whole world. I have never forgotten one of my children, aged three, asking some baffled Turkish children on holiday, 'Do you go to Molly and Ros's too?' Their group *is* the outside world: the only thing beyond home. So if it is a frightening or belittling place the whole world

45

is full of terrors; and if it is a place where you have fun and feel powerful and competent, the world is your oyster. Enjoying a pre-school group is the first step to enjoying school, and the wider society for ever.

So for heaven's sake, if it really doesn't work (after a fair trial of a few weeks) or if you have doubts, end the experiment. At least for a while. Prove to your child whose side you are on. If you can't juggle work round this crisis (and it is probably a short-term crisis) then call on a grandparent, a partner, a friend at home with a baby. It may be inconvenient, it may mean losing a term's fees, it may mean losing face among the sickeningly complacent parents of carefree children who think that group is absolutely fine. Never mind. This is your child and you know best.

And if the staff pooh-pooh your concerns and try, hawkishly, to get you to change your mind, then you will know that you were indeed right, and that they do not have the welfare of individual children in the forefront of their minds. It may be extraordinarily difficult; the nursery may be part of a primary school where you hope your child will go eventually. But if it is a good school they will understand, and honour you for putting your child before your convenience. If it isn't, to hell with it.

Coaching Days:
Starting them young

There is virtually no sport or skill that somebody, somewhere, is not trying to impart to waist-high children. From the cello to motorcycle scrambling, someone is manufacturing miniature equipment and training up impossibly tiny tykes to master it. The British upper classes have a staggering track record of introducing their children to formal pastimes in infancy. A fair example is Sarah Ferguson, Duchess of York, who was put on a horse at two, swam at three, and skied at four. Others, of all social milieux, may be spotted whizzing around in little nutshell sailing dinghies alone when they are five, talking about their tennis trainer at six, and throwing other chunky little figures in white pajamas around on judo mats before they start school. Beginning to learn a musical instrument at four is no longer regarded as remotely precocious.

All together now: *so what?* If you joined in that cry with confidence, skip this chapter. You are a well-adjusted parent with a certain grainy confidence in your own methods. You probably skipped most of the nursery chapter, too.

However, if – like the majority of us – you began to twitch with nervous guilt during that first paragraph, and looked outside at your own children charging one another with plastic swords or throwing stones at the wall in a seriously unstructured manner, be brave and confront the issue head on. What do they need? What can you offer? And are you sure of your motive for wanting to?

Many parents, under social pressure, rush around getting their children into countless 'courses' and coaching sessions in much the same way as owners of dubious old cars keep buying cheap bolt-on accessories, go-faster stripes and flashy aerodynamic spoilers. 'Oh,' they say, meeting rival mothers, 'Nicky's absolutely loving his tennis coaching, but of course it's the tae kwon do which is so marvellous for developing coordination before the ski season, and I think it helps his cello, too.' The other mother responds instantly. 'Well, it's the swimming that's so serious for Samantha just now, and what with voltige riding on Wednesdays and gymnastics on Thursdays, I'm not sure that it wouldn't cut too much into her drama if we started martial arts now. There may be a slot next year.' Nicky and Samantha are four and five respectively, and their parents ought to be ashamed of themselves. In a couple of years, these two overloaded tots are going to be victims of a syndrome which teachers in prosperous areas are starting to report. One city teacher told me, 'I get kids who can hardly keep their eyes open at assembly, and they aren't the ones who help in the family shop either. It's the gang who never get an afternoon without an extra-curricular activity. Middle-class victims. Parents have no confidence that they'll do anything unless it's organized and paid for.'

This chapter is not about parents who let their children be over-coached in serious sporting activities. They are a special case: experts in sports medicine are alarmed by the number of burnt-out ten-year-olds in fields like skating or gymnastics, which is ironic considering that for the wide majority of British children the opposite – lack of any exercise – is a greater problem. Yet there does exist a parallel and less visible situation in which privileged infants are overloaded with activities, perfectly good in themselves but adding up to fatigue and bewilderment and children who lose the art of entertaining themselves by mucking about, dressing-up, and devising long, wonderful imaginative games together.

Of course, we know why we do it. We do it because otherwise we are afraid they would do nothing but watch television. But the answer might often be just to remove the television time, rather than replace it with too many heavily structured activities. A few of these are fine but should not be confused with playing, or socializing. What goes on when you are 'doing a course' is different in quality, whatever age you are.

If you are thinking of enrolling very young children – under eight – in any kind of course, remember this. Children taught specific skills in groups become competitive and develop

48

pecking orders with chilling rapidity. They know who is best at it and value them accordingly. Children in a mixed group amusing themselves have a different system: in the freer and more original atmosphere of ordinary play every child contributes a different talent. 'Matthew's brilliant at drawing machines, but I'm best at inventing what they're for. Rose can get right up the climbing frame and pull things up, because Sally's good at tying knots at the bottom.' It is true that learning a specific skill can build a young child's confidence; but there are other things to learn about life, and they need time too.

So take a deep breath and say to yourself the first mantra: *six is soon enough to start anything*. For some activities, seven or eight is soon enough, and for some children all special skills – even sports with rules – can wait a good deal longer. If you are already past that, skip on to teenage chapter, p.187, which deals with this subject from a different end.

Of course, there are exceptions to the 'six is early enough' rule; they are obvious and natural. Swiss and Scandinavian mountain children learn to ski as soon as they can walk, because it is the natural family thing to do. Horsey families always plonk their children on ponies as soon as they can sit up; sailing families give the tiller to the toddler as a matter of course, and parents who cook well, or do woodwork at weekends, often pass on remarkable skills to very young children. The point is that sensible parents who do this are not doing it because they think it is educational, or desirable, or smart. The snow or the fat old pony or the boat are there, and the children want to copy their parents in the same way that they might make cars out of cardboard boxes.

Where the special skills become suspect is when they are part of social ambition, or of the boring modern pressure on parents to 'develop' their children incessantly and by force; it is almost as if they were trying to build on a kitchen extension or a conservatory, striving as they are to increase the 'value' of their small child by having it taught a set of adult skills.

Examining my own conscience over the years, I have devised a set of awkward questions to ask yourself:

Does my child want to do it? Has he/she shown the faintest aptitude or interest – patted a horse, built a toy boat in the garden, been rapt by classical music on the radio, danced since she could walk?

If so, move cautiously ahead. But also ask yourself, has this plan got anything – anything – to do with the fact that the sport in question is rather chic and trendy?

Is it possible that I secretly want to be a kid again and go to the class myself? Am I compensating for memories of a damn dull childhood? If so, can I honestly say that the boredom began as young as four?

Just because you longed for a pony when you were ten, that is no reason to plonk a nervous and unwilling toddler on a riding-school nag at five.

Has this plan got anything at all to do with the fact that my neighbour put her Jason in the class and claims he got a bronze medal in it last month?

Or has it anything to do with the fact that I long for an hour off from childminding on Wednesdays, so am craftily disguising it as education undertaken for the child's sake?

Ask, answer, decide. Meanwhile here are some fruits of assorted mothers' experiences of the most common courses:

Swimming lessons Clearly very useful. Of all skills, this is the one to encourage positively.

However, once the child can swim adequately, he or she may lose interest in formal lessons and prefer mucking about with sibling (loosely supervised by you) to formal lessons designed to produce the next Duncan Goodhew. Stock up on ointments for verrucae and athlete's foot.

Riding lessons If the child doesn't like it a lot, then stop immediately. It is too expensive and dangerous for unwilling amateurs to carry on. Never mind that you have spent £100 on clothes and hat. Sell them.

If you carry on, check insurance, BHS accreditation, etc. Only remember that the accreditation schemes are concerned far more with the welfare of the horses than with any skills the staff may or may not have in dealing with young children.

Skiing lessons Same principle. Some small children love it, some hate it. There is no disgrace in reverting to a sledge.

Sailing lessons Same principle. Buy the child a neoprene wet-suit before you start: a cold wet child can't concentrate. I would never start a child sailing until he or she begged to do it, because I sail myself and I am forty-nine years old and sometimes I *still* hate it. However, if the child really enjoys it, it brings a sense of mastery and independence which is pure gold dust. As with the pony world, watch out for over-competitive parents trying to wind you up about how much better their child is doing than yours. Smile, though your heart is breaking . . .

Skating, motocross, tennis, martial arts, voltige, gymnastics If the club concerned doesn't allow single trial lessons, don't consider it. Never, ever, buy the full kit before you are sure that this is an enriching and enjoyable thing for your child to do. And if there is a governing body or accrediting council, make sure the course is approved.

Music lessons The difficulty here is knowing whether to be a laid-back parent, as above, and let the child drop out when it wants, or whether to go by the received wisdom that once begun, an instrument must be given time and practice in order for any breakthrough to be made. It is pointless letting a child give up too soon; on the other hand, if he or she never wanted to start in the first place, it is a bit harsh to force week after week of hideous scratching violin on someone who will never make a decent sound, let alone a tune. Remember that some music teachers are not very good; if nothing seems to be happening it is worth discreetly asking around.

If it still doesn't happen, give up for a while and go together to some good concerts instead. The world needs concert-goers as much as musicians.

Drama classes Watch at least two before you enrol. Or else ask other parents – the kind you trust, not the kind who always say everything their child does is brilliantly well-run. There are some pretentious idiots running drama classes for four-year-olds which are an utter waste of time; and some brilliant, life-enhancing, happy classes too.

Dancing classes Very good for developing discipline, co-ordination and an ability to point one's toes to order. For some strange reason, children fresh out of a dancing class are always in a dreadful temper, and kick their mothers. Something to do with relaxation of discipline, I suppose. Keep them in ballet shoes until the mood passes.

Foreign languages Tricky. We all know that the British and Americans don't learn enough of these, and that it is absurd not to start teaching even French until after eleven when puberty strikes and children are rightly embarrassed to be heard making foreign noises. We all know that small children soak up languages like sponges, and enjoy it. If there is a good language club for small children in your area, and especially if you might have a foreign holiday in the appropriate land, it might be worth encouraging your child that way. But if it doesn't work, it doesn't, and there are worse things that could have happened. Lose no sleep over it.

As with so much else, arranging coaching is a matter of keeping balance and a sense of humour. And above all, retain a sense of your own child's individuality. A few children don't like being taught at all, preferring to make their own explorations of the world, and can only just tolerate school. Some of them turn out to be geniuses. Comfort yourself with that thought next time Jason hides under the bed rather than be ferried to Tai Chi class.

The First Outsiders:
Babysitters, bachelors & co

The first three years of parenthood are devilishly hard work, but there is a rather soothing, sheltered quality about them nonetheless. In retrospect, anyway.

The outside world recedes, at least from your home life. You may complain about doors too narrow for double buggies, or restaurants that hate children, but on the whole you live and travel in a cosy, frantic little nursery bubble of buggies and wet-wipes, teddies and tears and damp, grubby, chubby little arms round your neck. I look now at friends whose children are under four, and rather envy them this private world: they smile, harassed but happy, through clouds of talcum powder, wiping away tears and turning aside tantrums with a hug and a joke. Their children ask easy, if rather wearing questions, like, 'What is dat?' and fall asleep suddenly, like cats.

In these early years, you have control over your little family world and create an ambience and a moral framework within which you all live more or less contentedly. But the time comes, at the age of four or five, when the child turns outwards from the family and towards the wider world. He has friends you don't know, at school or nursery. I have never forgotten the shock when my son, aged five, walking through the village, suddenly waved delightedly at a lady across the road. 'GOOD MORNING, MRS SAXBY!' he bellowed. She was one of the school helpers. The shock was only partly of pleasure; to see one's child turning outwards towards the big world is a mixed, bittersweet joy. For a child to have other child friends is easy; other adult friends may be harder to accept. But this is an emotional weaning, the moment for which the baby began rehearsing years ago, when it used to turn away from your breast in a crowded railway carriage to beam hugely at all the other passengers (leaving you horribly exposed, but then babies have no consideration).

So who are these outsider adults? Start with the species already most familiar to you:

Babysitters The odds are that while your children were very small, you had a small circle of well-known babysitters. Grannies, aunts, trusted neighbours, a childminder or a nanny. Such sitters are priceless. Women with young babies suddenly find themselves taking a new interest in certain sectors of the population, evaluating the local teenage girls with as much concentration as any teenage boy. Good babysitters are worth their weight in gold. Bad ones do not bear thinking about.

The most important thing about any babysitter is his or her brain. Don't look at the punk hair, the miniskirt or the chewing gum; look for intelligence. After all, only a very wicked person would knowingly let a child come to harm, but a stupidly well-meaning one is every bit as dangerous, and far more common. If your friend's teenage daughter (or your cleaner's aunt or whoever) looks seriously gormless to you, then don't let her babysit even for half an hour while you go next door. One of the prime signs of real stupidity is not knowing when to call for help; another is the tendency to panic and throw water on to a burning chip pan, or waste time trying to make a poisoned child vomit, or laboriously telephoning parents and getting them called out of the cinema when it would be obvious to the meanest intelligence that the only number worth dialling is 999. A good babysitter is not only friendly and fun but has a sufficiently morbid imagination to stop a child of any age going to bed cuddling a length of strangly rope, or to pick up a plastic bag blowing around on the bedroom floor. He or she will also disbelieve your child's wide-eyed, candid assurances that he is always allowed to suck boiled sweets in bed.

When children are old enough for social chat, a babysitter becomes an event, something to look forward to. Teenagers are highly glamorous beings to young children, and new adults of all ages represent a bracing challenge. 'Hello, Suzy. Are you a teenager? Do you go to discos? Shall we have a disco here?

Would you tell us a story? Do you want to see my acrobatics? Do you want to see the bubble trick that I can do with a straw?'

Faced with a nice, kind, cosy, middle-aged lady, small boys in particular like to test the boundaries of her tolerance in the same way that horses go round a new field leaning on all the fences to see if they are electric. I have a friend who left her two perfectly nice little boys, aged seven and five, with a new babysitter for one hour in the afternoon, by way of a test. She returned to find the house upside down, drawers emptied, toys scattered, furniture upturned, rude words written on slips of paper everywhere and the babysitter looking vague and worried while the boys rampaged. She was cross with the children, but equally cross with the babysitter. Adults have to know when to slam the brakes on, and have the confidence to do it: someone who was wonderful with your baby may come back three years later and be a disaster.

On the other hand, over-strict babysitters sometimes make children reluctant to let you go out at all. It is not easy to gauge what exactly is going on, especially if you have a hyperbolic child. 'Mummy,' says the little girl, 'Katy is dreadfully cruel to us.' Mummy panics inwardly, envisaging child abuse, chainings, beatings . . .

'Yes, darling, what does she do?' she asks as calmly as possible. Child announces, 'Well, I apsley hate her. She does awful things to me.' Mummy (shovelling down Valium): 'What, darling?' 'Well,' says the child, pleased to have such close attention, 'I was getting undressed for bathtime and she told me to put my vest in the dirty basket. She said I had to pick it up myself. And she said she wouldn't get my rubber duck off the shelf unless I picked it up.' Half an hour's questioning having failed to elicit any further evidence of unnatural cruelty, Mummy decides to leave Katy on the babysitting list after all.

The greatest bugbear of parents seems to be the Mating Pair of babysitters. They spend the evening with an uncomfortable vision of Katy and Jason snogging passionately while the children shriek for help. A friend who lives in an area where you can't get babysitters unless they bring their boyfriend too (largely for protection) offers the following rule-of-thumb:

'Check up with the parents. If your house is the only place where Katy and Jason are going to be alone, don't do it. If the teenagers have plenty of other chances to chew one another's ears, then risk it. A nice girl who is a safe babysitter isn't going to turn into a monster just because she's got a bit of company. Only do listen to what your children say about them afterwards.'

With babysitters you have not, quite, ceded control. They come into your own house and become temporary, family members. The next level of outside society that impinges on a child is more far-flung.

Parents of friends From babyhood onwards most children get quite accustomed to staying for hours, meals, occasionally nights at their friends' houses. The first 'sleepover' is a vast adventure, involving bagfuls of furry animals, special cuddlies, last-minute misgivings and whispered instructions to the other mummy about lavatory habits. The home-based mummy tends to sit by the telephone all evening in an agony of concern. Some children sleep happily at their friends' houses at the age of two or three; others never pluck up the nerve until well after seven. But it is a godsend to be able to hand a child over for the night; not only does it ease the babysitting problem for very late nights, but it means you have easy and untraumatic cover for any emergency that might befall you (or a sibling) and involve a night in hospital. It is good for children's morale, too; after a night at a cosy friend's house they come back with a swagger you can see from the other end of the path.

Ways to smooth the way to a trustful sleepover are:

Only do it with parents whom you and your child know pretty well. Don't ignore any signs that your child actually dislikes or fears a certain daddy, or mummy, even if you know for sure there is no sinister reason. Everyone has a right to their dislikes.

Tell the other mother every detail of your child's idiosyncrasies: lambskin fleece, teddy bear under the head, light on the landing, pyjama jacket on back to front, dry cornflakes for breakfast, whatever. Don't assume that every family eats when yours does; you might drop off a child at five thirty, unfed, because you eat at six and then discover the next morning that he had no supper at all because they had eaten at five and he was shy to ask.

You may pass on any current fears or nightmare subjects. It is very reassuring to a child when a comparatively strange adult seems perfectly au fait with his feelings about Rottweilers, trapdoors suddenly opening, or Nu-killer explosions. But if you are going to do this, be sure that the other mother is not the sort of dingbat who, at bedtime, well-meaningly starts mentioning the said Rottweilers, bombs, etc.

If you say you will be there straight after breakfast, or even before it, be there. One betrayal may mean a whole year before the child tries again.

When it is your turn to be the hostess, remember:

Leave lights on all the way to the lavatory.

Know that even the toughest and most macho little boy likes to be offered, at least, a bedtime kiss. Even if it is just so that he can say 'Eeugh! Not likely' and get a laugh from his friend in the other bed.

If your child and the visitor decide to share a bed, or lay out mattresses on the floor and camp, or practise some other eccentricity, then give it a trial. This is an exercise in independence, after all. Don't fuss.

Don't do it before a schoolday if you can help it. There is a rough equation whereby for every extra child-age-year under ten in a house, the whole lot sleep a full hour less.

The wider world Beyond the cosy circle of home and school and Other Mummies, there is the wider world. In my view, the wider and more eccentric a child's circle of acquaintances the better. I do not see that there is any advantage for a child in growing up with the belief that everyone in the world has a steady job, is married with children about his age, and belongs to the same social class.

If you happen to live somewhere reasonably comfortable and affluent, it is not too difficult to present a child with a never-ending procession of sensible mummies, old ladies, new babies, friendly daddies, and other children. But there are other sections of humankind too. With a cautious parental eye in the middle distance, young children can make great friends with elderly men, teenagers, the eccentric, the single, the mentally handicapped, nuns and monks, restless travellers, gays and lesbians. Within the family, some of the best relationships are between children and their bachelor uncles and aunts, who make no concessions to the cosy child-centred world but introduce a wholly welcome element of mayhem, irresponsibility and fun ('Aunt Susie,' wrote one child, 'always brings us things like bubblegum-flavour lip ice or jam from aeroplanes. Once when we had a meal at Covent Garden we couldn't find a parking space so we parked on a double yellow line and every five minutes me or Susanna had to go out and check there wasn't a traffic warden about. She paid us five pence every time we checked. She's a super aunt!')

Every well-regulated, well-disciplined, responsible family needs occasionally to find a bachelor uncle or friend unexpectedly snoring on the sofa in the morning with a crashing hangover but still willing to teach a nephew how to make a banana into a convincing model of a pig being sick. Some of the happiest memories of childhood in autobiographies seem to concern friendships with tramps or eccentric relatives. Now that the extended families have dispersed, there is a real risk of bringing a child up too bland, too safe, too utterly Mothercare. The soul, as well as the body, requires roughage.

A lot of these friendships need, I repeat it, middle-distance parental supervision. Perverts and paedophiles do exist; often they seem to be very nice people, and often the 'grooming' process of seduction lasts months, even years, before anything untoward happens. Later chapters speak more of this. But in addition, even the moral philosophy lessons dispensed by a certain class of bachelor uncles may need a bit of discreet counterbalancing ('My Uncle Neddy,' a child once remarked to a horrified acquaintance of mine, 'told me the Rule of Life was, never nick a thing you can't flog. I don't think Jesus would approve of that, do you?'). But their importance is immeasurable. To ensure a balanced view of humanity, a growing child's world must be populated by varied but likeable and trustworthy people if only to counterbalance the need to warn about:

Strangers It is axiomatic that children, growing independent, should be told not to talk to strangers. It is also very sad. It has corrupted public manners and loosened social cohesion; has made it impossible for respectable adults to upbraid rude or disruptive children in a public place, the way they used to, and encouraged children in the habit of turning aside in fear and detachment from the elderly, the unfortunate and the handicapped who may accost them with no ill at all in mind.

In more innocent times, lonely old people in parks could chatter happily to children, telling them their life story and enjoying harmless casual friendships. Some parents consider that it is enough merely to tell children never to *go* with strangers, especially in a car. But even so, a lot of expert opinion is that this won't do. A friendly child who has been drawn into conversation, harmlessly, perhaps more than once, is going to forget that this person is technically a 'stranger'. For children under nine or ten the only safe rule is no talking at all, unless a parent or guardian is present. As they get to the older end of this spectrum, however, children can be allowed to sort out 'safe' conversational arenas – for instance, to understand that there is no harm in a group of children on a bus joshing with the conductor, or in offering to pick up shopping in a busy precinct for a harassed lady who has just dropped it all over the floor.

The Bad Stranger warning is a horrible one to have to give, just when your child is expanding into love and interest for the whole world. But you can't shirk it, and it would be madness to water it down too much. Some formulae for giving it are:

'Remember the wolf dressed up in grandmother's clothes? Well, unfortunately, there are some people a bit like that. They seem friendly and look nice, but inside they are as bad as wolves. So don't talk to strangers, just in case.'

'Most people are friendly to children, and wouldn't harm them. But there are a few – who look just the same – who have got a sort of illness that makes them want to take children away from their parents and hurt them. So don't talk to strangers, just in case.'

You don't have to give a child nightmares by spelling out the atrocities which have happened to other children: the threat of 'being taken away' is quite terrifying enough to ram the message home. The point to keep stressing is that most people are good and kind BUT that you can't judge by appearances.

It is also worth stressing to your child that you would never send anyone to fetch him without telling the teachers, and doing, or sending, something to prove it was the right person. This may be over-effective, but never mind. When I was eight I flatly refused to go home with someone from my father's office in Lille, although Reverend Mother and three other nuns knew it was OK and tried every tactic of persuasion they knew. I hid my small brothers behind me and stood my ground like Joan of Arc.

Casually, in conversations, also mention the following:

'Sometimes bad strangers might pretend to be your parents or teachers, when they are trying to drag you off. Nobody would blame you for rudeness if you ran away, screamed "He's not my daddy!" or even bit them. Call out to the good strangers to help you. Policemen are safest; or lady shop-keepers, or traffic wardens.'

'Sometimes people you know quite well, and who are usually very kind, might ask you to do strange things which you feel are wrong. You don't have to do them. You belong to yourself, not to anyone else. Even your parents.'

'Bottoms and willies are private. Nothing wrong with them, they're just private. You don't have to pay any attention to anyone who wants to show you his willy or see yours, unless he's a doctor and your mummy or daddy are there.'

There is a fine balance between encouraging friendliness and lack of prejudice, and safeguarding a child who is sometimes outside alone. Most of us err on the side of caution, but there is a real risk of painting the whole of the world outside the family as a nest of murderers, perverts and child-killers.

I happen to feel strongly about being open to other people beyond a closed circle of friends and relatives; you may not be so inclined. You may be a bit of an isolationist and not mind the risk of producing a mistrustful, xenophobic child. You may lay the warnings on thick, with no watering-down at all. Well, fine. But beware: bear in mind the risk that your child will one day find out that one stranger is perfectly friendly, not monstrous at all. And knowing your horror of strangers he might not mention this to you, but quietly and disastrously assume that you were wrong about all the other strangers, too.

The Dawn of Discipline:
Sense, slaps and self-defence

Oh dear. I have not been looking forward to writing this chapter, not one bit. The first time I wrote about children and discipline was a decade ago, and the subject has got no easier in the interim.

To use the word 'discipline' is the quickest way to rattle, disconcert, or infuriate other parents. You suspect that they think your child is either unmanageably spoilt or unnaturally repressed. You make excuses, but all the time you are thinking much the same about theirs. The only thing that gives both parties temporary relief is uniting in a sort of ritualized Two Minutes' Hate against some other parent in the newspapers that week, like the wretched idiot who got himself arrested and put through the courts after he lost his cool and smacked his daughter's bare bottom in the dentist's waiting room. But after that, any two families will drift apart again, because there are no two families with an absolutely identical approach to discipline, order, family crime and punishment. It is a snake pit.

This chapter is mostly about younger children. Some of the basic principles endure into teenage years, others become ridiculous. But as the question of teenagers comes up later on, it is simpler to consider the beginnings of family law and order, with inexperienced parents, children changing and developing at breakneck speed, and major considerations of safety and rationality causing parents to lay down far more rules and prohibitions than they ever would with a great thumping teenager.

Begin, though, with the reflection that there are many styles of family life. If you will forgive me, I will plunge back into nice easy stereotypes for a moment.

Imagine a street, or block of flats. At No. 1, Mr and Mrs Careful always make the children write thank you letters, eat up their spinach, stand when a visitor enters the room and switch their reading lights out at seven. They are not allowed to put their feet on the sofas even though they have separate indoor and outdoor shoes. They look wistfully at the crocodiles of scrubbed little children from the nearby private school.

Next door live the Reckless family. Their children dash about with uncombed hair, climb on the furniture with Wellington boots on, go to bed when they feel like it and call their parents names. However, they are avid readers and very musical. Their parents would rather like to send them to a bohemian 'free school'. They sit down and eat together every day.

At No. 3 live the Grumps. Their children likewise have no bedtime, never eat at table but live on a running buffet of crisps and sausage rolls, and play in the middle of the road with a homemade go-cart constructed of all the wheels missing from local prams in the last six months.

Now, the pecking order here is more complicated than it looks at first sight. Obviously, Mr and Mrs Careful think the other two families are appalling; on the other hand, they do slap their children quite often, which is very shocking to the Reckless family. The Recklesses never slap, nor do they let their children hit anyone: it is the only solid rule in their chaotic, artistic household. They think it is uncivilized when Mr Careful endorses fighting – 'They've got to stand up for themselves,' he says.

The Recklesses look down on the Grumps, largely because the Grump children spend too much time watching television and kicking tin cans up and down the street. But the Grumps despise the Careful children because they tell tales on each other, and the Reckless children because they use rude language. Also, the Grump children clearly have their heart in the right place: they were the only ones who went on the latest charity walk and raised money for the Save the Children Fund. The Carefuls were worried about their children getting too tired, and the Recklesses forgot the date.

The only thing that unites all six parents is a deep contempt for the Nouveaus, in the rather bigger house up the road, because they delegate the whole question of behaviour to a hired nanny and an expensive boarding school. It need hardly be said that the Nouveaus think all three of the other families are bringing up ghastly little hooligans.

With such widely diverging styles of family life, who is going to say what 'discipline' consists of? In one of those families a rude word is a heinous crime but a punch-up isn't; in another it would be a serious offence to get in late for family tea but perfectly all right to enthuse about Mahler even if you did have your mouth full. And so on.

As the second part of this book explores further, family life has to find its own tempo, its own code, its own private kind of strength. Discipline is part of this; not just teaching children a code of reasonable behaviour, but ensuring that parents share the same values, and recognizably sing from the same sheet.

If you look at discipline in this light, it becomes less puzzling and alarming an idea. The man in the dentist's waiting room was out of order, not because he slapped the child but because he lost his sense of decorum and proportion. She had a painful tooth, the place was public, and she was a girl old enough to mind about bare bottoms. He, frankly, was panicking. Had the courts not become involved, this was a situation which should have concluded in the father apologizing to the child, and all concerned having learnt a salutary lesson about what extreme provocation can do to otherwise loving family members. The relationship could have been (perhaps was, in the end) strengthened by the moment of disproportionate weakness.

So, discipline. However much I haver on about family cultures and loving relationships, I fear there is no getting away from the awful fact that you, the parent, are in charge of behaviour among your tribe.

Here goes.

How soon do you start?

There are still a few batty authoritarian midwives and nannies around who truly believe you can discipline a new baby – 'stick to four-hourly feeding and let her cry, dear, she's got to know who's boss'; there are even more who regularly slap children under two (pointless and unkind). You and I know they are wrong, but we also know the sort of weak-kneed family where the doctrine of demand feeding for new babies gets extended, year by year, until parents (oh, all right, mothers) are providing demand washing-up after spoilt teenagers, and eventually demand lending of the family car five nights a week without thanks. We shrink from that, but on the other hand we don't want to be ruthless disciplinarians, do we? A family, after all, is not the Chinese Army. The answer is that you start gently, humorously, as soon as a baby is to be observed looking at you to see what you think of a particular activity. Not far short of two, in my experience. Before this stage you just lift the child clear of the knife, or electric plug, saying the N-word if you like; after that, you try a 'No' and be prepared to have to do the lifting bit as well. For quite a while.

What is discipline, anyway?

A dangerous word, certainly. Politicians bang us over the head with it whenever someone throws a beer can off a football terrace: 'No parental discipline,' they say. On the other hand, earnest liberals intone platitudes about 'instilling self-discipline rather than obedience to petty rules'; while back home, fathers struggle in exhausted from the office and roar, 'That child doesn't know the meaning of discipline!' when a chippy five-year-old won't go to bed.

And all the time we are haunted by a vague Victorian bogey of merciless discipline: by Mr Murdstone and Wackford Squeers and the image of sobbing tots being shut in dark cupboards for hours.

So let us strip the humbug from the word. Discipline is a word closely allied to 'disciple'; it is about learning. It is the individual's ability to order his conduct. It needs to be taught. Get that straight; discipline is that element of good behaviour which has been instilled from outside, however gently, and is endorsed by the reason of the individual.

It is NOT the same thing as the natural kindness, or quietness, or interested concentration on a task which we often see in

65

a child. When a timid child doesn't run away from Mummy in the road, there is no discipline involved. He just doesn't dare to. On the other hand, the child who is fearless and curious and struggles successfully to control his impulse to dart off is worthy of high praise and reward. There is nothing necessarily 'good' about a naturally quiet child who is happy to draw pictures for hours on a long, dull train journey; he is being no better and no worse than the brat across the aisle who runs up and down and bounces on the seats. They just have different natures, and as they grow older, each will have to learn to control the instincts that nature gave him. Discipline will drive the bookish child out into the fresh air to get a bit of exercise; discipline will keep the rowdy one sitting quietly over his books to get a bit of learning. Two children may be behaving identically, but one is being 'good' with great effort, and the other is just doing what comes naturally but which suits adult convenience at that moment. It is necessary to notice effort and praise it; that is why early behaviour should be affectionately supervised by someone – parent or carer – who knows the individual child very well, and can give credit where it is due.

How do you teach children that there are rules?

Obeying rules is only a small part of self-discipline. Rules are necessary to keep society together and individuals safe, but real self-control goes deeper than that.

What we are talking about is the process of learning three things: self-control; consideration for others; and how to wait for what you want. ('Delayed gratification', the psychologists call it.) A brand-new baby has none of these things; it screams when it is hungry or uncomfortable, doesn't care what effect it has on you at three in the morning, and is incapable of waiting. Over the next five or six years, he is going to have to grow out of this screaming selfishness, and you are going to have to help. But most parents, unless they have been teachers or Scoutmasters or regimental sergeant majors, have no experience of imposing discipline on other human beings; besides, they love this little creature to death and can't bear to see it sad.

With a child under about two, there is no point at all in getting cross: you just keep on removing the forbidden thing. However, when the stage comes when the child goes for the light socket while glancing over its shoulder at you, or even giggling, then you can inject a bit more steel into your tone. No violence is necessary: a really serious, fierce 'NO!' is as shocking as a slap to a baby that is used to affection. About this stage, too, comes the beginning of the vital lesson of delayed gratification. A child learns that it has to wait for its supper because you are still making it.

Again, you have to gauge very skilfully whether it is worthwhile ticking a toddler off for whining and pestering for the food; a child could be desperately hungry and totally out of control on one occasion, and on another behave the same way just as a whiny try-on. In the earlier stage, losing your temper is fatal: it frightens without teaching anything. You have to maintain a Pollyannaish sort of gentle firmness, even if it means you walk out of the room occasionally and have a good swear at the cat. Once it becomes obvious that the child knows it is winding you up – usually over three years old – I personally think it does no harm to shout occasionally. Children have to learn sometime that Mummies have feelings too.

But never sulk with a small child: they forgive and forget in a matter of seconds, and so must you. There is nothing illogical about the occasional sequence of 'SHUT UP! Come on, pet, into the bath, whoops, there's a lovely girl!' uttered almost in the same breath.

It helps the process of discipline if you take the trouble to explain things. 'We can't go to the playground because the plumber's coming. If he doesn't come, we won't have any hot water for bathtime. No, we have to have baths, else we'd get so dirty we might get poorly,' etc., etc. It also helps if you point out something which children can't be expected to know before they start school, which is that everyone has to obey sets of rules. The average four-year-old is utterly fascinated by the idea of laws, police, prisons and the rest of it, and it cheers him up to think that his all-powerful parents also live under some sort of outside control.

In a casual way, you can also point out when you yourself are doing something you don't particularly like in order to help someone else: 'Oh dear, better take this heavy old washing to the laundrette for Mrs Biggs next door, she's a bit poorly.' 'Better pick up all our picnic rubbish and throw it away, it wouldn't be nice for other people to find, would it?' (However, it takes a certain skill to do this without giving your child the idea that other people are nothing but a blasted nuisance.)

At all stages, the best guideline is to know your own child very well. My son, for example, went through an infuriating phase at four when every time we refused him anything he would shout, 'You poo-face!' and storm out of the room slamming the door. From an older child this would be grounds for chasing after him and exacting an apology ('Don't speak to your father like that!') but what was actually happening was that a very small child was accepting a rule, stopping his demands, and then suddenly letting off steam in the only way he could think of. So we decided to overlook being called poo-faces.

In the end, the only kind of discipline worth having is self-discipline; otherwise, once the brakes are off, there is nothing to stop a grown child from running wild. The offspring of dreadfully strict homes often go seriously off the rails, once Father or Mother or Nanny or Teacher is well out of sight. Self-control is the only reliable control, and you'll never have self-control until you accept the idea of 'delaying gratification'. This is exceptionally difficult to instil today, in a fairly affluent society where adults are constantly wooed by credit firms and shops to 'take the waiting out of wanting'. However far down this primrose path you have gone yourself, you owe it to your child to keep at least some of the waiting in his wanting. It doesn't have to be repressive: the good old principle of 'reinforcing good behaviour' is perfectly effective. Every time a child saves a sweet for later or waits with dignity for a birthday treat, you can let him know that you find it, and him, more special for that perseverance. If he then shares it with another child, no praise is too lavish (only do it privately, later).

Some common battlegrounds

Whingeing Whingeing, whining, moaning, call it what you will, is worth treating as an offence (unless the child is very small, very tired or very stressed). For everyone's sake, campaign against it from the start; for whining brings a parent nearer to smacking point than many graver misdeeds. From earliest years you can – lightly – insist that anyone asking for something in a whiny voice should ask for it again, in a nice voice. Even if you do this religiously from the age of two, however, the sound of aggrieved whingeing will still be with you for some years. It can be difficult to know how to treat it, since its only real fault is that it drives you, personally, mad.

Some people have a system – which I dislike – of pretending the child has changed identity. 'Oh, where's Timmy? There's a horrid little boy come instead who whines. I wish Timmy would come back . . .' There is something creepy about this popular line.

However, I have at times resorted very successfully to a claim that my ears have been fitted with 'whine filters' so that I actually cannot hear demands made in a complaining tone of voice. With a bit of convincing acting from the parent, a child will half-believe this – he knows it isn't real, but acts as if it were. It is also a bit of a joke, and saves resorting to punishments or antisocial roaring. However, beware of the DIY-minded child who comes at you with a toy hammer and screwdriver to disconnect your whine filters.

Eating If there is one truly futile battle in this area, it is the battle over 'eating up'. Eating should not be a matter of virtue or naughtiness, only fuel or pleasure. Children use odd eating habits as a lever to annoy parents, but they also have genuine oddities of preference. Either way, do not rise to provocation. A lump of brown bread and peanut butter followed by a bit of fruit is a balanced meal. So are many other combinations and snacks. The only actual rules worth trying to enforce over food are: no junk between meals except on special days, and no sweet or pudding until you've had some protein and something green.

Try not to scream aloud when your child goes to a friend's house and keenly tucks in to meat and two veg he wouldn't touch at home; try not to be neurotic about junk food at parties and on outings. In ninety-nine per cent of cases it does no harm as an occasional treat, however depressed you may get at the luminous orange stain around your child's mouth.

I am not going to attempt to treat the complex subject of anorexia right here; merely to observe that it is a very stupid and dangerous habit for parents to nag at either the slightly plump child or the slightly skinny one, and particularly dangerous for fathers to betray any sign at all that they think their daughters are less than utterly gorgeous. If you really do have a circular daughter, help her eat sensibly but *do not mock.*

Fighting All children sometimes fight. Wouldn't you, if you didn't have the vocabulary to make your case verbally against aggressors, and hadn't developed the sort of long view of life which helps you to stay your hand when it itches to slap a spouse, or boss, or unbearably slow and rude counter clerk? Children have to learn the practical and moral limitations of physical action, that is all. It is done little by little, in the family circle and the nursery, by adults who must be willing to sound like Joyce Grenfell a great deal of the time ('George. Don't do that'). Eventually the message will get through. It helps to have some ground rules. A very useful one is to insist that any object which has been used as a weapon will be taken away for the rest of the day. This should apply to all members of the family; if Daddy should happen to do a bad-tempered thing with the wooden spoon, banging the worktop in frustration, a great and comedic show should be made of taking away the wooden spoon. This total weapons ban helps to limit danger in any sibling fights that may break out.

It helps also if any object fought *over* – like a disputed toy – gets taken into protective adult custody, made a sort of ward of court, while the rights and wrongs of the situation are calmly discussed. Some parents swear by making children formally 'make it up' and shake hands; others use 'down time', putting protagonists into separate rooms to cool down. I have never

70

done much of this, partly because I am the kind of nervous parent who does not like to be left wondering what a small, emotionally unbalanced child might get up to all alone, but largely because at the age of peak sibling violence we happened to spend a large part of the year on a small sailing boat with our three- and five-year-olds, and there was nowhere to put them anyway. This compelled us to sort out problems on the spot, and I think it was no bad thing. The same effect can be achieved in a monsoon downpour on a caravan site.

Whatever your tactics, remember that as a parent you have to be the peacekeeping force. The best peacekeeping forces are mature, moral, fair, and above all utterly immune to insult or ingratitude. If you start getting emotional and screaming like a four-year-old yourself, just get the hell out of the room for a minute, or stare at the ceiling, and get a grip.

Smacking Here the ways divide. Some countries already ban all parental smacking; Britain is undergoing a furious debate as to whether we should follow suit. Everyone except a few mad floggers is in broad agreement that you shouldn't hit babies or tiny toddlers, that you should never give more than one sharp slap, and that you should in no circumstances, ever, hit a child on the head, or with an instrument – stick, spoon or strap.

But a vociferous lobby still demands that 'any hostile physical act against a child', including restraint, should be illegal. I have done quite a few interviews on the subject, and the main proponents of this idea, I would like to tell you, have teenage or adult children and distinctly short memories. When you try to describe what it is actually like living with a stroppy four- or five-year-old, they merely look blank. But the arguments have been fascinating to follow.

Basically, the case against smacking is: it doesn't work; it leads on to harder hitting, even child abuse; it is symbolic of a bad attitude to children, that they have less than full human rights. We don't hit prisoners, or even murderers, any more. The alternative that they suggest is to 'reason' with the child, or to 'withdraw your approval' – a pompous phrase.

The case for smacking is: it does sometimes work; it doesn't need to lead on to harder hitting. For every thousand families where children are occasionally smacked, perhaps one descends towards real violence. Mother cats do it all the time. It is not symbolic of anything, but instinctive and as natural a part of mothering as a cuddle. It is a good way for children to learn that they can drive you that bit too far.

Advocates of the odd smack also point out that 'reasoning' can turn into remorseless nagging, and that 'withdrawing approval' can cover all sorts of chilly mental cruelty. Children are impulsive, dramatic beings and as the writer Lynette Burrows put it, 'the brief spirited drama of a slap' can knock them back on course a great deal faster and less depressingly than endless nagging. I have slapped my children now and then, and its main virtue is that it sometimes brings a rapid end to an episode which would, under any other system, have lingered unpleasantly on. 'I said you don't kick babies and you don't spit at people', accompanied by not particularly violent swipes across the bottom can sometimes seem a better solution than: 'Now then, you mustn't kick, you know that – how would you like it if she kicked you? She did kick you? And take your car? Well, she's a lot younger and you should have told me, not kicked back . . . no, you mustn't spit, it isn't nice – no, it isn't, don't be cheeky or no pudding for you at lunchtime – Frederick, you must never ever call me that again. Go to your room.'

If Frederick will not go to his room, his mother will have to shout, or take him by force (restraint might be illegal, though, remember?). By lunchtime he will have forgotten what he did, and withdrawing his pudding will seem a very petty and nasty thing to do. He will feel a vague, generalized resentment all day. If you had lovingly, exasperatedly, slapped him (and then given back the car his wretched sister stole), the whole thing would have been over in seconds. OK, you have affronted his dignity as a human being, but at least in his mind kicking and spitting will forever be associated with a loss of personal dignity.

But whatever you think – and there are half a dozen other valid ways of handling the tiresome little scenario above – the real damage done by the anti-smacking campaigners has been to the already low self-esteem of parents – mothers, in particular. Frankly, most of us are driven to a smack now and then: either instinct tells us it is right, or weariness and exasperation make us do it – not very hard – to relieve our own feelings. So when respected childcare gurus say smacking is a bad, bad, wicked thing and 'invariably' leads on to child abuse, we panic. Our instincts are all wrong! We are Bad Mothers! We always suspected we were, from the very first moment our natural childbirth turned into a forceps drama. We are cruel harridans, who need the Law to keep us in order. It takes very little, especially in the cold Nordic cultures, to make mothers feel wretchedly inadequate, and it does no good. From what I have seen in normally loving families, what happens is that there is a short phase – from about three to five – when smacking happens naturally. After five a child begins to develop a certain additional dignity, and if your antennae are sensitive to the reality of that child, somehow you hesitate to shatter that dignity with a smack. If you are still smacking a seven-year-old, it is worth reconsidering matters. For one thing, he or she is more amenable to reason, bribes and threats. You can withdraw privileges by now without being unfair, simply because of the child's longer memory. Once children start getting pocket money, you can use fines to great effect. (Kicking and spitting, 5p per offence. But one is not heartless. You can win back your 5ps by deeds of great kindness, helpfulness and consideration.)

Other punishments are various, and depressing to list: deprivation of television, of treat food, sending to bedrooms, banning friends coming round for a week, and so on. The more complicated they get, the more depressing: remember the awful aunt in the Saki story who whenever one child was bad would invent a wonderful treat from which only the criminal was excluded. The only thing to say about any sort of punishment is STOP IT FROM ESCALATING. All human conflict has a fatal tendency to spiral upwards if it is not stopped by one strong-minded participant; that is how smacking turns into beating, and reasoning turns into mental cruelty. Usually parents stop it getting out of control; it is when they use the power of parenthood to vent emotions which are not much to do with the actual child that disasters occur.

Whatever you do, don't let things escalate. If for some reason you are alone and friendless, or feel it; if your rebukes are turning into furious shouting half the day; if the pocket money fines reach weeks ahead and you lash out mindlessly before considering the justice of the case, then take steps. Get out of the room, brush your hair, give yourself a small treat. Look at the photographs of your tormentor as a beloved baby, and cry if you feel like it. Then look at the present and realize how well you have actually done so far, to raise a child healthy and bonny and bright and defiant. Even the defiance is a tribute to loving and non-violent upbringing.

And if you have reached such a catharsis of unhappiness and conflict, remember something else. Love is better than justice. Having a punishment cancelled out of love is not, as some would claim, a sure recipe for a spoilt child. It can be the best lesson of all. Never mind that the little demon got clean away with breaking the bathroom mirror in a temper, ripping up a new book or calling you a stupid old cow for the fifteenth time in a morning: if you have had a dreadful row, then have the grace sometimes to drown resentments in a hug and a laugh. Even apologize for your own temper. How else can a child learn to do the same?

Snips and Snails:
Are boys different?

Well, yes, they are. Of course they are. Their body chemistry is different, likewise their musculature and the physical wiring of their very brains. Even if you dress them in identical dungarees and cut their hair short, the difference between a very masculine little boy and a very feminine little girl is fully apparent by the time each is two years old.

Among more average children there may be more blurring of the line, more cheerful confusion of roles: little boys have tea parties, little girls have war games, and in the dressing-up box it is a toss-up who gets to the Scheherezade spangled veil first, and who the Hussar's jacket. By nursery-time some boys and some girls have withdrawn into voluntary purdah among their own kind, while others are still making best friends irrespective of gender. At school, you watch them grow gradually apart, one lot to the hopscotch corner and the other chasing a ball; later, they eye each other up from the safety of their respective gangs; still later, they pair up in earnest and become friends and lovers.

But they are different. Despite all the vast intellectual and emotional common ground, despite the advance of women and the way that every calling is now considered equally open to either sex, in some important respects girls and boys will always grow up differently. Parents need to admit this to themselves. It has been difficult, these past few decades, because quite rightly parents were urged not to force their boys and girls into narrow, constricting stereotypes of the kind which caused so much misery and frustration in other times, when gentlewomen could not earn their living or men show their emotions. It is right that we should pause before assuming that girls want dolls and boys want cars, or making girls do housework while boys do not. But there are differences, and we ignore them at our peril.

75

Many of those differences are scattered all through this book, and sometimes the he/she pronoun is used one way or another for a very good reason. Here, in a sketchy impressionistic form, I have just tried to round up some of the most important, and most widely noted, differences which affect the way you look after them. Every rule I cite will have its exceptions; but as caricatures they may be helpful.

In babyhood the differences are not important. Some say that boys are cuddlier, but some boys are most definitely not. Equal scepticism should meet claims that girls are quieter and less prone to tantrums. Didn't apply to mine, I can tell you. However, every experiment ever done shows that parents respond differently to a baby depending on what colour ribbon the experimenters put on it. Boys are encouraged to physical endeavour and not to cry – 'Ah, brave boy! Go on, pull yourself up! Whoops, only a bump' – while girls are coddled and treated as pretty objects – 'Who's Mummy's beautiful princess? Careful, don't fall over . . .'
This is obviously not a very good idea. Watch it.

From 3 to 5 real differences start to appear in the way that children play. They are not the ones that cliché would expect (dolls versus cars) but subtler. Girls seem to be hard-wired to be interested in relationships and feelings. Their imaginary world, and their daily friendships, start to use the language of emotion more freely than boys. Teddies, Duplo set firemen, plastic dinosaurs etc. are 'sad' or 'happy' or getting married. They speak of Best Friends and change them, often, making portentous announcements about which friends they hate that day. The idea of concealing feelings, or being duplicitous generally, starts to appeal to them. They also, as a rule, come earlier to a sense of how they seem to the outer world. Some go so far as to preen, many indulge in tears for show, and most do a certain amount of flirting.
Boys are more straightforward. If they have enemies it is temporary, and pragmatic, and they are more ready to fight physically, and more ready to forgive and play with the enemy

again. It is not true that only girls tell tales, but boys are slightly more likely to settle their problems themselves by pushing the offender over.

With this refreshing directness, though, comes a tendency to what we now call 'emotional illiteracy'. They are slower to sympathise than girls, and less likely to empathise with the suffering of other people or creatures. Of course some boys are naturally gentle, but others – otherwise perfectly nice – need careful watching when they are with animals or insects which can't fight their tendency towards cruel experiment. It is stupid to ignore this possibility, but fruitless to get upset about it. Just because your child did something awful to a frog does not mean he is necessarily a psychopath. But he needs teaching.

5–11 Schoolboys really do start to be different from schoolgirls quite early on. One difference is physical: their bodies demand to run and jump, especially early in the day, and they truly suffer if there is no outlet for this fizzing energy. Primary schools where the children are delivered by car and go straight into class report that boys are disruptive. If they let them run hard round the playground three or four times before they came in, things would improve.

Girls, meanwhile, have a parallel overpowering urge to socialise. Their pressing need is ten minutes' chitter-chatter with their best, second-best and auxiliary friends.

Boys are generally first to offer a challenge to authority, or at least to distance themselves from it and enjoy the sensation of breaking rules. They are shocked and horrified to find knots of little girls in the primary school playground together, testing one another on their times tables. This, to boys, seems plain revolting.

Girls – because of their interest in feelings and relationships – are often more voracious recreational readers than boys. Boys may need to be wooed with non-fiction books about spacecraft or ships, or with bloodcurdling thrillers about heroic chaps defusing atom bombs with their teeth. It is plain cruel for schools to force boys to read *Jane Eyre*. The damn book has no hero. Girls, on the other hand, love reading stuff about orphans and Little Princesses being hard done by.

Very boyish boys like risk, and dislike thinking things through to their consequences. Even if your son is a quiet sensible sort, you have to watch out when his friends come round. When you get two or three of them together they do crazier and crazier things, egging one another on. Girls, on the other hand, are much safer *en masse* than singly, because one at least of the group will urge caution. Both genders need outdoor and physical education but broadly speaking it is for different reasons: with boys, lessons on safety equipment and the right way to do things makes them safer, with girls it overcomes any natural timidity.

Growing up Girls, we all know, are particularly prone to peer group pressure and a desire to match the skinny, moody images sold by glossy magazines. Or, at best, to be just like their peer group and the right size to swap clothes with them. But these days, there are so many sharp positive role models for women, from media to industry, and such a preponderance of strong-minded women teachers, that girls' level of confidence is generally pretty high. Higher than my generation's was, for certain.

Boys, on the other hand, may go very short indeed of good role models. There are a lot of absent or neutral fathers, a great shortage of male teachers especially at primary level, a prevailing social contempt for establishment leaders like politicians (who are mainly male) and a terrible load of stupid inarticulate yobs offered to them as models on pop radio and pulp films. Even the famous sportsmen are rarely very helpful role models any more, being often petulant, unfaithful, drugged or pig-stupid. This is a real problem. If your son shows signs of having a hero who *is* a hero, facilitate study of this person as much as you can . . .

The identity crisis of growing boys – and the creeping feminization of education – has led to a situation where in the middle years and often right up to GCSE, boys lag behind girls in academic achievement. This is so often written about that it depresses boys terribly; try to be aware of this so that you can help counteract it. Something else which helps girls do better than boys in school is the shift of emphasis away from the short, sharp, virile challenge of the examination room and towards the meticulous slog of 'coursework'. Boys are more likely than girls to be invigorated by deadlines. Girls are more likely to panic at exam time. Both need help.

Puberty is experienced differently by the two sexes. Boys may get a sense that their bodies are outrunning them, and be baffled and awkward and hulking and surly as a result. Girls go into dreams of perfection: perfect love, perfect success, a perfect body, beautiful friendships, and get disappointed every time. But the result of this difference is that brothers and sisters may annoy one another unbearably during the period of galloping puberty; boys by jeering at their sisters' pretensions and girls by being haughty about their hobbledehoy brothers.

It helps – it *really, really* helps – if both parents are at hand, and living civilly and affectionately together during the period when boys and girls painfully metamorphose into men and women. It is yet another very good reason to avoid divorce, at almost all costs.

It isn't that they want to be just like you (ugh! gross!). But however scornful they seem of your clothes, values and sa-aa-aad lives, it is good for them to know that there is at least one fairly reasonable way that someone with the same sort of genes as theirs can be a viable grown-up.

It is, at least, a fallback position.

Nobody's Got No Class: What is good behaviour, anyway?

There is a wonderful song in the musical *Chicago*, delivered by the two most reprehensible characters in that dark, cynical story of jazz age murder and dodgy lawyering. Together, Matron Mamma Martin and jailbird Velma Kelly sing:

> Whatever happened to fair dealing and pure ethics and nice manners . . .?
> Whatever happened to 'please may I' and 'Yes, thank you' and 'how charming'?
> Why is everyone today such a pain in the ass?
> Whatever happened to class?

And so on, with the coarse and venal pair lamenting that there ain't no gentlemen to open up the doors, nor any ladies now but only pigs and whores; and that, in short, nobody's got no class. It is one of my favourite songs, right now; seeming to get to the nub of a bewilderment as vivid now as when it was written – in the sixties, about the twenties.

What is it, this 'good behaviour' that we all seek for our offspring? It is not precisely the same thing as morality. The inculcation of moral responsibility, non-violence, honesty, etc., is something which runs through every part of our dealing with our children, and every chapter of this book. It is not just a matter of drilling and discipline, either. Good behaviour is vaguer than that: it takes in manners, and language, and deportment, and the way we react to trouble, and our response to strangers. It involves not only innate goodness, but self-restraint and a degree of acting. Yes, a bit of benevolent falsehood is necessary to smooth everyday dealings, and make society mesh together. Everyone, in every setting, needs a bit of what Velma and Mamma would call Class.

80

Yet today, powerful forces militate against such elegant pretences. We are told that it is healthy to express our feelings, especially anger. We are counselled against repression and bottling-up of antisocial urges. To use language sweetly and restrainedly is reviled as pretentious; to pretend pleasure where we feel none, as hypocritical.

So in teaching our children how to behave we send out a mixed message. They see us behaving hypocritically, because from earliest years their beady eyes sees the different way we carry on in company. They bask in our pleasure when they first learn to talk and describe, and then are bewildered by our horror when they use their verbal gifts all too accurately ('Mummy, – why has that lady got big bazoomas?' 'Daddy, has that old lady got a baby in her tummy?'). They discover as they grow up that certain words have a magical power to dismay and disrupt, and use them with glee. Arriving at their teens they realize that there are other codes, as strong as the parental one, which they can choose to abide by instead of ours.

The first rule of inculcating good behaviour is to admit the double standard, and let even a very small child know that certain things are OK in the family circle but disastrous outside it ('Granny doesn't like people talking about bottoms'). The second is to convey to the child that bad behaviour is an assault on other people, who deserve more kindness. Even the youngest child quite likes to be kind and chivalrous; if you praise thoughtfulness and generosity, even the small generosity of waiting patiently while you listen to Grandad's oft-repeated fishing anecdote, children are glad to have it recognized. It is also permissible to laugh about the situation afterwards, and admit that it was a joint sacrifice for both of you. If a child grasps that good social behaviour is a sort of gift to the world, it takes off some of the mysterious, oppressive pressure of abiding by adult rules.

It also helps if people bother to be polite to the child. Talking across them, referring dismissively to them in their presence, interrupting a serious communication or bumping them aside in a crowd is rude. It teaches rudeness. Adults should not do it, and parents should make it clear that they will not tolerate it. I once sprinted along a railway platform to berate a man who had swung his briefcase into my four-year-old's head and walked on regardless; I asked him to apologize to the child. It seemed as important a lesson about manners as any amount of nagging about elbows on the table.

There is more about older children's and general family manners in Part II; but for young children, here are some flashpoints.

Table manners There are really very few which matter in the first years. It is hard for a short child not to put elbows on the table sometimes, and the mastery of knives and forks, 'though useful, and to be gradually taught over years, is less important than avoiding gross piggish stuffing, noisy slurps, hunching an inch from the plate, or open-mouthed chewing. These should have ceased before the age of six. Frankly, the best cure for all the really ugly habits is – if gentle requests fail – to place an upright mirror on the table in front of the offender. Or to mimic him or her, movement for movement.

But do these things on a day when everyone is feeling strong and confident about life. It is not worth spoiling a cheerful family mealtime with endless nagging.

Another thing which improves toddlers' table manners no end is either to go to a restaurant, or sometimes to lay a beautiful formal table, with a candle and some flowers and real wineglasses, and have a grown-up formal meal together. Once, aboard a small buffeted boat in a windy anchorage, our five-year-old demanded that instead of the usual stuffed-in supper we have a 'grand dinner'. We must have told the children about some dinner we had been to at a yacht club or wherever; at the end of a strangely dignified little meal the eldest rose to his feet and drank a toast: 'Thank you for coming, Mr and Mrs Heiney, and we hope you enjoyed your dinner. God save the Queen.' Well, why not? If you happen to be on a foreign holiday where stylish little bistros are as cheap as fast-food here, then take the family and splash a little wine into everyone's glass. You will be amazed by how well they behave, from the volatile six-year-old to the surly sixteen.

Social manners

You will have your own standards, which may not be identical to mine. Different families have different ideas about such things as thank you letters, opening doors for ladies, elbows on the table and whether to discuss money and politics at mealtimes. The bare minimum is:

Say please and thank you.

Don't barge into people or get in their way without saying 'sorry'.

Don't make offensive remarks, even if the subject is supposedly out of earshot.

Be aware of your impact. Not everyone likes noisy shrieks and laughter in a confined space, like a train carriage, that they can't easily get out of.

This minimum ensures that your child is, at least, not seen as revolting by other people. You can refine it with even better manners, as they grow older:

Offer your seat on the bus to anyone who looks as if they might appreciate it – tired, laden, pregnant, old . . .

When you laugh with friends, be aware enough not to seem as if you are laughing at a stranger.

Don't exclude one person from a conversation when you are in company.

Try and make conversation rather than grunting at visitors or people at parties.

Use your imagination and offer help to people who look as if they need it.

Simple stuff. Keep it simple, and good-hearted, and leave etiquette for later.

Flagrant disobedience Hmmm, tricky one, this. The concept of obedience as a virtue has rather declined these past decades. We are all so attuned to the dangers of child abuse that we hesitate to boost the old-fashioned notion that children should obey adult orders, without judging them. However, within a family nothing is so infuriating as constant ignoring of straightforward instructions like 'Tidy your room' or 'Please make sure that the washing-up is finished before you go out'.

The two questions to ask yourself before you blow your top are a) was it a reasonable request? and b) did the benighted child hear and understand it?

This last is particularly relevant with teenagers, who appear to have some bit of wiring loose in their heads, so that understanding clicks on and off like a faulty relay switch. It is very easy to appear to be always nagging, nagging, nagging and then yelling, making no attempt to understand.

However, a series of instructions, backed up by Post-it notes, repetitions, messages by younger siblings and (according to one American manual) e-mails from your computer to theirs does eventually constitute an undeniable order. If it is then disregarded utterly, you are within your rights to take reprisals. But try and keep your temper and sense of proportion, and avoid emotional blackmail about how hard they are making your life. Always remember the great exchange in Stella Gibbons' *Cold Comfort Farm*:

'Do you want to break your mother's heart?'
'Yes,' said Seth, with elemental simplicity.
    The porridge boiled over.

Tidiness Even trickier. The trouble is that when children are very small you tidy up after them – unless you are an infinitely patient Montessori mum who tidies up *with* them, very very slowly. So you get in the habit, and before you know it you are tidying up round a perfectly capable eleven-year-old . . . then a teenager . . . then *aagh!* suddenly one day you storm into his filthy, permanently curtained room, see the great lout reclining like a lump of molten lard amid layers of torn paper, dirty glasses, broken computer bits and abused CDs which cost you a fortune as treats and birthday presents, and SNAP. You shout. You bitch. You nag. You become an Awful Mother who Doesn't Understand.

There are two solutions. One is to insist that the offender keep his (yes, usually it is a he) area tidy, and be prepared for endless battle. The other is that embraced by my good friend Nicki, who simply gave her teenage son the attic room and herself did not set foot in it for several years. He went through a phase of deep-litter husbandry, but eventually cleaned up. So some parents simply resign themselves to having one unspeakable room in the house, on the principle that it contains the mess (strict ban on letting it spread) and that eventually the offspring will tire of it.

This tactic, however, causes great embarrassment all round when you show prospective buyers round the house. Invest in some storage chests and fork-lift the rubbish into those for a spell.

Talking Proper:
Language foul and fair

If this seems an odd sort of topic to you, since children's speech is quite natural and not something to worry or pontificate about, then congratulations. You are laudably self-confident and come from a classless society.

For most parents, life with young children is shot through with moments of alarm at the way they speak: expressions, accents, profanities, euphemisms all ringing faint warning bells. And if you think that is trying, life with teenagers can turn into one long inner shriek of alarm as the carefully-spoken parent tiptoes through a minefield of 'Orright', 'Yer, right', obscenities, hideous glottal stops and estuarial grunts.

Some parents make major, and hilarious, drama out of it at both stages. The first sign of an alien or vulgar turn of phrase and they come on as if their child had had its soul stolen by the Devil. The British are particularly prone to this terror – there is truth in Bernard Shaw's observation that an Englishman cannot open his mouth without making another Englishman despise him – but every nation has its version. You can make a Bostonian very uncomfortable by teaching his child a sharp Bronx twang, and a Parisian will flinch at broad Provencal expressions or suburban vulgarities from his precious little Lyceén.

How far should you insist that your children talk in the way you personally consider correct? If a child comes home from a Norfolk school sneezing and saying 'Ow, this win'er weather, that hent noo fun', or from a Yorkshire one feeling 'reet mardy', is that cause for panic or amusement?

Where pre-teens are concerned, the first thing to remember is that they are natural mimics, and like to try out a range of imitations; and that if they see a lot of you, then it is you that they will mimic above all. So it does not do to worry too much about occasional departures into wild accents picked up from admired contemporaries at school. Teenagers are a slightly different matter; they are beginning to find their place in the outside world, and may be using the bewildering slang and pronunciations of that world as a form of camouflage. They know very well how you get placed by your accent, so English public schoolboys will frequently be found slopping around saying 'Er, yeah, brill, magic, lads' in an accent never heard on sea or land (somewhere between Liverpool and California, with overtones of Eton), when they want to disguise themselves as democratic proles. Others make doomed effforts at black rap speech. For years I said 'Yup' instead of yes, because I was terrified that 'Yes' would come out as 'Ye-ahs' and everyone would guess I had been brought up in embassies and consulates instead of the chic sixties background of a cobbled street well north of Watford. Today in Britain the vogue for the young royals has swung the pendulum back a bit, and many teenagers have no objection to sounding Sloaney and saying 'Yah, reahhly' a lot. Poor kids; they need compassion, not scolding.

The third point, and by far the most important, is that children naturally love language. All of it, without prejudice. Words are a new country to the growing baby, and he revels in it. Try to teach a baby to say 'cat' for too long and he may lose interest; try 'Rimsky-Korsakov' or 'Supercalifragilisticexpialidocious' and he will bravely have a go, and laugh. A two-year-old loves rhymes and easy puns, a three-year-old is enchanted to learn a few foreign words. (English children say 'Mercy Boko', for thank you, with the same delight that French children say 'Sankyoo'.) They play with words: a four-year-old boy (not mine) once pointed at the sea and said, 'Fish and ships!' before doubling up. My own daughter said, 'Granny's got over her pneumonia, now she's an old moanier!' It is part of the natural delight in language, the highest of human achievements. When a five- or six-year-old comes home from school laughing, it is to tell you some terrible, terrible joke; the odds are that it will be based on verbal ambiguity or deceitful use of language:

'What animal can jump higher than a house? Any animal, houses can't jump.'

'What sort of animal tells the time? A watch dog!'

'What did the one wall say to the other wall? See you on the corner!'

'Knock knock! Who's there? Teresa! Teresa who? Trees are usually quite tall.'

'Knock knock! Who's there? Banana. Knock knock! Who's there? Banana. Knock knock! Who's there? Banana. Knock knock! Who's there? Orange! Orange who? Aren'ja glad it's not another banana?'

Well, you know the genre. They are a tremendous sign of progress. You should cherish them. As children grow into teenagers, the sharing of jokes – sometimes very sophisticated, verbal jokes – is one of the best ways of communication. There were periods in my own growing-up when the only form of conversation possible with my mother took the form of quotations from *Cold Comfort Farm*.

Children also need to be exposed to wonderful language, to ceremonial, grand, beautiful words. It is a great shame that we talk down to them so much, in books and prayers and poems for children, and thereafter leave them stranded between the moronic wittering of pop culture and the jargon-ridden management-speak which infests the education establishment. A six-year-old has the capacity to be thrilled by the language of the King James Bible, by snatches of Milton. C.S. Lewis wrote that the line 'Thrones, Dominations, Princedoms, Virtues, Powers' once kept him happy – in an unhappy childhood – for a week. It need not be archaic language, but it should be rich. While they'll still listen to you reading (it can last until early secondary school age, especially if they are ill or tired, and thereafter can be taken over by audio cassettes), read them books with some style about them, and don't be afraid of the long descriptive passages unless the children obviously are restless. Try old-fashioned books sometimes, or fairytales told in the old grand manner. Turns of phrase, fine words, will creep into their vocabulary painlessly and be brought out at times of need. I have never forgotten the night when my daughter, still almost a baby, suffered a night terror and my son of five came up and put his hand on her shoulder and said, earnestly, looking her in the eye, 'No, do not fear. No stranger comes.' Where he picked up that lovely iambic sentence, that dramatic inversion, from what story or rhyme, I do not know. But he needed it, the specialness and poetry of it, to meet the emotion of the moment. On another occasion Rose sang a song to us on the boat, mingling every element of grandeur that she could find from song or carol or story:

> The glory of the West in the sunlight
> In the ranks of South Australia,
> Spanish ships sailing the East Coast
> Going West
> Sailors sailing, sailing to harbour
> In the ranks of Beth-le-hem!

I am not fondly bragging. Every child – *every single child* – has such moments of elevated imagination, and grabs words from its experience to express them. If they have heard words like *glory* and *miracle, majesty, ancient, echo, despair, rejoicing*, they will use them. Wrongly, on occasion, but with great gusto and appreciation. If all they ever hear is a banal vocabulary of 'nice, super, brilliant, great, good boy, uh-uh, naughty, bad, eat your supper', they will be impoverished. Language is communication, but it is also music. Find them decent books, not the zap-pow macho nonsense of *Masters of the Universe*, nor the pretty-pretty blandness of money-spinning fairies and little ponies whose spiritual home is on duvet covers rather than book-shelves. Buy or borrow classics, old and new. Read Erik the Viking and Beowulf and E. Nesbit, Narnia books and Linnets and Valerians, Margaret Mahy and the better books of Roald Dahl. Take them to the theatre if you can, or let them watch classic children's serials on television as well as (or instead of) the inverted snob, yobbish 'yer, fantastic, loadsamoney, motor-mouth' kind. Declaim from an old-fashioned poetry book.

Though less intense than Lewis, I remember walking around for months as a small child saying to myself, 'The Assyrian came down like a wolf on the fold, and his cohorts were gleaming in purple and gold.' I did not know what an Assyrian

89

was, or a cohort, but I knew they must be grand. Even if you are not a great reader yourself, you can give your child an inheritance of dazzling words, dazzlingly deployed. And – here you may think I enter the realms of fantastic optimism – it lessens the need for, and the frequency of, swear words. A child who is equipped to call you (as I once called my brother) a 'monster of iniquity' is marginally less likely to call you a bloody old cow.

And are you really going to ruin this joyful initiation into language by nagging your offspring about pronunciation, or grammar, or 'common' expressions? Don't do it. Don't let Daddy or Granny do it. Or at least, not until they reach their teens. The only words worth fighting for, in that depressing way, are 'Please' and 'Thank you'; let the rest run free.

There is only one certain way to give a child the gift of clear and acceptable speech, and that is to converse freely and well yourself. In whatever accent you happen to have; that hardly matters. Don't correct, just discreetly show the way. It is the same principle that you used in early talking lessons: if he said 'I saw a mixmenter', you said 'Oh, where was the cement mixer? Was it in the road?' and got the message through that way, without reproof. Children can take hints. The same applies at this older stage, even more so because their feelings are so easily hurt. If you jump on every incorrect or unfortunate expression, they will give up trying new words on you at all. If you care about accent and pronunciation, then watch your own grammar and vowels (and be sure to say interesting things in your nice voice, and tell good stories). Cut down on slang if you must, but more importantly cut down on boring, meaningless phrases like 'Know what I mean' and 'This is it'. If you hear your child keep saying 'Well, this is it', you know where it probably came from as surely as you know why he shouted 'Oh, shit!' when his Lego failed to hold together.

Vocabulary, communication, and enjoyment are all more important than accent or correctness any day. If you are really worried that your child at six or seven doesn't express himself clearly, there are games that you can play, without pressure. One is storytelling, where each member of the family stops a story in the middle and the next carries on. Another very good one is to get on the floor with some Lego bricks, giving him an identical selection, put a visual barrier between you (like an armchair) then ask him to make a building and tell you exactly what he is doing so you can build an identical one. It helps the child to use spatial words, describe colours and shapes, and sort out concepts like 'opposite' and 'sideways'. And the huge advantage of it is that if he isn't very good at it, it is you who fail – your building is the wonky one. It may even produce a new word for the language. After a session of this, a friend's mildly handicapped girl rose to peer over the sofa at the mess her mother had made under her directions. 'That,' she said, 'is not a house like mine. It is a scrambunctious mess.' Not bad.

Below the Belt:
What matters, what doesn't

Be warned. The second part of this chapter is full of perfectly
brisk, sensible, generally acceptable stuff about sex. That is
because it is about older children and teenagers. But the first
half is stronger stuff. Do not leave it lying around where
innocent bachelors may see it. It contains strong language,
unsuitable for those unaccustomed to sharing premises with
persons under eight years old. It may involve bottoms. Also
willies, poo-poos, and the breaking of wind. We are dealing
here with the kind of people who deliberately indulge in
shocking, inappropriate and abusive language: small children.

There is no getting away from it, they just love smut. Not the
kind of glamorized, eroticized smut that adults go in for. Sex is
a matter of glorious indifference to small children, who prefer a
roistering Rabelaisian line in scatological filth. They walk
around shouting, 'Farty party, farty party.' They chant, 'Smelly
knickers at the vicars.' They know poems in which tasteless and
unsavoury rhymes are found for 'Mum' and 'Billy'. They open
their innocent rosy lips and carry on like something out of *The
Canterbury Tales*.

Researching the issue of potty talk, the most interesting
discovery is that absolutely nothing seems able to ward off
the phase. Even families which are grittily enlightened about
bodily functions and walk around naked explaining the childbirth process seem to suffer it. The most liberated, intellectual
North London family I know – forever chatting gaily about
Tampax to their four-year-olds – have been regularly mortified
by a hilarious shrieks of, 'Piddle in the pot, nice and steaming
hot!' when visitors call round. 'No, darling, there's nothing
funny about urine,' they plead, but still the little minx giggles.

Psychologists are reassuring. They insist that it is a normal and
healthy part of children's coming to terms with their bodies. It is a

useful defence mechanism, a child's way of reducing the big frightening adult world to absurdity. They are probably right. I have a relative of tender years who shouts 'Smelly bum' at all the scary apparitions in Phantom Manor at Disneyland. On the other hand, psychologists don't have to pacify mothers-in-law who have had raspberries blown at them in church.

My own strategy was a trade-off: no rudery in public, but no holds barred at home. Since we had a few prim neighbours who refused to allow their children even to use the word 'bottom' within the family circle, our house rapidly became the poo-talk capital of East Suffolk, forever echoing to the indecorous shrieks of liberated infants discussing Hippopotto's smelly botto. I knew it would pass. It did. These days it is me who gets told to watch my tongue.

But then came a great and wonderful discovery. After I wrote my original chapter on foul-mouthed tots, as years passed it got translated. I stuck the foreign editions on the shelf and forgot them. Then one day, recovering from flu, I heard an old Flanders and Swann song on the radio. I had quoted it in the chapter – the one where in falsetto tones they sang: 'Mother's out, father's out, let's talk rude/ Pee, po, belly, bum, drawers!'

Suddenly I wondered how on earth all the translators had coped with this? I got up, collected the dusty books and began to search. A wonderful, feverish world of international toddler smut began to open in front of me.

The robustly British cry of 'Pee, po, belly, bum, drawers!' comes out in German as '*Pinkel, po, Hintern, Furz*'. In Spanish it is '*Pis, caca, tripa, culo, calzoncillos*'. Do not think that Italian bambini are too refined for this kind of thing either: '*Pippi, cacca, sedere, mutande*' to you, Papa! The French translator rendered it as '*Pipi, caca, boudin!*' – but by that time was enjoying herself so much she added a whole different poem about *zizi*. The Dutch did the same, rendering 'Pee, po, belly, etc.' crisply as '*Pies, poep, pens, kont, onderbroek!*' and then gratuitously adding a rhyme about '*poep in de soep*' which leaves little to the imagination. In Norway when you want to embarrass your parents you shout '*Tis, puha, vom, rov, unterhylere!*'

I read on. Another rhyme I had quoted in my examples, the one beginning 'My friend Billy had a ten-foot willy', comes out in Norwegian like some heroic Viking saga. As well it might; you may recall that in the poem he 'showed it to the lady next door; She thought it was a snake and hit it with a rake And now it's only six foot four.' So flitting from book to book, I traced the troubles of My Friend Billy through the languages. *Mi amigo Tito*, he became, and the operatic-sounding *il caro Billy*; and *Alfred* who *avait un quequette de trente centimetres*; and *Mijn vriend Peter had een pik van drie meter* . . .

I cannot tell you how liberating it was. Every translator – for even serious, academic translators come from families – added his or her own rhymes and ruefully remembered baby ruderies. There were *bambini* with smelly *sorpresas* in their *pannolini*, there was *caca* and *poep* and *puha* galore. It was as if the shrieking, hilarious, reckless, anarchic infancy of Europe had determined to teach me all the words which don't find their way into the Berlitz guides. It was a United Nations of poop. My only grief was that I couldn't find my way through the Japanese or Arabic alphabets to decode their versions.

And the happy thing is that it reinforced my firm belief – the belief that carried me through many an embarrassment: it doesn't matter. It is healthy. It is just a small child's way of invoking the most basic, smelly animal functions to prick the pomposity of the adult world. I once found a huddle of six-year-olds, unaware of my approach, speculating evilly on whether the Queen ever breaks wind.

I feel a lot better now because I know that all over the world similar small children are asking similar questions about *el Presidente, der Reichskanzler, M. le President, il Re,* and the *Konigin.* Nation shall speak filth unto nation. It is a whole new spin on the brotherhood of man.

Bum to you, too. How to cope

Play it cool, but point out the social limits and do not be ashamed of doing so. Few spectacles are more hilarious than a liberated, open family which keeps telling its children that there is nothing wrong with the body and nudity, suddenly faced with explaining precisely why one does not, in polite society, take out one's willy and wave it at Great-Auntie Flo. The best approach (which is also the best anti-molester message) is: 'Bottoms are private.' Not wrong, just private.

Speech, however, is free. And another limit worth considering is on the words you teach children. When they are seven or eight, and developing a decent sense of modesty, they may as well learn the right ones: penis, vagina, anus, and so on. But, before then, consider: is it not better to use childish words for purely social reasons? Here I diverge from advanced childcare gurus, but considering that small children are going to use scatological words as insults anyway, would you not rather be called a 'poo-face' than a 'shithead'? And will Granny not respond more forgivingly to a cry of 'I hate your smelly bum!' than to one of 'I hate your rotten old vagina!' (That is a real example. The child didn't mean anything, just knew the word was something bottomy. But it took the daughter-in-law two years to live it down.) Think about it.

Another useful motto is: 'Bottom jokes are only all right in the family', although this may lead to some hair-splitting about grannies, aunts of varying susceptibilities, and whether it is all right to say 'wee-wee' to an uncle by marriage.

Early sex talk

The old way of tackling the subject is to leave it strictly alone until puberty, and then harrumph a bit about birds and bees and Impure Thoughts. This no longer works, for the simple reason that if you won't answer a straight question, their schoolteacher will, or the television will convey a confusing idea that babies come from kissing people with your head sideways, or some schoolfriend will give your baffled chick such a tangled picture of reproduction that she vows (as I did, aged eight) to observe perpetual celibacy.

Par contraire, the post-1960s way of teaching sex is to bombard the child from an early age with technicalities, medical words, and cheery little books that say an orgasm is 'like a great

95

big sneeze' (speak for yourself). Here, the drawback is that the child will get bored and stop listening, or else cause violent embarrassment by discussing big sexy sneezes with inappropriate adults.

The third way is simply to answer questions in a pleasant, straightforward, unembarrassed manner as and when they occur to the child. Unfortunately, they generally seem to occur in the middle of a supermarket checkout queue, in a chemist's shop full of cross old ladies, in the doctor's waiting-room, or on a bus. You could always fob the child off with 'I'll explain when we get home', but it depends on the child. The only safeguard against unconvincing floundering is to run through it on your own before the subject ever comes up. Ready?

'Women have a little house in their tummy that the baby grows up in. It's called the womb. And they've got special places called ovaries, and once a month a teeny weeny egg . . .'

'Men grow special seeds in their bodies, and the seed can come out of their willy and meet the egg in the mummy . . .'

'When a baby's big enough to be born and live safely, it has to get out of the mummy. It comes out of a special hole . . .'

Difficult, isn't it? I would not dream of putting words into anyone's mouth, but a private run-through in your own mind will save a lot of confusion and floundering when you get asked. The trick is not to answer anything which hasn't been asked: leave the Fallopian tubes, testicles, ovaries and perversions for a bit later, and stick to such topics as babies growing up in mummies' wombs, seeds coming from daddies, and the fact that mummies and daddies love each other and want to build a baby out of that love (astonishingly accepted by all children I know, even when Daddy is nowhere in sight).

As to discussing the act of sex itself, I may be stoned to death by sexologists for saying so, but after a cursory and boring explanation of the mechanics ('The seed gets into the mummy by a special kind of hug that only grown-ups can do'), when dealing with under-eights I have always loftily tried to convey a general sense that sex is something grown-up mummies and daddies do, which is not particularly relevant or interesting to children. After all, there are many odd things adults do which

96

their offspring wouldn't fancy: drinking bitter coffee, talking to yakky ladies in shops, writing out cheques, listening to the weather forecast. One more peculiar taste is neither here nor there.

However, schools today will tend to have a sex education programme even for children this small, and you need to keep an eye on it. There is considerable muddle about what sex education should be today; some programmes for very young children could be quite seriously upsetting if there has never been any simple acknowledgement of the facts of life at home. Stay in tune with the school.

One other thing, before we leave the small children and move to the stormier waters of adolescence. If you are anxious yourself, or unsatisfied, or under sexual siege in some way; if you are equivocal about sex, or angry at the mess it has made of your life, or merely fascinated by it all day long, then that is your burden. *It is not your child's.* To lay it on him, or her, or to let any child grow up in a hothouse atmosphere laden with sexual innuendo, is a form of abuse. And it may lead to other forms: all children are at some risk of sexual abuse, but 'knowing' children, unhealthily fascinated by the sex all around them at home, are at graver risk than most.

And treat with caution anyone – even a therapist – who goes on too much about the 'awakening sexuality' of young children. Far safer to stick to the boring old lines: you belong to yourself, you don't have to hug anyone you don't feel like hugging, or in a way you don't feel like doing it. And bottoms are private.

Even if, at times, comic.

Children growing up: sex education

There will come a time – and the age will vary – when the bum-poo-willy stuff stops and a certain unexpected modesty becomes visible in your child. Bathroom doors start being shut. Piggybacks while wearing skirts are graciously refused. Boys get tongue-tied with strange women, especially strange busty women; girls seem warier of men. Then – again at varying times – puberty strikes, with all its physical awkwardness, growling voices, uncontrollable bits, breasts, periods, spots, greasy hair, unrequited love. If you need guidance as to whether these are occurring in the proper medical sequence, look to a medical expert. All I can tell you is what you already know from your own memories: that they happen, and are both unnerving and exciting.

Now the question of sex education crops up in earnest. All secondary schools are meant to provide it, in some form; but you can *not* rely on it being either sensible or balanced. You cannot leave something this important entirely in the hands of teachers. On the other hand, a lot of teenagers in perfectly happy, balanced families find it excruciatingly embarrassing to discuss sex with their parents, ever. You may be lucky, and have one of those households where everyone lets it all hang out; you may not. Therefore there may be a problem, and you have to use subtle methods to make sure, absolutely sure, that your teenagers are getting the right message.

There are three basic components of sex education, and the balance between them is crucial. These are:

1) Biological facts, mechanics of reproduction, and methods of protecting yourself from pregnancy and sexually transmitted diseases.
2) The nature of relationships and the ways they can succeed or fail; the need for love, consideration and responsibility towards partners as well as potential children.
3) How to do it well and make it happy for both partners.

If 3) has just made you hit the roof, squawking in alarm, note that it is actually seen as quite important by a lot of sex educators both in schools and clinics and youth groups which run 'drop-in' centres where your teenager may well drop in. These experts feel that a proper understanding of pleasure, especially in female sexuality, is a vital part of teaching young people about sex. They say that it empowers girls and – by making them understand that they have as much right to enjoyment as boys – actually makes them more able to say 'no' when they want to, and not be pressured or blackmailed into having sex.

But you may have reservations about strangers chatting away to your fourteen-year-old about her clitoris. Just as you may have Roman Catholic scruples about lessons on contraception, or traditionally moral scruples about the implication that experimenting with sex outside marriage is a natural and inevitable part of growing up. You may be worried about what they will be told about homosexuality, particularly about how early adolescents can 'tell' if they are gay or not.

If so, then sort out your own thoughts good and early, check with the school what is taught, and put your own point of view across to your child, lightly and in passing whenever the occasion arises. If you regularly converse with children, watch television with them (very useful, soap operas are) and go to the cinema together, there are plenty of opportunities to put your own view of love, sexuality, and marriage. I heard a doughty old campaigner recently observe that she commented to teenagers in her care about the famous scene in *Four Weddings and a Funeral* where the heroine tells the hero how many men she has slept with. 'Would have had chlamydia, at least, three or four times by now,' said this lady mercilessly. 'Film should have mentioned that.' Well, one can see why it didn't. But a parent needs to work out whether or not to make a similar point after the film; or just to say 'sad'; or to observe, lightly, that films are very far-fetched about what is normal. Teenagers are not daft; if they are not left alone to the mercies of television but grounded in reality and warm normal family life, they can work out quite well that just as nobody is quite as thin, perfectly groomed and constantly witty as the cast of *Friends*, equally it is quite likely that the people they live amongst will not fall into bed quite so casually either. And that if they do, they ought to take precautions.

Most importantly, remember that beyond biological lessons the main source of sex education – the important part of it, which is to do with love and respect – is your example. Parents who are affectionate, considerate, laugh together and hug one another are sending a powerful and important message to the children who run in and out of the family hug, from infancy to adulthood. They may go 'Yuk!' they may distance themselves, they may mock you, and they certainly do not want to know that you actually still 'Do It.' But every time you ruffle one another's hair or flop exhausted into your partner's arms at the end of a trying day, they take in the message that the truest use of sex is to reinforce tenderness, belonging, and the kind of shared physical and mental ease which is the basis of marriage and family. If they know this, then there will always be a safe counterweight to the excess and craziness of early passions.

Another useful thing is a rather racy aunt or uncle. It is easier to ask embarrassing questions of non-parents.

Protecting children from abuse

Small children only need to know the basic rules, that bottoms and the rest are private matters, that you need not show or share them with anybody, however great their authority (doctors and nurses should be very careful about intimate examinations for this reason, and punctilious in asking permission and explaining and having a chaperone). Also they should know that nobody has the right to tell you to keep a secret about something which makes you uncomfortable.

Beyond that, their safety lies in your vigilance and sensitivity. There are child molesters in the world (fewer than you would think from the newspapers) and most of them are not violent, but seductive. The children these people target are often emotionally needy or confused. Happiness and confidence are a good armour against them. If a young child ever does come to you – or to someone else – with a disquieting remark, then keep calm, act unsurprised but interested, and try to draw out more detail.

If the person accused is close – your brother, uncle, father, partner – then the effort to keep calm will be superhuman. Still, do it. Listen. Give the child a chance. Even if it does turn out to be a lie or a fantasy, there will be something – TV, something seen, even a verbal suggestion from someone else entirely –

which triggered it off. You need to know what. It is not unknown for children to say that one person touched them wrongly when in fact it was quite another; but nevertheless, something untoward happened.

Above all, give the child a sense that he or she still has security, credibility and all-encompassing safe love from you. And if – God forbid – it gets that far, do not let any professional investigators do anything, or conduct any questioning, which your honest instinct tells you is damaging the child further. If – God forbid again – you are jointly under suspicion by some authority, and have to be out of the room, then do your damnedest to ensure that the child has a familiar carer to hand: granny, aunt, babysitter, nursery teacher, whoever.

As children get older and bigger, different dangers arise.

Girls You have to point out, with a suitably light touch, to a tall girl of thirteen that the peril is no longer just the kinky paedophile (by this time they know all about such things) but the ordinary rapacious chap who doesn't quite realize – or does not let himself realize – how young she is. Since fashion may induce thirteen-year-olds to dress routinely in the way that only hookers did a few decades back, it is unfortunately necessary to spell it out to growing girls that certain clothes may have their message misread by certain men. They will rage at you, mock, deny it and accuse you of being hopelessly out of touch, but it is still your job to point this out. Most teenage girls, in fact, are strangely modest these days (except when clubbing) but there will always be surges of fashion which cause problems. And you cannot ignore that.

Feminism has made things more complicated for our generation of mothers, because we were taught to chant, 'Whatever we wear, wherever we go, Yes means Yes and No means No.' And of course it is true that no costume or appearance constitutes an invitation to rape. But we live in an imperfect world, and a teenage girl should know that the skin-tight outfit which she is wearing – merely out of pride at having lost ten pounds and acquiring a flat stomach – may be misread and spell out E-A-S-Y.

It is tough for today's mothers. One very liberal, gently-spoken woman of my acquaintance pleaded for half an hour with her daughter (crop top, hipster spray-ons, tousled streaks, puce lipstick, everything bar a stick-on rhinestone in the navel) to cover up, at least in the street. No dice: streams of abuse about how daughter's life was being wrecked because of mother's ignorance, sad fashion sense, jealousy of younger beauty, etc.

Finally gentle liberal mother snaps, and barks, 'The reason you can't walk through the streets like that is that you look as if you're bloody gagging for it.'

Shock. Silence. The mother's descent into the street language rattled the poor daughter, who stamped upstairs and later went out, without another word, wearing a Puffa jacket on top of the ensemble. I am not necessarily recommending shock tactics, but on that occasion it did work.

Boys Diehard feminists reading the above will be fuming: what about telling the boys not to take advantage and 'misread' signals, eh? Well, of course. But even in a perfect society where all teenagers were taught sexual equality and sexual courtesy as a matter of course, there would still be older men to leer at underdressed teenage girls, so they are in a specially vulnerable position.

Naturally, maturing boys should be told not to judge girls' availability by dress or manner, and to take no for an answer. But there is something else they should be taught too, and that is their own vulnerability. Male rape, and the seduction of teenage boys by older men, is undoubtedly less common than heterosexual abuse, but it does happen. To warn boys about their own vulnerability is uniquely hard, and even harder to do without prejudicing them against gay men in general. But it should be possible. Just as with the far younger child you carefully warned against strangers without making the whole world terrifying, you need to work out ways to respond to questions, and constructive ways to comment on the subject when it crops up in news stories or books or TV drama.

If you are naturally rather shy and reserved about these

things (or, indeed, dreadfully shocked at the whole idea of homosexuality) then you need to think about this well in advance. Ideally, a father should be able to talk rationally to his son about the danger that may be posed by a few – a very few – older men or boys. If that is impossible, a mother, or other relative has to, or you have to make sure that the school discusses these things in good time.

But with discussions involving either gender, and any form of sexuality, the key thing is to keep it all as matter-of-fact as you possibly can. The seven-year-old in the back of the car who hisses, 'I know a bad word – *prostitute!*' is trying very hard to shock you, and should not be gratified. The best response is a studiedly tedious reply along the lines of, 'Yes, that means a woman who agrees to have sexual intercourse' (or whatever phrase your family uses) 'with a man for money. It's a pretty dangerous way to live, and sadly a lot of them do get beaten up or murdered, and most of them get diseases from it. But not always, obviously. Some of them take the risk and make a lot of money.'

If you offer all the information you have, courteously translated into language the child can understand, the morbid thrill of talking dirty will fade quite fast. Similarly, teenagers who try to shock you with fetish gear will rapidly get disheartened if you launch into a musing history of the genre, from de Sade to Helmut Newton, and let them know that there is nothing new under the sun ('Your Auntie Suzie was terribly keen on PVC thigh boots back in the sixties. Very sweaty, she said, and the heel came off halfway down the King's Road.')

However, if a child of any age gets too obsessed with any of it, it does no harm to express your own views and revulsions, again in a reasonably mild tone, e.g.: 'I suppose some people find whips and ropes exciting, but it doesn't show much respect for the other person, does it? You're sort of treating them as a toy, really, aren't you?'

Outside influences: video

We are bombarded with warnings about the vile, horrible, sadistic, sexually explicit films children can get hold of from video shops and satellite channels; and, indeed, increasingly of late on terrestrial TV drama in peak time. Our paranoia on this subject is aggravated by people telling us that they'll see the stuff round at friends' houses anyway, so they cannot be protected at any age.

Nobody should ignore these warnings, but nobody should overreact either. Once a child is at secondary school age, eleven and over, it is certainly hard to police what they see at friends' houses. You can make it quite clear to other parents that you prefer them not to have contact with anything carrying a higher certificate than their age, but other parents may not be at home, or frankly may not care.

The child's best defence against this tacky world lies within itself. If they have watched films and television with you, discussed levels of violence and sadism and immodesty, and been helped to consider why people make these things and whether it is really so clever to be taken in by them, they will have that defence. A child of eight is a natural satirist, quite capable of laughing with proper contempt at the fact that people in Hollywood and elsewhere are making huge fortunes out of filming other people's naked bottoms, or making actors pretend to pull other actors' innards out.

The same applies to violent TV and computer games (see 'Computer gaming', p.154). Don't let the fantasy world draw them right in: be there sometimes with them, analyse it, laugh with them at it. Relate it occasionally to real life. I was told a wonderful moment in one household where the father was watching a TV play with the children and a particularly far-fetched and explicitly brutal coupling on a character's office floor startled them all. There had been a family event the weekend before, and rather than express shocked disapproval of the gratuitous and violent scene, the father sighed deeply and said, 'Don't see *them* getting to their golden wedding, not unless he gives up pushing her over every time she tries to get her spreadsheets organized.' It brought the house down.

Younger children must know, above all, that there is no shame or wimpishness involved in refusing to watch really nasty videos, in walking away, or expressing their view that a particular film is silly, unpleasant and perverted. Self-confidence helps; and so does knowing, quite clearly and happily from the family background and family viewing, that there is a better way to use a camera and a script. If, together, you have loved watching things which are wholesome, fun, true and inspiring – and that includes thrillers with a moral core and restrainedly handled violence – you are better able, even at ten years old, to reject those which are tiresomely tacky and exploitative and leave a bad taste in the mouth. The children we read about in the shock-horror tabloids, the ones who become addicted to extreme violence, sexual explicitness and morbidity are generally those who have never learnt to enjoy anything else, and who have been alone too much with televisions.

Do not worry unduly about phases in which young teenagers watch moderately sexy (i.e. not hard porn) films with a terrible obsessiveness. They are trying to work it all out. Your best contribution is not to shriek in horror and take the plug off the machine, but to hire some irresistible and more romantic love stories on video. Even the most sex-obsessed teenagers can get carried away by *Sense and Sensibility*, or the bittersweetness of *Truly, Madly, Deeply*. If the general atmosphere of the family, the small world closest to them, is healthy, balanced and loving; if enough time is spent talking and laughing with real, three-dimensional people outside the family, it will be hard for mere videotape to corrupt them.

I suppose all this may sound laughably naive and idealistic. But simple ideals are often the best way to counteract complicated decadence. And while, undoubtedly, times will come when you have to say, 'No, you are not going to watch *Driller Killer Sex Machine III*. Go to bed,' those moments will be much easier if you have taken a broad-minded view at other times.

Things and Creatures:
Toys and pets

You think that having children adds nothing to the household but the actual children? Think again. That baby whose toys can be tidied up into one prettily painted chest will gradually fill your entire home with things, and (unless you are very strict) introduce the odd living creature, too. Toys and pets must be considered. And controlled.

Toys

Toys are joy, and toys are junk. The first time round, I saved up writing this chapter, deliberately, until our family was halfway through moving house. I wished to speak from a position of authority, that is, standing knee-deep in broken plastic legs, defunct spaceships, squashed crayons, dollies' fridges with the doors hanging off, half-finished model windmills, legless Lego men and gappy jigsaws.

Of course, that stage does not last. Today I am readdressing the subject after an exhausting three hours assembling IKEA storage units in the desperate hope of bringing some kind of order to my son's dusty maze of CDs, moribund electric drum kits, diving equipment, and bits of old dinghy. And to my daughter's world-record collection of horse-related detritus and bygone birthday presents.

It can fill you with despair, at any stage. Look at it, the toy box of any moderately prosperous household: so many bygone treats, thrilling presents, guilt offerings, surprises from Santa and pocket-money treasures lie around us, reduced to a sea of unwanted plastic. We feel guilty of environmental vandalism. We fear we have spoiled our children, and resent the sense of having given in to a massive commercial confidence trick. Many is the day when I have struggled to tidy up a nasty

106

sea of plastic while both children were upstairs playing rapturously with a tent made of bathtowels, or a set of model shops which I made – rather sketchily – out of matchboxes during a rare fit of creativity three years before. At such moments it is tempting to say that all the rest was pointless waste.

But it wasn't. The truth is more complicated, and resentment at the mess and muddle only obscures the real issues. The subject of toys is very difficult to disentangle from other dangerously emotional aspects of parenthood.

For one thing, toys point up our fear of spoiling children. For another, they play on our educational hang-ups and our deep unadmitted aspirations. We all desire children to live up to certain intellectual and personal standards: see the disgust on a scholarly father's face as his son fires off plastic jellies from his Masters of the Universe gun, or the feminist mother's discomfiture at the sight of her little girl lovingly putting a nylon frilled wedding dress on to an orange rubber pony with a Lurex mane. There is plenty of harmless merriment to be got from watching a tasteful upper-middle-class household at Christmas time: here is the Liberty-decorated Christmas tree, here are the impeccably restrained Swedish baubles and the recycled-paper crackers with wildflower seeds in them. And here, beneath the tree, waiting to assault the parents' delicate sensibilities, are a Ponysweet Dream Beauty Parlour in appalling colours and tacky fabric, a Sindy doll in bondage leatherwear, and a gruesome reproduction Kalashnikov machine-gun.

Poor parents! Torn between sense and taste and a praiseworthy desire to let children choose for themselves, they gave in. No wonder they are drinking so much wine. It is depressing to buy all your nursery fabrics from Colefax and Fowler, only to have plastic Bart Simpsons plonked down on them.

The toy industry is, quite frankly, rather a revolting one, at least in its internationalist aspects, and where it deals with the over-fours. Younger children's toys are not too bad. By law, they are strong and safe, and many are extremely well designed: a Fisher-Price farm or Tomy push-and-go toy will last out your children's time and sponge down beautifully for the playgroup jumble sale. Also, toddlers are not style victims.

107

They really don't care whether it is the model before last they are playing with.

But the world of toys for older children is a none-too-pleasant jungle. If you want to know how these people, the manufacturers and marketers, really think then visit a commercial toy fair: listen to them talking about ninety-eight per cent market saturation targets and 'aggressive marketing'; see them drool at the thought of 'tying in' with a television cartoon, or getting a celebrity to 'write' a range of bland little books about some cynically, deliberately designed merchandising character. You cannot separate toys from books and television in this area: pallid, bland creations are foisted on us with a complete marketing plan which has designed the duvet covers and pencil boxes with far more attention than ever went into writing the books.

Toy manufacturers have a strong commercial interest in colonizing our children's minds. They push 'collectable' ranges, hoping to addict them: you must have the full set of everything, plus accessories. Toy shops, even some of the most famous, tend to go along with this because it is more convenient for them to have predictably packaged and well-established ranges on their shelves than to scan all the catalogues, chat up independent, quirky manufacturers and carry an original range. As a result, it is possible to walk round some of the biggest toy shops in the Western world and not find a simple child's drum or set of wooden bricks. A spokesman for Hamleys in London once told me: 'We are governed by what people want, and I suppose they are governed to a considerable extent by what is on television, or advertised strongly on television. Some of them are tacky, horrible things but they just do sell. We try to carry handmade toys, wooden toys, but you know how it is . . .'

I do, I do. But after a while, during the toy stage, I took to frequenting specialist shops like Tridias of Bath of Hawkin of Harleston (both do mail order) where they stock an extraordinary range of toys from all over the world. This does not mean very expensive wooden toys or self-consciously traditional ones; one of the most successful battery toys we ever had was an inter-galactic missile-firing chicken which Tridias discovered. It is a lifesize plastic rooster which strides across the carpet, flaps its wings and shoots off plastic missiles in all directions. The owners of Tridias told me modestly: 'We found it at a foreign toy fair, and it seemed to be the ultimate answer to the problem of aggressive war toys.' It certainly is: it is a fat yellow chicken, but can outshoot anything from the nursery NATO arsenal and send itself up rotten at the same time. Anyone who gets depressed with grey and khaki plastic tanks and little children nursing rocket launchers needs a missile-firing chicken to cheer them up.

But here endeth the sermon against capitalist exploitation of children. There is joy here too. Among the tatty dross lie treasures, whose value is in the eye of the small beholder. Even some constituents of the most offensively oversold ranges of toys are actually very well-made.

Children are also rather well-made, and have a great inborn capacity to mix the toys together, break the manufacturers' rules and play precisely what games they want to. I saw several hideously macho, muscle-bound plastic figurines lying in a frilly doll's cradle being nursed by a teddy bear and a rag doll. 'They're poorly,' I was told. 'They're being made better. Then they'll have a holiday on the beach.' Considering that the patients were all still wearing their ammunition belts and SAS scowls, I thought it a most commendable leap of the imagination into a more peaceful world than the designers would have liked. (And no, it wasn't a girl speaking. Boys need dolls too: why else do you think the toy soldier was developed?) After that, I gave up my vain attempts to ban guns and war toys at home, and was rewarded by the spectacle of the tank being used as a tractor to pull a toy plough, and by a gradual decline of interest in guns except during certain brief, vicious, all-boy interludes with particularly hawkish visitors.

There are three useful principles to use in managing toys during the years when you still have to.

The first thing is, periodically, to *put things away*. Any set of toys becomes boring; rather than keep buying new ones, rotate them.

109

The second is to have periodical *blitzes* (just before birthdays and Christmas are good times) in which you, as the managing director of this household, firmly reassemble all the sets into different boxes, getting construction sets and play people and doll's house things and soldiers from the fort sorted out. Cross-fertilization is a good thing in play (see above) but can end up in sordid chaos, out of which no decent creative game could ever emerge. By seven, children will begin to be able to do this job themselves, but it is too daunting beforehand. If inspection reveals that your children clearly have too many toys, this is the time to Put Away or – even better – Give Away.

The third principle is *try not to buy things too early.* Just because you always longed for a Dublo electric train set is no reason to give one to a clumsy four-year-old who won't be able to fit the trains on to the rails properly. Just because you remember the joy you got from your John Bull printing set, don't foist a lot of fiddly rubber bits on a child who can barely spell out CAT. If a child gets given a toy for which it clearly is not ready, then put it away, almost immediately. Otherwise it will be dispersed and ruined before the time is ripe to use it constructively.

Also, don't give presents so lavish that they only baffle the child. There is a terrible temptation to do this, especially if you are a mother guilty about being out at work. The child's capacity for awed wonder is something so marvellous to adults that we sometimes – selfishly – try to jack it up for our own pleasure. If this five-year-old is so delighted at finding a dewy cobweb in the garden, we reason erroneously, just think what he will say when we give him a scaled-down Lamborghini Countach with Briggs & Stratton four-stroke petrol engine and working gearbox! If he is so thrilled with his teddy bear, just imagine what he will say when he finds a fifteen-foot tall furry giraffe with light-up eyes peering into his bedroom! This way madness lies, for both of you. Fortunately, most of us cannot afford this particular form of child abuse.

The final – and most important – thing is to remember, especially when you begin to panic about spoiling a child, that there are two types of toys (irrespective of quality or long-evity).

Some are *tools*, and some are *luxuries*. The tools are obvious if you look what you gave them at a younger age: you would not deny a baby his rattles or a toddler her bricks. If you couldn't get them, you would make them. In the same way, growing children need certain types of play for their mental and manual development. Never feel guilty about buying a really good construction set (even if it doesn't get used every day), or a jigsaw, or a set of basic plastic play people, or drawing and painting equipment. Remember that children actually need things with wheels, things that float, things that contain other things or tessellate with them to make patterns. They don't have to be over-elaborate or expensive, but it helps to keep it clear in your mind that you are buying the basic tools of the trade for a child who is a professional developer of his or her own mind and body. It is not the same thing as lavishing all the latest Pokemons on a child (or indeed pandering to your own sentimental memories with handmade jack-in-the-boxes). These are luxuries.

The best advice on actual toys that I can offer takes the form of two lists. The first is of things that you will never regret buying, although you do not need them all; and the second list comprises things that you probably will regret, bitterly.

You will never regret:

Ample, simple, drawing and painting equipment. Basic colouring books.

Decent construction systems. Lego for architecture perhaps. Meccano or Brio Mec or Fischer-Technik for old-fashioned mechanical engineering. Lego Technik or Capsela for modern versions and the working of gears and motors. Only make your mind up early: don't buy a starter set of everything on the market.

Some truly excellent series of figures and small accessories, such as Playmobil. The important thing about them is that they

111

are just detailed enough to excite a sophisticated six-year-old, but not so 'finished' that there is nothing left to imagine. These series tend to come in small units, but are not oversold as 'collectable' – each box is a worthwhile toy in its own right.

Balls. It is amazing how some families seem to have every kind of climbing frame and elaborate outdoor toy, but no football in sight. Perhaps a ball would merely underline the fact that they don't give their child enough playmates, adult or child.

Kites. Simple ones. Controllables come later.

Good board games, which you and they actually play.

Good children's tools. Carefully designed saws, hammers, planes, and so on, if kept in a separate place from other toys and used under discreet supervision, are a better guarantee of future safety than a mere hysterical ban on all sharp blades.

Jigsaws of the right level, which can be hugely variable. Ignore the age group on the box.

A basic doll's house for which furniture can be bought or made in stages.

A fort with soldiers. Call it history, if you must.

A toy theatre. But for heaven's sake don't get carried away with frustrating tangly puppets. There is a Czech type where the head is supported on a wire, with just two strings for the arms. This is as complicated as you should get before the child is ten. Believe me.

Glove puppets and finger puppets.

Dolls that your child actually wants and loves and chooses herself (or himself, come to that).

Very good quality 'sets' that you couldn't possibly have assembled yourself: shape-printing sets, junior embroidery frames, a basic safe chemistry set perhaps, a pinhole camera kit.

Peculiar, offbeat science kits that don't cost much: the cardboard models you build and power with a solar cell, the clock which runs off a potato, and so on. But for most science learning, alas, there is no substitute for the patient parent and a good children's book. Nothing is more irritating than to buy an impressive box marked 'make your own weather station', only to be ordered to get a jam jar and a balloon and a straw to make a barometer, something every boy scout ought to have known anyway.

Very cheap, rather silly, possibly short-lived, but highly amusing novelties: magic tricks from China, Czechoslovakian wooden oddities, tiny torches with a spray of optic fibres coming out of them making sparkly patterns with their tips. I look out for them all year, and keep a stockpile in the attic for party bags and to help out Santa.

Stuffed toys with pleasant expressions on their faces.

Just scraping, by the skin of its teeth, into this list is: a decent computer. See 'Electronic Children', p. 148.

Here are the ones that you *will* regret buying:

Silly little paintboxes, with brushes whose bristles fall out the first time you wash them. Also felt pens (only rare children put the tops back on each time, and they dry up). Also very expensive and beautiful crayons like oil pastels which the child squashes and loses. If you can afford such luxuries, it is nice to give children good colours instead of garish crayon colours, but there is a middle way. Conte crayons are excellent.

Anything whose only appeal is that it belongs to a set of merchandised figures, heavily advertised on television. If it has other merits, which are obvious (solidity for one), you won't regret it so much.

Superior kites that only Daddy understands and, even so, they get him into an awful temper.

Anything that you buy out of guilt because their maths/ spelling/reading doesn't seem to be good enough, and the packet promises it will teach them. It probably won't.

Overcomplicated jigsaws. But you can always do them instead.

Vast railway layouts, again leaving nothing for the child to invent, yearn for, and collect personally.

Elaborate dolls your child hates the sight of. Also simple dolls, ditto – but at least you haven't wasted much money.

Con-trick 'sets' which don't list the contents on the box, can't be inspected open in the toy shop, and prove to consist largely of printed instructions and over-priced bits of plastic moulding. They make their money exploiting the academically minded but bone-idle parent who thinks that by getting a 'Young Electrician' set he is somehow putting his child on the road to being the new Clive Sinclair. You can do better for a quarter the price at a good model shop with a sympathetic assistant.

Computerized toys which only do one thing – such as testing spelling, or sums, and which talk at you in a harsh grating American voice.

Remote control aeroplanes for under-eights. They will fly away and not come back, because your child is much too young for them. Remote control cars at least don't get so far, so fast, but are rarely a favourite toy for more than a week.

The first list may sound expensive but some of the things can be made, and some can be saved for. And the second is, in fact, very nearly as expensive. A few well-chosen toys, supplemented by coloured pebbles, are a better foundation for life than a sterile nurseryful of luxurious nothings. And it is worth putting some thought into the business of toys, because they are – at their best – agents of joy and fascination and growth of the spirit. And at their worst, bringers only of disappointment, cynicism, dust and ashes. They matter.

Pets

. . . are sharing a chapter with toys but are *not* toys. They are, however, sources of education, joy and frustration alike, which is why they are here.

There is, no doubt about it, some special relationship between children and animals. Watch a child pat a horse, or pick up a complaisant kitten, and you know it. Observe an even smaller child colouring in the white patches on the family dog, or a toddling baby using the family Labrador as a walking frame. Grown men wax sentimental at the memory of a childhood cat, and I myself carried a curl of bull mastiff hair in my locket through all the traumas of adolescence. (I was forever having to open the locket and turf out the ginger, black or mousey hair of swains who didn't come up to the mark. But the wiry curl of sand-coloured dog hair stayed inviolate.)

Furthermore, when asked to write about a 'sacred early memory' for some charity book, I found the typewriter mysteriously producing data I had not consciously examined for years: the story of Birdie the cage bird whose remarkable life spanned years of my childhood. Oh yes, animals matter to children. A cool and unsentimental look at the whole subject is required, however, or you will end up with a bitten child or a bored one; or at best with a psychopathic cat, a ruined carpet and a tankful of dead goldfish.

If you are already a confirmed pet lover you don't much need this chapter. Except for one heavy warning which everyone needs: *existing pets, however sweet, may deeply resent a child.* Dogs are especially jealous; never, ever leave them alone with a small child until you are a thousand per cent sure of their benevolence. Don't rely on them, ever; remember that a dog which didn't mind a baby, or a comparatively slow-moving toddler, may get edgier as the child gets older and starts to assert his human right to be Master. It is rare – most dogs gloomily knuckle under to any human authority, doing 'sit' ten times in succession for bossy visiting children – but unexpected attacks do happen. Even greater caution is needed round other people's dogs when you are visiting: a child's face is placed too low to risk even a brief bad-tempered snap. And beware of cats' claws. Most cats will do anything to avoid confrontation, but if grabbed by the tail they will panic in a big way. Make children treat them with all the deference that you do, and hammer home the message that just as they themselves don't have to kiss and hug anyone they don't want to (modern anti-child-abuse message No. 1 as taught in all good schools), cats don't have to either.

If you've never had much to do with animals but are being nagged for a pet and feel your child would benefit, here is a beginner's guide. I have made it as depressing as possible, purposely to counteract the cuddly, furry, sweet-eyed trusting appeal of the animals which are trying to get in and live with you. Give the furry brutes an inch and they'll take a mile. I speak as one who has a kitten on my shoulder, another one eating my left shoe, a pig snorting outside the window and a moribund baby hedgehog stretched out by the kitchen stove.

Dogs Everyone knows their good points: one forgives them a lot because they are so sickeningly devoted and uncritical. But until a child is over ten, and capable (depending on your neighbourhood) of exercising a dog herself, it is madness to buy one unless you want one for your own parental sakes. Dogs need a lot of rather expensive food, daily exercise and regular worming, especially if children are around (the Toxicara canis worm is a serious menace which can cause blindness). Also, in many areas you will quite rightly be expected to clear up the dog's messes yourself. Carrying little white spades and plastic bags around is not everyone's idea of spontaneous enjoyment of the natural world.

116

If you do get a dog, pay attention to the breed. Big ones are often, oddly enough, better-natured than small 'toy' dogs, and it is a truism that mongrels are nearly always more pleasant than thoroughbreds. Show dogs have been bred entirely for appearance, and not temperament, so a vicious, untrustworthy bitch will be allowed to breed if she is beautiful enough. Mongrels, on the other hand, are bred for company or else by accident; the result is calmer and friendlier.

Inexperienced dog people should avoid taking 'rescue' dogs; there may be a very good reason why they got abandoned in the first place, or they may be confused and traumatized. And do *not* buy a puppy unless you are allowed to see it with its mother, and its siblings. Dogs with unnatural puppyhoods, from horrible puppy farms, do not get the handling and the affection and security they need before eight weeks. Result: they often seem very sweet until puberty kicks in several months later and they become difficult or dangerous.

If you really are a dog beginner, take advice. And get a professional to give the pup (over six months) at least some training. Take the whole thing seriously; this is a wolf descendant you are letting into your house.

Cats are independent, cussed animals. They can be very frustrating for children because they insist on choosing for themselves whose knee they sit on, and they prefer people who don't move around all the time.

If you get a kitten, choose the boldest and brashest of the litter. Two will be more amusing than one, because they wrestle and pounce and buoy up one another's confidence in the face of big looming children. House cats need no exercising, but flit in and out of the cat flap; however, if you insist on keeping one in a flat, you must bravely face up to the question of cat litter. Litter trays, as used by adult cats, are Not Nice. They are especially Not Nice if you have a crawling baby or are pregnant yourself (they are a disease risk to pregnant women). Litter costs a lot. So does cat food.

On the other hand, small children can get a real relationship going with cats. Kathleen Hale, creator of the Orlando books, says that she observed with her own children that the cat made a comfortable halfway house between child status and the bewildering world of adult authority: the children liked the cats' rugged independence and naughtiness. My children used to go carol singing to our late cat Nelson at Christmas, saying, 'If you had a mince pie or some money, you'd give it us, wouldn't you, Nellie?'

Rabbits and guinea pigs are small, portable, furry and vegetarian (therefore their droppings are not too nasty). They can live outdoors in hutches, so you don't have the smell in the kitchen. What could be nicer? Well, it would be nicer not to feel so guilty. They are transparently, chronically bored in hutches. They want to run on the grass. So you make a run, and the next-door dog jumps in and kills them. Or they tunnel out and you have to spend hours crawling round the hedge because they might die if they spent the night out.

They also – and here is the crunch – need daily handling to keep them tame enough for children, and both species scrabble in your hands, which alarms shy children and makes them drop (and possibly injure) the animal. After the first rapturous week a child will grow tired of them anyway, so you have to tame and handle them yourself. It is necessary to read a few leaflets about these animals, as there are all sorts of strange rules one might not know about. Did you know that guinea pigs need daily vitamin C? That Dutch Miniature rabbits mustn't overdose on lettuce? Is there really room in your mind for these facts?

Having said all that, it is possible for a family with a garden to get a rabbit, let it hop round the kitchen from babyhood, totally tame it, then let it live out of doors. I know one family with a hand-reared tame rabbit in the garden. It has brought in, and tamed in turn, a succession of wild ones. The family play and garden surrounded by friendly, strokeable bunnies. It is an idyll. Sheridan did it, and good for her, but I didn't manage it; and only you can judge whether you would.

Guinea pigs can never live free for long, and have, frankly, the most boring temperament of any animal I know.

*   *   *

Gerbils and hamsters Even smaller and more portable, and they inspire less guilt because at least they have a wheel to go round in. But gerbils in particular have to live indoors. Do you have a corner where the cage won't get knocked over or trodden on? Do you have children who will keep it clean, and the water changed?

As far as children are concerned, these small rodents are better winter entertainment than rabbits because they are always visible. However, they are frail creatures and die more readily, which is harrowing.

It is certainly fun for children to handle them, but they do tend to let them go, and then you have to get them back from under the wardrobe. Once an elderly Russian hamster escaped for good (they live in colonies, so you always have rather too many). It crept into the leather case of my laptop computer to die. Some weeks later I put the computer in the case after it got back from the repairers, and went to work. On the train, as I took it out, from the bottom of the case tumbled a flat, ancient hamster carcass, to lie on the train table like a miniature tigerskin rug. It was very hard to pass off gracefully.

The same goes for mice, except that in my experience once a mouse gets away it stays away. Sometimes it mates with your own wild mice and you get intriguing piebald pests going through your larder for years afterwards, and you don't feel like poisoning them because you are, in a sense, their granny.

Rats put a lot of mothers off. But they have all the good qualities of the group above, and a lot more intelligence. You can teach a rat tricks, at least. Still, I wouldn't recommend them wholeheartedly for under-tens. Ours went psychotic and used to lunge at us through the bars whenever we entered the room. Not a success.

Fish Don't buy goldfish or tropical fish, however much your child pleads, unless you actually like the idea of a handsome tankful in the house. A lone, sad goldfish in an unfiltered and unoxygenated bowl is a miserable sight after a while. It is also a bad example to your child of care for living creatures. So you

119

have to fling yourself into the business of getting a proper bubbling machine and a big tank and giving them plants to swim around. The trouble is that a young child may well lose interest halfway through this process.

We bought fish because the children begged for them, and developed a curious problem. All the fish died, except Albert. Every time we put more fish in with Albert, they died too. Albert flourished. We decided he either had a form of fishy AIDS, or was a murderer. So we spent a whole year with one lonely, murderous fish alone in a vast tank, wasting electricity and light. In the end we put him in the garden pond to sink or swim. He lived there until the great drought of 1989 when one must assume he perished. The children had forgotten him by then, so we were at least spared the carpentry of making an Albert Memorial.

Birds The guilt problem arises again. Nobody has ever established that birds don't mind being in cages. I think they do. I suppose if the cage is big enough and hangs in a window, or if you have a proper aviary, and the bird has plenty of millet and a bell and a piece of cuttlefish and music on the radio to sing along with, it isn't too bad a life. Check that you are not buying a species which ought to be protected (like the African finch). Children will enjoy the bird, in a half-hearted sort of way. But if you know someone who keeps racing pigeons, get them to go and help out with those instead. Animals doing a job are far more interesting and rewarding than mere pets.

Ponies Unless you are horsey yourself, think very, very carefully. Neglected backyard ponies are now a serious problem in Britain. A pony means feed, stabling, tack, shoeing (more expensive than shoeing an extra child), and unexpected vet's bills. Only a dedicated riding child, who has proved his or her keenness, should be given a pony. If it has not got a decent -sized paddock, it will need exercise every single day. Even when it is proved to be nothing but a liability, the child will be fond enough of it to make a dreadful fuss when you sell a pony or pass it on.

Farm animals Penelope Leach has pointed out that six months of hand-rearing a lamb or calf is more educational and memorable for a child than a lifetime of cleaning out rabbit cages. However, this option is not open to you if you live in a third-floor flat in town. Also, adults have to be really clued-up and dedicated to manage farm animals, especially since a half-grown sheep which wants to sit on your knee is a problem in anyone's terms. It may be better to opt for visits to a farm park or a city farm. Also remember that farm animals a) die unaccountably and b) get sent to slaughter eventually anyway (except milch cows and farrowing sows). Children have to accept this.

On balance, pets are worth it. They teach children gentleness and respect for living things. They are pleasant, uncritical companions in a world peopled by figures of authority and, with their short life cycles, they provide a good way to learn about death. Too often, television and games and Hallowe'en grotesqueries portray death as violent and gory. A child who gets the chance to bury a pet rabbit and make it a wooden cross, or stroke a dead cat for the last time and feel it as lifeless as Plasticine beneath the fur, is getting a clearer, calmer idea. One day in January we watched together over a sick orphan lamb slipping peacefully into its last sleep by the fire. It was sad, but there was a reality about it which we were glad, in the end, to share with the children.

Although – did you guess? – it was barely a week before the next one turned up.

Money, Clothes, Status

Amazingly early, children find out about money. Two-year-olds drop coins into slots crooning, 'Munghymunghymunghy!' They know it is 'of value', not like pebbles in a bucket. These clinking discs are kept in special places, always put away, protected by zips and flaps; they are urgently sought for in shops, looked at with care, shut away in ringing tills.

Munghy! It has an aura of power and mystery and carefulness. It is the tribal totem. Later on, they hear parents use the word anxiously, gleefully, gloomily: 'It's a lot of money . . . fine if you've got the money . . . did you bring any money?' It is a universal excuse for deprivations, absences, frustrations: 'Too much money . . . can't afford it . . . Daddy's got to go away to work, to earn money . . . Mummy does a job while you're at playgroup, to get money for nice things . . .'

Psychologists have traced children's awareness of money. First a child gets the principle of exchange: sweets for coins across the counter. Gradually he develops some idea of scale (can't buy a Ferrari for 40p). Then of divisibility (one small girl quoted in research didn't realize yet that you can still have a 10p lolly even if you've got 20p). Next comes the idea of earning (money for services), or circulation (Daddy gets money from his boss to give to the milkman), and finally such concepts as profit (shopkeepers charge more than they paid out) and value-adding (buy a stick and cloth, make a puppet, make a profit). Finally the child grasps interest and saving, and is well on the way to credit cards, tax avoidance, Eurobond trading and a numbered bank account in Switzerland. So much for the intellectual understanding of money. The emotional and moral aspects are tougher.

Somewhere, a child has got to find answers to the following questions, answers which will last for life. How do you decide

122

how much money different things are worth? Or how much different jobs are worth paying? Does paid work make people worth more? How much profit is it fair to make? When is it right to get into debt? Are rich people better than poor people? Or worse? Or neither? Why do some people have no money at all, and starve, while others waste it? What is the difference between being a saver and being a miser? The answers to all of these will be implicit in things you and other people say, in a child's hearing, in what you do and how you do it.

At any level of income, you can mess this one up. Poor but honest families can give the wrong messages every bit as much as rich and careless ones. I tend to indulge myself in a romantic idea that growing up in a poorish family builds character. Part of me believes this, yet I never can forget George Orwell's devastating description of the Comstock family in *Keep the Aspidistra Flying*: they were poor and careful with money, and 'The first effect of all this was to give him a crawling reverence for money. In those days he actually hated his poverty-stricken relatives – his father and mother, Julia, everybody. He hated them for their dingy homes, their dowdiness, their joyless attitude to life, their endless worrying and groaning over threepences and sixpences. By far the commonest phrase in the Comstock household was "We can't afford it".'

The key word here is 'joyless'. Dozens of autobiographies record a different picture of growing up in a relatively poor family: of fun and laughter and enjoyment of the free pleasures of sunlight and moonlight and public parks; of children reading their way through the public libraries and building ingenious go-carts out of old prams. Children like these, brought up not to be defeated by poverty, are by far the best and happiest custodians of money when they do have it in later years. The ones who splurge and debauch, or turn mean and snobbish, are those whose parents have treated it as an obsessive and burdensome worry.

You and I may know that money actually *is* an obsessive and burdensome worry; the trick is not to make the children old before their time.

The opposite peril is the over-monied household. How are

you going to stop your child being inadvertently wounding, patronizing and otherwise nasty about his own lush Christmas presents? How are you going to dissuade your daughter from swanking offensively about her new pony, or your son about his state-of-the-art games console? On the whole, the amazing fact is that you don't have to do anything, except shut up and not make things worse by trying too hard.

Up to the age of about ten, unless they have been corrupted by a particularly materialistic family or school, children are hazy about monetary value. They won't be offensive about possessions unless you encourage them to be – there are very few children who don't have something to swank about. Be neutral. 'So Lisa hasn't got a Pony Castle? It's lucky that you have, it'd be boring if you had the same. Do you think she'll let you go round and see the trains rattle by her window again?'

Avoid the emotive word 'poor' when talking about anyone you know; it conjures up visions of Little Match Girls and everyone sleeping in a hovel around the family pig. I have heard of children solemnly offering their pocket money to the parents of friends who have been incautiously described as 'poor'. At least they got a first-hand experience of how strangely touchy adults are about this curious stuff, money.

On the other hand, there is nothing wrong with letting young children know about poverty further afield. Television appeals are always met with a blaze of young generosity: passing on toys, raising money for Third World children or Kosovan refugees and writing them letters are all sources of real and lasting joy and understanding.

The real problem comes when children ask, directly or implicitly, why some people are poor and others rich. Why isn't life fair? The temptation to give a trite answer is overwhelming; after all, it is one of the biggest and saddest mysteries in the world: the rich man in his castle, the poor man at his gate, and whether it was indeed God who set them high and lowly and ordered their estate. You can explain about famines and droughts and earthquakes; you can talk of 'luck', or try some basic global economics (or Marxist theory, if that way inclined). You could even, though heaven forbid, try and stand

124

up the shaky theory that good, hardworking people never end up on the breadline.

But it is hard to do more than be honest about the unfairness, frank about the bafflement, and reiterate that money itself is neither a god nor a demon, but neutral. Some people deserve it and don't get it, others have it handed to them on a plate by inheritance. Some enjoy it, some let it ruin their lives. You can say that it doesn't matter, isn't everything, and can't buy you love; but on the other hand it would be madness not to teach children to respect it and save some up for a rainy day. Shake the kaleidoscope, make your own philosophical pattern, only don't leave anything out.

Pocket money is the first practical application of your philosophy. A curious aspect of this, in Britain at least, is that surveys show that the wealthier the family, the less pocket money the children tend to get. One TV personality gave her children, at eight years old, only 1p a day. In the homes of manual workers the children may get up to £2 a week.

I regard this with great cynicism. In the well-off household, the children get bought a great many things by their parents anyway. But it seems crazy to me to give a child only 7p a week, or even 10p. At present prices, he or she has no chance whatsoever of learning to handle money. It is not fair to make a child save up for two months for the price of an ice lolly or a comic. Pay silly sums like that and you are encouraging the child to think of his money as different to yours – as a sort of toy. You exaggerate your power: if you buy a moderate toy for £7, you are underlining that an adult has a hundred times the spending power of a child, over and over again. The child feels powerless and aggrieved.

On the other hand, give a child £1 and he or she feels a sense of responsibility. He sees, dazzled, that if he didn't buy anything for a year he could save for a whole electric car set. He makes decisions, he divides it up; he splurges 50p on a toy space monster, then learns the bitter feeling of wishing he hadn't. He puts the money in a savings account, and sees it visibly growing. He gives 25p to charity and is told that it has bought rice for a whole family in Ethiopia and put them two days further away from death by starvation. He gets a small taste of power and responsibility and the dilemmas of money. On the whole I favour pocket-money on the generous side, if you have it.

Earning is another useful concept. There are few legal openings for a child of seven to earn, but parental doses of pocket money can be earned or docked with great profit to all. Dock a few pence a time for swearing, spitting, hitting and such behaviour during the week, and you encourage a grasp of subtraction; pay small sums for household jobs beyond the normal call of duty. (Beware: children can grow very mercenary around six, and start charging for table clearing and bedroom tidying. Don't be taken for a mug.) Earning one's first money is a great and solemn delight. Do not ruin it by indulgently giving your child double the agreed rate: the sense of really having *earned* 5p is better than the sense of being patronized with 20p.

Spending of one's own first money has to be free. Some families control it far too dictatorially. Obviously, really foul sweets or dangerous objects have to be controlled or banned, but otherwise it is a child's prerogative to waste his own money. The cold, hollow sense of having been cheated by a shoddy, over-packaged toy is something we all yearn to protect our children from, but we have no right to. In the catch-phrase of British politics when a chancellor resigned, 'Advisers advise and ministers decide.' Parents are only advisers, and it is hell. One of the most arduous task of middle motherhood is standing around for ages in toy shops while an anxious, half-miserly and half-yearning child peers at all the price labels and tries to make decisions. Grit your teeth. Take a paperback. Only don't take over.

Swapping I take an unconventional view. I do not think parents have much right to interfere with the curious inter-child commerce of the pre-teen years. If your child is one of the sort who swaps a £50 state-of-the-art supertoy for two marbles and a piece of chocolate, then let him. (Unless you are quite sure he has been bullied into it: speak to both children, if necessary.) If the child (usually a boy) actually wants the rubbish, then say goodbye to your money and learn your lesson: it is not fair to impose adult value systems upon young children. If you really cannot bear seeing vital tools, like construction kits, leaving the house then say that without special permission he can only swap things he has bought himself (not presents).

Giving is a more difficult area. On the whole, for a quiet life and level relations with neighbours, a good rule is that children under sixteen never take money from anyone outside the family without your knowing, and never give them any either – unless via a proper charity. Nor should children under about eight too freely lend or borrow; it too quickly becomes un-trackable, out of control, and a source of resentment all round.

You may get it all entirely right. But I can tell you one difficulty that still might lie ahead.

Teach a child to handle money sensibly, and you find yourself saddled with explaining that people who fall on hard times with no reserves are not necessarily (*pace* a few right-wing theoreticians) feckless or stupid. One well-heeled child I knew stopped once in front of a tramp near Charing Cross and loudly asked her mother, 'Why didn't this man open a Young Saver Account when he was little?' Glares from dosser in cardboard box, a guilty fiver from Mummy failing to appease his dignity; and off fled Mummy and Young Saver down the Embankment, the sound of harassed explanations fading in-effectually on the chill evening air.

Clothes

They fit in quite well here, because a) they are a visible sign of status and relative affluence and b) they are one of the most visible, easily understood forms of expenditure and thus one of the first that children become aware of.

127

The beginnings Sometime between leaving off Babygros and being fitted for a wedding outfit, children develop a dress sense. The later it happens, frankly, the luckier you are. If you have a child who wishes to wear the same pattern of tattered unisex tracksuit, in ascending sizes, from the age of four to the age of consent, then your only problem is getting that child smartened up occasionally for a few hours. This may be an ordeal at the time (I well remember going rigid and screaming when someone tried to force me into a red velvet party frock with lace collar) but it will save you money and, on balance, save you irritation too. Children look adorable in fancy clothes, but an overly clothes-conscious infant is a pain in the neck as well as a drain on the purse.

Not only is there the logistical problem that whatever such a child fancies wearing at any given moment is either in the wash, too small, or costs £70, but a small child constantly preening herself in the mirror is not a seemly sight. A healthy, active, unselfconscious rag-bag is easier to live with. Most children fall between the two categories, not caring overmuch about anything except comfort, but enjoying brief crazes for certain favoured sweatshirts, or threadbare jumpers with pictures knitted into them.

Whichever temperament of child you have, it is obvious that in the three to eight age group the clothes business is substantially different to what it was before. Nappies are only a memory, sick-ups are rare, and most importantly of all, the child is beginning to become independent in dressing. This precious independence (precious to you, I mean, because you can get a cup of coffee in the mornings) should be cherished and encouraged with easy slip-on clothing, wide necks and elastic waists. Little boys look wonderful in real shirts with cuff buttons, but the drawbacks are obvious. Children at this mucky, active age need a lot of clothes, often a daily change of everything including the sweater; there is room for perhaps one or two fidgety 'best' outfits at most.

What there is not room for, at their bewildering speed of growth, is fashion. If you are wise, you will set your face against it and never *ever* recommend anything to a child so young on the grounds that it is 'trendy' or 'fashionable'. To quote one harassed urban mother with a smart sultry moppet in tow, 'Everything she has which isn't outgrown she says is out of date, and vice versa.' Her daughter is six years old. Fashion will, of course, influence what they wear because fashion decrees what the chainstores carry, but to encourage it wilfully is madness. It is also, in my admittedly slightly eccentric view, madness to encourage little girls this age to be 'feminine'. There will be time enough for that later on; for now let them run and rip and swing unselfconsciously in boyish clothes. It is, after all, a freedom many women fought to gain for them.

If you have been jogging along happily with handed-down baby and toddler clothes until now, you should know that there are clearly stratified levels in the lucrative children's clothes market, and be aware of which kind of shop you have strayed into. Here is a cynic's guide:

Top of the tree Largely thanks to the fertility of the British royal family, there has been a renaissance of very grand children's clothes. In any big city now there is somewhere selling cream woollen coats with velvet collars, embroidered shirts in fine cotton lawn, unwashable Fair Isle sweaters, and raw silk ballgowns for little girls of four. The boys' shorts will be long, with turn-ups; the shoes will be soft leather. Everything needs ironing or steam-pressing with care, most things need dry-cleaning.

These clothes will break your heart. They are designed for parents with nannies whose mission in life is to starch and wipe the children four times daily. They cost a lot, and their only advantage is that they can be handed down through the family (indelible stains permitting) for fifty years. It must also be said that those beautiful cloth coats with adult detail in the seaming are damned uncomfortable and stiff around five-year-old arms. I know, I used to wear one.

Très très trendy Whereas the shops above are targeted at social climbers and fogey sentimentalists, this lot is more likely to

129

attract the new establishment: pop stars with accessory kids who are always being photographed in magazines, actresses with massive guilt complexes about being on tour for weeks, and people who somehow think they will feel better about their lifestyle if their children, too, look vaguely as if they were on the way to Annabel's. The shops sell ra-ra skirts, layered fifties petticoats, drainpipe jeans for boys which hardly go over their poor little ankles, combat pants, multicoloured patchwork jackets from Bali, sequinned DJs for two-year olds, and every kind of tarty dancewear and impossible bodysuits for little girls. These clothes are expensive, but none of the designers will have taken much account of lingering toddler pot bellies, washing machines, or the need to go to the lavatory in a hurry. They will snag, fade, run and rip in a week. But it doesn't matter because they will be out of fashion by then, and if you bought them you have more money than you need anyway.

Upmarket sensible Many of these will come from Italy or America, and be beautifully made and designed and priced accordingly. They will be in classic styles with an original twist (like pink corduroy dungarees), cost a lot but wash beautifully, and be passed down through the family for years. If you buy them, buy them a shade too big or your heart will be broken the moment the child grows out of the garment. Actually, the most trouble-free way to enjoy really good quality children's clothes is to have an affluent and good-natured neighbour with an only child a year older than yours and immaculate taste. For several years my daughter was thus equipped with wonderful clothes: comfortable, beautiful and easy to look after. Then she grew six inches and outstripped the older child. Curses.

Whereas only caprice is likely to make the ordinary mother buy from trendy or upmarket shops, this expensive category is worth considering occasionally, especially with a big family or a collection of nephews and nieces to pass on to. Many of the clothes are so good they can be sold on if you are broke.

Chainstore Probably the mainstay for most of us. Tracksuits, T-shirts, sweatshirts (preferably without advertisements for naff toys all over them), trousers with elastic backs so lazy boys don't have to use the button and zip, T-shirt dresses for little girls which pull on easily over the head, six-packs of knickers and socks – these are the essentials of the working wardrobe. And children ought, on the whole, to be thought of as manual workers: their clothes should be tough and cheerful and for-gettable. We are, in the West, well served by chainstores. The only irritations are the creeping sloganization of clothes (why should an innocent three-year-old want to walk around la-belled Surf City, or Cool Dude?) and the utter failure of chainstores to understand that children grow at unpredictable rates. They still assume that if you want cold-weather clothes you will stock up on them in September, so by January (when it really gets cold) their shelves will contain nothing but spring dresses and Hawaiian shirts.

Mail order Gets better and better. Since the pioneering days of Clothkits, this sector has boomed. For country dwellers and working mothers and all who hate shopping they are a boon and a delight. Children enjoy catalogues, and the measuring systems are effective. The order forms, however, are cleverly designed to make you spend more than you meant to.

Downmarket Most supermarket chains have a children's clothes section, and in the cheaper chains this is the home of the really downmarket clothes, cheap to buy but cheap in fabric (and sometimes made in dubious sweatshop conditions by Third World children, which is something you might like to check up on in your favourite chain). If children are growing a good deal faster than your bank balance can take, you will be thrown back on these; but approach them with cynicism and give the sleeves sharp, unforgiving tugs in the shop. Often you can get far better value at:

Jumble and second-hand sales In affluent districts of big cities, the most amazing clothes (often from the royal-ish shops) turn up as jumble or in 'opportunity shops'. No parent should be ashamed of using them. Rose's best beloved party dress for

131

three years cost me £1; I snapped up some wonderful shorts and T-shirts one summer for 50p the lot, pure cotton and nicely styled.

Homemade We all think this will be the best value of all, if one can be bothered; and so it might. One cautionary tale, though: a girl I know set out to make a fleecy tracksuit, spent three hours and £8 on fabric, and then saw a virtually identical one for £6 in an upmarket shop sale. Virtue is not always rewarded, after all.

However, if you are original and craftswomanlike (as is one of my sisters-in-law) you can make fantastic waistcoats and wild, wild pyjamas which go down very well right into the tall teens.

Getting older: status dressing Teenage ways (q.v.) start very early, these days. Peer group pressure at school is very strong, and by the time a girl or boy goes to secondary school they know what they like in the line of clothes. And shoes. What they like, because of complex commercial pressures, may be very expensive: £70 trainers, £60 sweatshirts, etc. Very similar items will be available at a third of the price, but you will be told that they *will not do*. If Adidas track-pants are the only possible kind, or a Kookai vest top is demanded, any attempt to fob the wearer off with virtually identical items from the Supersave shop will be met with shrieks and tears. Logos matter, tribal identity matters. It is all immensely frustrating to parents worn down by responsibilities and the boring demands of common sense. It is one of the issues that make you feel very, very old.

One of the best answers is to declare a clothes allowance, monthly, and pay it into an account. It seems to work best (from my researches) when the deal is as follows; parents buy the basics – underwear, socks, a few plain T-shirts, a best outfit, school stuff, simple sportswear. Anything beyond that has to be found, costed, and bought by the wearer out of the allowance (which is set according to what the family can afford). Application may be made for extra funds if the subject is buying something which is both dead cool and practical (e.g. a waterproof jacket). Valuable lessons are learnt because money frittered away on ghastly bangles, illegal alcopops and unauthorized nose-piercings becomes unavailable for the purchase of wicked combat trousers and rollerblade repairs, unless more is earned by washing the car. And so forth. Be reasonably fair, allow as much leeway as you can possibly bear to, and bite your lip before uttering unkind criticisms of other people's clothes just because those people happen to have grown in your womb fifteen years ago.

But remember: you don't have to handwash or iron any garment you absolutely hate. That would be asking too much. With freedom, children, comes responsibility . . .

Parties, Treats, Outings

Parties

Children's parties are the stuff of dreams and nightmares. The dream sequence shows a dozen little faces around a long table, a cake shaped like a train with Swiss-roll wheels, the soft light of candles and the piping of childish voices singing 'Happy Birthday' before filing out to Pass the Parcel with little squeaks of happy (yet somehow well-controlled) excitement.

The nightmare is of an invading rabble of screaming, cake-throwing delinquents. It is that you will be left single-handed with a fighting scrum of uncivilized infants, with the local asthmatic being crushed at the centre and your own birthday girl wailing dismally on the fringes.

Now, I like parties, and incline to optimism. I also have spent parental life in houses which suit children's parties (old, battered, devoid of fitted carpets and not too recently painted). Before the party phase ended we clocked up eighteen birthday parties, nine Christmas teas, several impromptu children's garden parties in summer and, best of all, a special mini-party held at ten minutes' notice for those younger siblings not invited to someone else's sixth birthday party.

I liked them all. I rationalize this with a lot of high-flown stuff about how children need to get some idea of formal social occasions as young as possible, in case one day they get asked to Buckingham Palace. But the truth is that, given a Thomas the Tank Engine tablecloth and a boxful of party squeakers, I throw myself into the proceedings with indecent zest. You may feel quite differently, but because it is hard to avoid having at least some children's parties, I offer what I have learnt. There are ground rules to observe, and I have broken them all in the past and suffered. Putting a lot of young children in a room with some balloons does not constitute an instant party. It will create instant tears. You need organization. A mother is an impresario, and a good party is a performance. It is a three-act drama, involving a lot of improvisation around a basic script. Here is that basic script.

Act I: The Games Invitations should always give a start time and a stop time – 3.30 to 5.30 p.m., for instance. Ideally, all the guests should arrive bang on time, and a game should begin as soon as their coats are off. This especially applies to four- and five-year-olds' parties; older children have more capacity for standing around chatting and opening presents without either losing their nerve or starting a fight. Mothers who dawdle along late are a nuisance. And if mothers have to stay (some younger children insist) they should refrain from chattering, interfering, or generally spoiling the ambience. You do, however, need to bag one of them as an assistant for taking children to the lavatory, retying hair bows on the fussier girls, and clapping plasters on wounds.

The first game ought to involve jumping up and down. This relieves tension, and ensures that anyone who wants to go to the loo develops the symptoms nice and early, before tea. Musical bumps, statues, or chairs fit the bill nicely. Next, for children over four I rather favour a more structured game, something that fits the theme of the party – pirates or circuses or ballerinas or whatever. (By the way, if you have a fancy dress theme party, make sure you have a few spare pirate kerchiefs, clown hats or whatever – there is always one child whose mother hasn't read the invitation or who has a new baby and keeps forgetting everything.)

These games are easier once the children have had a term at school; it is quite wonderful how, from being a big amorphous threatening mass, a group of sixteen children is miraculously turned into a Class. Once they have been at school you can have complicated games that need explaining; merely clap your hands decisively and say, 'NOW! Everyone is a pirate. There are two teams of pirates. Make two teams – red and blue, here are your rosettes. Now, the job is to find the treasure . . .' and so

135

on. Before school age, keep it simple. We had a howling success with a tracking exercise involving party streamers snaking around the house, leading them up climbing frames and down slides, through a makeshift tunnel, in one door and out the other, to a pirate island full of chocolate coins.

Once I went through a non-competitive phase and devised a game with no winners at all. The idea was that they were astronauts on a space mission to help a lot of wounded space monsters. Each child had a piece of card representing part of an octopus's tentacle. Each set of clues and stick-on green footprints led to a mutilated cardboard octopus in a different room, and they had to complete it by tessellating their pieces on until it was complete. Without every single child's piece the stages couldn't be completed, so the big ones kept a sharp eye on the small, confused ones who kept threatening to lose their bits of card.

The game was a success. I like to think it was because it brought out qualities of liberal cooperation, but reluctantly admit that the success could have something to do with the less idealistic aspect, which was that in one of the rooms they were pounced on by my husband, dressed as a six-foot-two green, furry, squawking parrot. It always pays to have a few surprises up your sleeve.

Act II: The Tea Anyone can lay on a children's party tea. I would not insult your intelligence by suggesting menus, except to point out that there are certain children who hate all sweet things and need sausages, crisps and cheese straws. Also that some children like sandwiches with no butter. Otherwise, do as you please: either spend eight hours making witches' hats out of ice cream and cakes with little faces on, or else nip down to the supermarket and buy the lot.

More serious is the problem of some children who have never had the experience of sitting down to a meal in company, because they are normally fed in front of the television or on the hoof. Such children may respond wonderfully to a pretty table with candles and crackers on it; or they may ruin everyone else's dignified formal tea by getting down and running

136

around. A touch of firmness is needed. I can confirm that a six-foot-tall, green, fur parrot is an invaluable disciplinary force: one squawk and down they sit.

The Cake is of course vital. Although, frankly, small children get so het up at parties that they rarely eat it, so you might as well ice a shoebox. Ask any child what it wants its cake to represent and the answer will probably be 'a combine harvester' or 'a ballerina on her points', and unless you are Jane Asher you are banjaxed. The trick is to steer the conversation round to something you can do, like a circus ring (round and flat) or a Swiss-roll train. My best effort so far has been a galleon – not as hard as it sounds. I got a friend to make two lumps of her patent ultra-dense sculptable sponge cake, shaped the bow and stern, lashed on the butter icing and Polo mint portholes, and rigged the whole thing with pencils and string (let nobody tell you that everything on a cake needs to be edible. If you are a genius with moulding-icing, then bully for you. Idle and feckless women like myself can get away with pencils, elastic bands, and bowsprits made of raw spaghetti. You're going to be supervising the eating of this cake more closely than any other of the year, so there is ample chance to whip off the inedible bits). The great moment was when we lit the candles and the rigging caught fire.

Act III: The Riot Tea is a jolly event, and it breaks the ice. However, ice can be useful stuff. It holds raging waters in check, and raging children too. If you rashly leave a game like Pass the Parcel until after tea, you may end up with your orderly circle turning into a heaving, struggling, shrieking mass of mixed infants and ripped newspaper. Pass the Parcel is a dodgy business anyway: they get bored, even if you put a sweet in between each layer. We jazzed it up by making it Pass the Octopus at the space party (pull off a tentacle every time, find sweet in tentacle) but even so it palled. Some jazz it up even further with silly forfeits like 'do a somersault', or 'sing a song'. But whether or not you play more games after tea, the Riot is inevitable.

There are two ways of handling it. You can hand the riot over

137

to a professional children's entertainer, with a Punch and Judy show or a collection of magic tricks. There is something ineffably soothing in hearing a voice in the next room saying, with that steely authority they have, 'Are you all happy, children?' and hearing an obedient chorus of 'Yeeeess!' However, under-fives may collapse in hysterical terror if the entertainer is even remotely frightening, and if he isn't, he may be unable to contain the seething, bubbling Riot that is waiting to happen. The only way to find a good entertainer is by personal recommendation, or by taking the risk of having your party end in chaos or anticlimax. If I could find a cheerful chap who would come with a guitar and lead a decent ordinary sing-song, I would opt for that instead.

The other solution to the after-tea problem is to channel the riot into a new direction of your own. One year Paul was dressed up as a bear and we inaugurated the game of chase-the-bear-and-tie-him-up in party streamers. It went very well, with shrieks of terror and delight in equal proportions. At another family's party, a wolf galloped about and the children were issued with water pistols to hunt him (it was in the garden). Once Paul was dressed up as a clown and the children were allowed to splat crazy-foam custard pies into his face. These events were chaotic and cathartic, as all good parties should be. But on the whole, I would not recommend starting them earlier than twenty minutes before official chucking-out time. When the mothers turn up and find their little darlings covered in streamers and foam and butter icing, they can take them away for a nice quiet bath.

Epilogue: The Party Bag This is a fine art. The trick is to put things into the bag which will give pleasure to the children, surprise them and keep them happy for a while, without spending too much money (even if you have it. Raise the expectations too much, and the other mothers will be justifiably cross with you). I worked on the basis of one small packet of sweets or chocolate figure, one balloon, a squeaker if one is left over, one incredibly cheap object (like a tiny pencil, or revolting 5p plastic bracelet) and one cheapish but very interesting thing. I collected these all

138

year round (still do, there is Christmas to be thought of, and auntly duties. The attic is always full of peculiar fibre-optic miniature torches, hopping false teeth, rainbow spectacles and impenetrable magic boxes.)

Finally, *The Guest Star* Somewhere among your friends' children, there must exist a child (often a boy) who is never frightened, never fazed, totally gregarious and ready for anything. Whether your child likes him or not, get him booked. I would never have a party without a certain Patrick, because I knew that if I said brightly, 'Now then, let's have a race pushing ping-pong balls with your noses,' Patrick would be down there, bum in the air, before I could finish the sentence. Say, 'Who can jump highest?' and your Patrick will be through the ceiling. If a smaller child doesn't know how to play musical bumps, she has only to watch Patrick falling like a stone to the floor, and she will get the hang of it immediately. Here's to Patrick, and all the Patricks everywhere. In years to come they will be the toast of some West End night spot and the darlings of the gossip columns; and who can grudge them their fame?

Treats and outings

Taking children on formal, old-fashioned treats becomes suddenly more rewarding after the age of four. Before that, their tolerance is short and you find yourself spending many a miserable hour at some fair which none of you is enjoying, or queuing in the rain for something the child would as soon not bother with. Early treats have to be close by, and brief in duration, or else something the adults so long to do that a bit of infantile whining does not ruin them.

But with four-to-eights, it becomes the shared fun you always hoped it would be. They have learned to look forward in anticipation, to be a bit patient in the car on the way, and to enjoy the thrill of collecting tiny souvenirs. They can, at small events, be trusted to go and buy their own ice creams (with you, needless to say, watching closely) and show other small signs of independence.

Common-sense rules apply: keep an eye out for signs saying TOILET even when nobody wants one yet; take a change of tracksuit in case of mud, rain, or accidents; and take your own fruit juice cartons and biscuits in case there is nothing to refresh the inner child. Prepare the ground, research the nature of the treat, and take advice more readily from fellow parents than from Tourist Board brochures.

One tip: now that children are well and truly beyond the age of reins and harnesses – and even strict hand-holding – if you go to crowded places you could dress each child of a pair in one identical garment – yellow sweater, the same anoraks, plaid trousers, whatever. That way, if you lose one you can brandish the remaining child of the pair and say to every passer-by, 'Have you seen another one wearing one of these?' It is amazing how effective this can be. If you lose both, you are really not concentrating and your only hope is to take a granny with you next time. Grannies are very vigilant. Unless, that is, they are the sort who wander off and get lost themselves.

Here are some good treats:

Theatre trips Of all the set-piece treats, these are the most worthwhile. Children are actors. Watch any toddler pull a pair of knickers on to its head and stare admiringly into the mirror. Hats and turbans are usually the first step to dressing up, because a hat is the quickest way to change your identity. The next thing is shoes. Beryl Reid says that the way she gets into a new part is to get the shoes right, and everything else follows. Any three-year-old clumping around in Daddy's Wellington boots could tell you that. It is a great day for a child, when it grows tall enough to put its parents' Wellingtons on without suffering too much discomfort around the crotch.

Next come jackets, cardigans, shawls, tablecloths, pillow-cases and masks. After that, if you have any sense, you provide a proper dressing-up box, generously filled with a jumble of old clothes (shirts with frayed collars, battered rain hats, and those little sequinned tops Mummy wore in her disco days, before breastfeeding modified her own little top beyond repair). I believe there are families who manage without a dressing-up

140

box, but I cannot see how. In our house, such a box is the only hope of stopping the children from borrowing every other garment in the house. The mystery remains why they will not dress themselves for school when they are so quick and skilful at deciding to 'do a play' by donning military jackets, plastic fireman's helmets, ragged pirate trousers, thick face paint and Hawaiian shirts with bits cut out for the last patchwork quilt. But I digress.

Drama is not a luxury, it is an instinct. It needs feeding with a few professional or good amateur productions, treats which inspire hours of games and performances on toy theatres. Living in deep Suffolk, we were never frequent theatregoers with the children; if we were Londoners, they would no doubt be whooshed from marionette show to Roundhouse, and virtually live on the South Bank. As it is, we might choose one or two really good children's plays per year, and otherwise rely on the pantomime to invigorate them every Christmas. Never, by the way, despise pantomime. A good one is a perfect introduction to the joys of theatre: spectacle, involvement, and the willing but knowing suspension of disbelief. You laugh, you tremble, you sympathize, and you wonder how they got the Giant Pumpkin on to the stage. It is grand opera, it is Shakespeare, it is circus, it is Greek tragedy, all reduced to childlike proportion. Sometimes, I grant you, it is reduced too far: even infants can have their intelligence insulted by some productions, and as David Holman's plays have proved, seven-year-olds are capable of taking in some powerful, non-comic drama as well. But on the whole, pantomime or a children's comedy is not a bad beginning.

Having enthused, let me warn. It is very unwise to take a child to its very first theatrical production without finding out all you can about it. Is it a noisy showbiz production full of rock 'n' roll and smutty jokes? How long is it? Is there a story you could explain beforehand? Reviews help a bit, but above all word-of-mouth recommendation is the key. The best bet may be a small local amateur production in a church hall. Small children get so fascinated with the whole idea of curtains going up and down and people being disguised, that they quite enjoy

141

the fact that they can see the stagehand's arm doing the winding, and that the villain is clearly the plumber who unblocked your drains last week. Also, church halls are less frightening for the timid.

Small children need some preparation for what will happen in a theatre. They need to know that the lights will go out in the auditorium; and that it is all pretend. The Demon King is someone's Daddy, dressed up for a laugh. They also need to be told that you have to sit quietly and watch, or whisper very quietly, or go out. Neglect all this and you may well be rewarded with shrieks, kicks, hysteria and profound embarrassment. Like I was. You also have to carry a yelling, terrified child along a row of seats while another hysterical, screaming child behind you begs to be allowed to stay and watch. First theatre visits work best with a ratio of one adult per child.

But it is worth it. After a theatre visit children act out plays and pantomimes together for months, learning essential lessons: that things are not always as they seem, that sometimes it helps to shout and express your feelings, that roles can be changed, pretences made and conflicts played out to a satisfactory conclusion. And that all of us, at least in our mirrors privately, have the right to be heroes and beauties who star in our own wonderful stories.

Cinemas Most of the same cautions apply. Cinema is less intense than theatre, more than television: a good halfway house. Films, however, need even more careful vetting than theatrical performances: some of those bearing a U certificate are really not fit for the eyes of under-thirteens. The worst fault of films, as far as little children are concerned, is their tiresome habit of allusiveness: they assume their audience to be totally plugged in to a particular stream of Americanized schoolkid culture and to understand all its references. A European six-year-old may be utterly baffled by most of it. The old Disney standards are always a success; Superman comes into his own at ages over seven, in my view, as do the Spielberg blockbusters.

One warning: cinema managements are very insensitive about young children, and often put on tacky trailers for '18' films and disproportionately frightening 'B' features with a soppy, gentle main film. The experience of trying to calm down three petrified little boys of five faced with *Peter and the Wolf* (big yellow teeth) when we had come to see *101 Dalmatians* and only prepared them for Cruella de Ville is something I would not wish to repeat. Ring up and ask.

Museums have suddenly discovered young children in the last decade. Gone are the rows of dull glass cases and the hushed, scholarly atmosphere; they are becoming almost too good, full of moving dinosaurs and feely-boxes and machines you can wind up yourself. The only trouble is that if you have a rather hushed scholarly sort of child, who actually enjoys staring into glass cases at the teeth of pterodactyls, he may get frustrated. In the City Museum in York we went to look specifically at suits of armour, and found that it was compulsory to walk round on a pre-set track, past all the reproductions of old shops, doll's houses, and everything else before we could get to them. It did nothing for anyone's temper.

The most successful sort of museums are sometimes local ones: either humble little displays you can explain at leisure ('Those coins were dropped a thousand years ago, and have just been dug up. Vikings used them. What do you think they bought?') or else the grander 'Heritage Centres' with displays which take you into the middle of a nineteenth-century lighthouse, or let you sit in the driving seat of a tram. Never assume that children will be bored by a very straightforward museum. I once took mine into Norwich Castle Museum for no other reason than to get out of the sluicing Norwich rain, and we spent two hours communing with stuffed animals and spelling out the labels on mummy cases. An extra frisson was added by the underfloor heating grilles, on which a little girl may stand and see her skirt blow up around her waist like Marilyn Monroe.

Museums can give children a very good graphic skeleton of history. In Portsmouth one day we saw the ships *Mary Rose* (sixteenth century), HMS *Victory* (eighteenth) and HMS *Warrior* (Victorian). Later we saw a Viking ship of the eleventh century,

143

in reproduction. For years, when the eldest wanted to put something in perspective, he said, 'Is that when *Mary Rose* was sailing? Or later? Before *Victory*, though?' All history is conveniently punctuated by the changing shapes of ships. You can do the same with castles, architecture, industrial inventions, anything.

Art galleries Again, surprisingly successful. Young children merely roam around, and should not be dragged to look at painters in a systematic way, or even to learn their names unless they ask. Children should be told not to run in galleries, and not to chatter about anything except the exhibits; beyond that, any attempt to curb their enthusiasm or hush their voices is probably doomed. Smile a lot at the attendants. Most are quite understanding, especially if children are really looking at the pictures: 'Look! He's got a lion on his foot! It might bite him! Specially with no clothes on!'

Theme parks We need them because of the decline of the funfair. Once – and still, in a few places – there were steam funfairs, paradises of gleaming brass machinery, gentle and beautiful artwork, flowers and gilding and baroque flourishes to sail past mounted on your pole horse or steam yacht. Modern funfairs are, on the whole, rackety, crudely coloured, violent in tone and often unsafe in fact. They are geared to teenagers, not children. So American-style theme parks are stepping in, with wonderful fantasy rides, friendly furry bears that wander about waving aimlessly at everyone, nice little railways, ample lavatories, and strict, strict regulations. Also, you can often ride on everything for the price of the entry ticket, which defuses the financial tension of parents. For a big day out, they are matchless. But they do cloy very quickly. One outing per summer is probably enough.

Steam fairs, horse shows, county fairs Each have their own local flavour. These events – rather nightmarish with toddlers – evolve into pleasant days out with older children. Especially if you have no overwhelming need to find any particular engine or horse, but meander along and let them lead the way. Choose the event depending on whether your children like steam engines or Shire horses best; the adjacent stalls, round-abouts, charity markets, bouncy castle and such will be much the same. Any event run by the local Rotary Club is bound to have decent Portaloos. Or so I have always found.

Battles Various societies of obsessives are in the habit of re-enacting historical battles – Civil War, medieval jousts, Viking scuffles. Even the gentlest of children seem to adore these. Just remember two things: don't sit too near the ropes, because not all of the participants are very good at hanging on to their flails, axe heads, or whatever; and be resigned to a houseful of a mayhem for weeks afterwards. Take the chance to impart some history, even if you have to read it up surreptitiously yourself from a children's encyclopaedia beforehand.

Holidays are more fully dealt with in '**Fun, Fun, Fun**', p.325. But while we are talking of smallish children, note that holiday travel becomes suddenly far easier after four. Children who can crayon, look at books or listen to Walkmans are manageable in cars and trains and aeroplanes. What is the best diversion depends entirely on your child, and I would not dream of prescribing them too closely: small toys help, board games for some, little prisms to distort the world for others, pencils and paper for all. The best toy for a travelling child is another child the same age: pooling families can make things far more pleasant. The only other bit of advice I would presume to give is *don't take too much*. I am a light packer, and yet I have never, ever, used all the children's clothes I packed. Not once. Pack the minimum, then take two things per child out. As long as one of them is not Teddy.

Children over five can quite well be fitted into exotic adult holidays. But it takes a lot of work, and for the children the rewards may be dubious, and not enough to repay the air fares. Beautiful Greek beaches may actually be made of gritty gravel and poisonous sea urchins, and hotels with romantic balconies may be death traps for bored clambering children. Even cruise

145

ships and flotilla yachts can feel like prison hulks to a child who prefers kicking footballs to any other of life's joys.

Also, think of what children actually say about past holidays. 'What did you enjoy most?' we ask. And they reply, 'Ooh, the best bit was when Daddy changed the tyre on the car going to the airport, and we helped with the jack.' After trying out various types of holiday and canvassing friends, I have come to the startling conclusion that small children actually prefer rather Spartan holidays, and that it is a shame that the crazy economics of Western tourism often make it cheaper for families to go on a package to a Spanish hotel than to wander about exploring their own country's odd edges. Doing the best from the child's point of view doesn't necessarily mean taking him to the biggest and best theme park, or on a plane to the Mediterranean. Children are not as sun-struck as adults, nor as blasé about entertainment. They like simple things, like jumping in puddles and watching waves crash over a seaside promenade in a gale. They are often more excited by the swooshing northern tides ('Oh Mummy, is that God doing that?' asked one, the first time a wave filled up his ditch) than by the gritty tideless beaches of the south, where giant vacuum cleaners have to clear the debris daily and you can hardly run around without falling over torpid, oily adult bodies.

In any case, for a young child three-quarters of the pleasure of a holiday is having the constant company of both parents. In modern life, children already miss out on one huge, vital chunk of experience because they so rarely see their parents working. The adult world, the adult mind, is a mystery. They may watch their mother overcoming everyday problems, and doing routine jobs at home, but they rarely see their father weaving a carpet or mending a plough for his living. Fathers tend to be shut away in mysterious offices and factories, doing incomprehensible things. So, more and more, do mothers. This makes early holidays doubly important, especially if they provide a chance to watch your parents overcoming real problems – tents that won't go up, or trains that leave you stranded. The times my children talked about for years were when we all trudged

146

across a bleak Irish beach carrying a little camp stove to make tea; when we climbed a hill together to a castle, and hid in the ruins from the British rain; or when we went on the Norfolk Broads in a dreadful houseboat and got blown into the rushes by gale-force winds. They have few memories of the packaged, group things we have done, just a dim sense of Mummy and Daddy waiting crossly and helplessly for the airport coach, along with fifty other herded passengers at midnight in a foreign airport. Parents passive, parents dependent on a bossy lady courier, parents made to sit in a row until the bus came, and hand over their passports: is that a holiday memory to enrich the rest of the year?

So if you are restricted by money to a hired caravan, or a tent on a windswept camping site nearer home, take heart. Children will get as much out of it, or more: discovering starfish and rabbit holes at your side, exploring local museums, learning the folk tales of the region, making maps and working out the next day's walk. And you will have real memories to share, of a holiday that may have been uncomfortable at times but was like nobody else's: your private family adventure.

Electronic Children:
TV and computers

The brave new electronic world is on us. Screens rule; the Worldwide Web has changed the nature of knowledge, computer games have altered childhood, television has become more important than parents. Some children are coming into school unaccustomed to real-time conversation even of the simplest sort; as they grow older, their ideas of human behaviour are partly conditioned by a medium which shows them fifty human deaths a week, and a set of games based on heartless, psychopathic remote-control violence. Culturally, emotionally, and neurologically, this is a disaster. Woe is us! We're doomed, I tell'ee, doomed!

Nothing is easier than to freeze the public blood and spread general dismay with statements of this kidney. As usual with scare stories, the net result is to make most of us screen out the subject entirely for most of the time, which does no good either.

This chapter cannot cover every aspect of electronics and children; there are whole books on that. But there are some useful ways to moderate the flow of pixillating pixels, and a useful overall attitude to take. This can be summed up as: *if real life is made attractive, real life will always triumph over the virtual world; and computers and televisions are only tools.* They are morally neutral. It is how you use them that counts. If you have a chisel in your hand you can use it to start building a great cathedral, or to stick in someone's eye. It is not the chisel's fault if you make the wrong decision.

Television

It is undeniably true that we have now created – in the affluent West at least – a situation where, for the first time in human history, children get far less than half their information about

148

the world from their close, primary carers. Michael Green, the comic writer, says that he dates the decline of fatherly authority from the arrival of television, when he was a boy. Once, your dad – who'd probably been in the war, and travelled a bit – was the most exotic source of information about the world you had, so you listened to his stories. Then the telly came, and you could *see* penguins and pagodas and foreigners, and it was all much more slickly presented than your dad's boring old stories – so you stopped listening to the old man, and that was that.

The process has intensified since then. If they watch a lot, and alone, it is the television and video which tell children about relationships, the uses of force, the importance of sex, the place of money in human life, the value of life itself. And you know and I know that by and large – with honourable exceptions – it tells them wrong. It is biased towards showiness, towards extremes, towards dramatic simple confrontations, towards empty fashionable agnosticism, towards cynicism. But it tells its stories well, and if there is not enough to counter them, it can begin to take over. In the playground little boys play at being Stallone and Schwarzenegger, and little girls preen and primp and flirt and cling to the boyfriend idea as expressed in *Neighbours* and in *Friends*.

That British children watch too much television is axiomatic; surveys suggest four or five hours a day is perfectly unremarkable even for five-year-olds who go to school. Research on pre-school children in Manchester has discovered a large drop in their average ability to pay attention, or distinguish real voices against the television. Even the most cautious psychologists are beginning to say that the habit of all-day television for pre-school children is measurably lessening their ability to listen properly, or catch the rhythms of speech. Where once nursery rhymes or tickling games would have been familiar, now the cadences in many children's heads are all TV cadences; and because they are not real, and can become background, the habit of not listening develops.

It is, however, curable. The same research showed that even when twenty or thirty minutes a day was spent playing with the small child, with the telly off, listening skill rapidly recovered. Even so, the instinct of most parents who think at all is to try and ration television at an early age. Why should a bright, keen, good-hearted and impressionable little child sit mesmerized by cynical rubbish on the television screen for five hours or more a day? One resignedly expects teenagers to lie around like slugs in the holidays, watching rubbishy films while the sun shines vainly outside; it is part of the mysterious process of modern puberty. But for a five- or six-year-old to be passive, uncritical and vague, sitting waiting for the next bit of trite or violent programming to be piped into his head, is a dreadful thing indeed.

So what do you do? What most of us do is get crosser and crosser and finally storm into the room shouting, 'Turn off that rubbish!' just when they were watching a rather good documentary about seabirds. This is our way of compensating for not having interrupted the preceding programme, (about obscenely bulging American superheroes zapping one another in the name of intergalactic brotherhood), because we were busy talking on the phone, and preferred distant spaceship noises to close-up whingeing of 'I'm bored, what can I do?' We are all to some extent guilty. What is needed is a Clear Policy.

To assist you in forming one, here is a set of guidelines. Some are my own family's, some borrowed; some frankly verging on the fanatical. Pick a few, formulate a policy, and stick to it:

Accept from the outset that some television is good for children. There are dramas, stories, documentaries, well-made cartoons and children's news programmes which make a positive contribution to their education. Let them know that you approve, and watch with them sometimes, uttering constructive criticisms. There is no point in regarding television as a mere vice. Taking the good from it is the first step towards rejecting the bad or banal.

Make a rule from earliest years that they always switch off the machine at the end of a programme, so that they can discuss it. Even when our children were allowed to see two consecutive

150

programmes, they still switched off for a moment in between. In this way, television is treated like a book, or a meal properly set at table: something to approach deliberately and intelligently rather than used as a non-stop tap of indifferent, half-understood entertainment.

If you can possibly afford a video recorder, get one. Use it to tape and keep programmes for children. Watching the same thing twice or three times doesn't hurt; it encourages a critical attitude. Even a five-year-old will start to wonder how the puppets move, or why they put a song in the play just there. Raising a new generation of critics has to be better than a generation of couch potatoes. A video also enables you to enforce time rules, such as, 'No television before lunch, ever.' And yes, it lets you use the television sometimes as a babysitter – when you are desperate for peace and quiet with a newspaper in the next room – because you can know that they are watching something worth seeing, which you have vetted.

If a young child really wants to watch a programme you regard as pointless rubbish (probably because everyone else in his school does), a good compromise is to agree provided that he subsequently switches off and writes a review (minimum 20 words) and draws a picture to illustrate it. The labour of spelling out the plot of 'WonderBarbie meets My Little Pony' may well dent its appeal.

Encourage a child to distinguish between programmes that make her think and tell her new things, and what my children called 'the brainlesses'. Everyone is entitled to one or two brainlesses a week, but they ought to know which ones they are. Mine is *Coronation Street*.

Watch with them for at least one session a week, and try to gauge how much they do and don't understand, especially of advertising. Explain what advertising is for, and how it tries to persuade you to want things. Analyse techniques (four is not too young to start). Children rather like to be one up on the

151

adult world, and rapidly stop wanting advertised toys so much when they have understood that someone is trying to trick them into desire.

Try to put off for as long as possible teaching young children how to switch on the television by themselves. I never fail to be amazed at the way some children of three and four will hammer downstairs at dawn to switch on pappy Breakfast TV. Switch the thing off at the mains, put a chair in front of the switch, don't make it easy.

Having said that, one very enterprising small child I know came down one morning alone, switched on the TV, didn't think much of the pictures and boldly replaced them with his own, with poster paints on the screen. His parents couldn't bring themselves to scold him, since he had shown such sturdy independence of the broadcasting industry. He had, they felt, the right spirit.

Keep the television in a common area – kitchen, lounge, whatever – even if you have two sets. Bedroom televisions are a really, really bad idea for anybody under . . . well, I say anybody under fifteen, but I am an extremist by modern standards. But I really do believe that encouraging lonely, unsupported, uncritical viewing of everything the networks throw out these days is asking for trouble.

Besides, genuine family viewing – with everybody sharing and cat-calling and laughing and gasping together, whether at *The Simpsons* or the classic serial – is one of the joyful and positive things about television. The conversations and jokes and arguments arising out of a good film, comedy, or documentary can keep you all going for weeks. They can also provide, without undue effort or such American earnestnesses as self-conscious 'family co-counselling' or 'quality communication time', a very valuable set of clues as to what children think about human relationships, moral values, and sex. I always find it rather heartening when in the middle of an Agatha Christie mystery or a frivolous James Bond film, to whose violence we have as adults become quite desensitized, a child suddenly goes all puritanical and says, 'Gross!' Or when they watch an adult row in a situation comedy or soap with narrowed eyes and then pronounce, 'They're both being really, really bossy and stupid, aren't they?'

But growing children will also want to watch certain programmes which you allow but which, with the best will in the world, you cannot face sharing with them. It could be football, or some computer-game quiz, or a brainless (but not particularly violent) cop series. In this case, if the children are under sixteen you ought to know something about the programme: dip into it, ask friends, check a film's rating. And you ought to ration, in a general way, the time that they are in front of the box. Just to keep the average down. 'You watched six hours yesterday. Let's leave it off. You can video something for the next wet day if you want' is more reasonable than 'Switch that rubbish off and get some fresh air!'

What that ration is you must judge, and agree, as a family. Possibly even with a bit of democracy involved. I cannot prescribe for anyone else. All I can remark is that it will be easier to ration television if your living area is not arranged exclusively around it; if, for example, there is a chair you can put in front of the screen looking inwards to a table where you sometimes play a family game of cards, or where someone sits and reads. If a room looks like a small cinema, that is how it will be treated.

Computer gaming

Over 85 per cent of British children over five play computer games regularly. Every now and then a fearful story crops up in the papers about some under-two who sits all day in his nappies bleeping and zapping, and screams when taken away from the screen. 'Computer addiction' is a condition increasingly referred to child psychiatrists. It is not difficult to get into a state where the sight of a Game Boy makes you burst into tears. Woe, woe! Is Mario stealing my baby's soul?

Let us dismiss the extremes, first of all. Computer game addiction usually manifests itself by playing excessive hours and, frankly, that problem has its root in parents having forgotten how to wield authority. Psychologists report, in slightly dazed tones, that affluent parents come to them with tales of a young child spending fifty hours a week at the screen and show surprise when it is suggested they should say no. I suspect, however, that these dingbats are the exception rather than the rule. Like the mother of the latest toddler 'addict' who stunned the nation with her artless line, 'I'm lucky. I have friends with children the same age and you see them clutching at their mums all the time and demanding attention. I don't get that with Sam.' You don't need me to comment on that.

But what has to strike you is that it is possible at all. Something is getting to little Sam, on a level that things don't normally get to toddlers. They won't colour all day, or do play-dough all day, or even tease the dog all day. Why will they computer all day? Is the uniquely computerish form of random satisfaction something genuinely addictive? The graphics these days are far better than they used to be, therefore more satisfyingly real in appearance. Judgement about whether some children are exceptionally vulnerable to addiction is something I leave to psychiatric professionals; I would submit that certainly among older children, it does not usually occur unless something else is wrong.

What else is wrong may be physical circumstances – children cooped up indoors because there's nowhere to play, or their parents are afraid of traffic and child molesters. It may be solitude, not enough peers, or siblings, or parents willing and able to keep company with them. We always kept the television in the big family kitchen, which had the games connected to it, until they were well into their teens. The games became sociable. We watched as we strolled through, cheered Supermario on his way and went 'Awwww!' when he got zapped. All the children I have watched playing computer games in company, like this, have been, after a while, self-limiting: they give up after a reasonable time and go in the garden to play with the dog. But then, we have a garden and a dog to play with. That's not universal. Safe play space is in shortage because of the pathetically short-sighted and grasping habits of British local and national government for twenty years.

Other things which seem to make them play or view longer, more intensely, and more worryingly are personal. In an untidy and hostile world there is something profoundly soothing about an interactive screen. It is a domain you can predictably control, a relationship without responsibility, a colloquium in which nobody judges you. If you are on the run from real life, there are certainly some very beguiling alternatives on the market. And those who are most at risk of getting drawn in too deep are on the run: from divorce, rejection, friendlessness, anger. Screens do not ambush happy people and wreck their lives. They are just there, available for the easing of pain and loneliness, as in earlier decades were trashy novels or booze or trainspotting or tarts or barmy religions. When a hostage becomes unnaturally obsessed with taming the beetles in his cell, we do not inveigh against the beetles. Rather, we deplore the cell.

So, more specifically, to children and games. These are some things which help:

Don't be bamboozled by the range of 'pre-computers' and pre-school toys with chips in. Some of them are good toys, some are bad. Their computer element, frankly, is often the least interesting thing about them. They are no more educational than a good construction set (see 'Toys', p. 107).

When children do get to the age for games consoles, try and know what they are playing. Computer games range from the highly educational, creative, delightful ones like Sim City, which is training a whole new generation of enlightened city planners, via games of skill like ski and flight and skateboard and sailing simulations, to pretty disgustingly violent ones like the Carmageddon series and Carpocalypse Now and Tomb Raiders, artfully designed to lure teenagers and alarm parents. It always amazes me to hear the parents of a nine- or ten-year-old saying, 'He's up playing computer games,' and when you ask which games he likes, they DO NOT KNOW. Would these

155

people, if asked who was babysitting, say, 'Oh, some guy from the park'? Even small children, under five, are often found playing very violent screen games, which is a bad idea because before a certain stage they can't really distinguish between fact and fiction. Some get nightmares of guilt when they have 'zapped' realistic people, or dogs, or whatever.

Keep the gaming area in one of the shared parts of the house; walk past, discuss what the game is about while you get on with the supper. Do not let it be a separate world. It helps if the children get used to playing the games most of the time with the sound off. The absence of booms and crashes and bleeps keeps the emotional temperature down. The general conversation, or the radio, or the cat mewing for its tea reminds them there is a real world out there.

Encourage sharing with other children. Any game using two controllers is better than a lonely one; even better are the sort of games which cause three or four children to gather round and whoop encouragement at the players.

Enforce screen breaks, for the sake of eyes and nerves. Give warning, let a level be finished, but enforce it.

Provide real alternative forms of amusement and keep computers away from these. Personally, I loathe and despise Game Boys and all portable computer games when they are brought on outings. They are harder to share, cannot be wonderful for even young eyesight, and most important of all, they stop children looking around at the outside world. There are few things more depressing than crossing the Channel on a ferry on a sparkling blue day, when children should be looking over the rail in wonder or running around the decks annoying people, to see scores of them hunched obsessively over their little plastic boxes.

Individual hand-held computer games, the cheap kind, are less pernicious (especially on holiday) because you soon get fed up with them. To have the full power and inventiveness of a big-scale computer game with you at all times is a different matter. A case for parental veto or rationing, if ever there was one.

It may be that you find all of the above advice hopelessly old-fashioned, that your children each had consoles in their bedroom from the age of three, and play alone for twenty-five hours a week while still excelling at conversation, home cooking, double bass and jujitsu. Fine. But if other things do start to go wrong – health, happiness, aggression levels – do the experiment of removing the computer-game element from their lives for a week or two. It has been known to have startling results.

The Internet

There is, obviously, an overlap here. The child who played screen games from five years old will, by the time the teens strike, be pretty damn interested in the Internet; not least because there are lots of games you can play on it or download off it. This brings up the whole subject of the new millennium's wonderful world of 'virtuality' and the fact that more and more parents are also plugged into some web or other, for both work and play. You need to think of the wider picture before considering how growing children fit into it. So let me digress . . .

Recently, a report in *Harvard Business Review* had the psychologist David Hallowell expressing concern for workers in offices who have 'fallen victim to virtuality'. Most of their communication is through e-mail, voicemail and the Net; even when they telephone someone they are met by one of those robot voices offering six options of buttons to press after the star key, and putting them on endless hold. A theatre or cinema booking, or a bank transaction, or any of the hundred small private affairs of any day is less and less likely to contain spontaneous human speech: nobody to make a joke with, nobody even to *pretend* to hope you have a nice day.

The result is that they lose the ability to relate to others in

157

what he calls an 'authentic psychological encounter that can only happen when two people share the same physical space'. Mr Hallowell recommends prescribed Human Moments during the day, when the workforce compulsorily practises encountering other real people. It's a lovely irony for those of us who had our first jobs in an era where the boss's priority was to try and stop us hanging around the coffee machine and flirting over the photocopier. Now the bosses are forcing us out there to practise authentic psychological encounters in the same physical space . . .

The point is that the electronic communication, at any age, strips out certain primitive, vital layers of humanity: conversation, charm, empathy, intuition, reading moods, tolerating bad ones, making a smiling immediate contact. The shy young man who once would have had to go to the local dance and suffer the agonies of making eye contact and risking rebuff when he asked a girl to dance can now cop out and spend his evenings talking dirty to invisible girls in Internet chat-rooms. There are fake alternatives to social life, just as there are fake alternatives to adventure. The tongue-tied fat girl can pretend to be a sizzling Monroe lookalike in her e-mail love affair, and the sluggish, cowardly, unfit young man can go down bobsleigh runs and leap from roof to roof and wrestle with monsters just by pushing buttons on a console controller.

On one level you can applaud that, and say that the virtual world frees the human imagination from the limits of the human body and of space. But of course the frumpy girl is not really getting what she needs: the acceptance of her human worth, in its true human state. And the young man is not getting any exercise, or any physical skills beyond the simple hand-eye co-ordination of the computer game.

The business executive who doesn't get out much is losing too – because gradually his skills at reading people, judging people, getting the hunch, evaluating the creative idea will go as well. It creates a business environment which is wary of new ideas and lateral thinking because it is so easy, now, for the top of the company to impose a matrix, a pattern based on past successes – and make people conform to it. One of the most alarming things is that employers now report a generation of salesmen who can't sell without a ready-made pitch, receptionists who don't know how to smile and say 'Can I help you?' as if they meant it, and new management recruits who walk round the factory floor with visible awkwardness whenever they meet a real employee, and only get happy when they're back in the clean white office scanning the 3D computer model of the line.

Well, that's the adult world. We're in the middle of a big experiment. It's exciting; it's technically brilliant. It has brought immense benefits, and enabled new ways of working for people like me, who can download up-to-the-minute information and write national newspaper columns from damp provincial farmsteads.

Its downside is starting to be understood better, now: the physical and psychological problems of virtuality, the loss of real human jobs, the limits of the electronic age. I don't get particularly worried about all those executives needing Human Moments programmed into their day. They're grown-ups. What we are thinking about here is children, and teenagers; and because they are not yet fully formed, the potential problem is much greater.

The cyberworld affects them in two ways: through parents, and generally. To take the first: I work from home, and when my own children were small, the phone often rang, interrupting play times and mealtimes with work queries from magazines and newspapers. There wasn't much choice, often, but to answer it. OK, so five o'clock is babies' teatime, and you all sit down together and have a joke and a chat over the toasted cheese. But if you've got a deadline, and the paper's printing at 5.30, a call at 5.15 may be to check a fact or query a line which is absolutely vital to your credibility and to your career and therefore to your very ability to put that cheese on that table for the children. So you answer it. And of course it isn't necessarily urgent at all, but still you carry on the conversation.

And goodness, the kids get cross. I've heard of a child of three who put the telephone in a bucket of water to drown it. Mine never went that far, but you could sense the angry

159

disappointment in them when I broke off talking to them to go and talk to the cold hard grey thing in the corner. Eventually, we compromised by leaving a loudspeaking answerphone on, so that we could decide. 'Shall Mummy tell the man what he wants to know? What do you think? Oh, all right then. Just quickly.'

Their instincts were right. It is right to expect that real breathing people, in the same room with you, should outrank distant interrupters. But it brought home to me how this process has been going on for many years: how readily we answer telephones in the middle of serious family conversation and allow the scheduling of television programmes to dictate our family evenings. It is a kind of alienation. Video recorders and answerphones reduce this dehumanizing effect but nevertheless we have all taken a step away from concrete, physical reality into an electronic virtual world, just by the way we live among machines.

A survey in Britain recently showed that of those who use the Internet, nearly half claim to be on it for 60 hours a week. Others spoke of 28 hours a week. That is a lot of hours. The university researcher who wrote the report asked, 'Would you rather be online than with your friends or family?' and over half of them said, 'Yeah, sometimes' or 'Quite often'. The people with high scores on her use and attitude scale were more likely to suffer from depression and introversion.

Admittedly, her survey was of only 445 users, recruited through a Web page; and there are seven million Britons who use the Net, and I doubt that we all spend such extravagant spans of time on it. But Dr Petrie said that as a psychologist she regards the Net as addictive because it delivers 'intermittent and random positive reinforcement'. In other words you don't always get what you want, but when you do it feels damn good. Most of these overusers were thirtyish; as many women as men.

Some of these thirtysomethings are parents. And what their children see – as well as the dominance of phones and television pictures – is adult people who constantly look for answers, not in the world around them, but in a screen. This must affect their idea of the world and of reality. Electronic stuff matters; real stuff, not so much. The Chief Rabbi Dr Jonathan Sacks spoke very eloquently lately of the threat to family life of these electronic tools: 'Eating the Sabbath meal together, celebrating the festivals at home, reading the Bible to our children – these are among the most powerful bonds between the generations. Present-day culture has no equivalent – the Walkman, computer games and the Internet we enjoy alone . . . families can only flourish on the basis of dedicated time, shared celebration and conversation . . . we must teach lost skills, restate forgotten values, and rescue parenthood from the bonfire of responsibilities.' I teased him in print, at the time, for overstatement, saying that any family life which can be blown apart by 32-bit technology must have been pretty rickety to start with. But he was making a valid point. Cyberspace must not come between us.

Children's own relationship with the Internet has been the subject of much public anguish because of the sites and newsgroups which are pornographic – often violently so – and the few but shocking cases where paedophiles have 'groomed' their teenage victims through the Net before arranging meetings. It is self-evident that parental responsibility has to be applied to Web-surfing just as it must to every other kind of encounter. If you have a teenager who spends a lot of time online, you probably need the software which records every site visited, and time spent; you may want one of the 'filter' programmes which cuts out dodgy sites. Unfortunately, these mostly appear to do caveman-simple things like cutting out anything with the word 'sex' in it, which can seriously rot up your A-level biology student's research material and cause undue resentment.

Probably the best guarantee against damage or confusion is the normal communication you have with your child. This, during teenage years, can be a problem but is always worth persevering with. If a parent or relative is around for enough time, slow to leap to judgement or hysteria, and willing to listen (leaning on the kitchen worktop while one of you has a late-night pizza, in the car, wherever) then important issues will eventually come up. If not, they won't.

161

Indeed, personal happiness and reasonable self-esteem are the best weapons against any kind of computer brain invasion. So is an alternative, sociable, physical pastime. We all know that a healthy small child gets more fun out of a sociable kitten than out of a Furby, and relishes a rough and tumble game with its dad more than a television programme. We need to extend that common sense into older ages too. The Internet chat-room may be a useful place to try out ideas and work through dilemmas and be listened to, but it should not be the only place available.

Computers, I say again, are only *things*. Morally neutral things. The choice is yours, not the thing's. Human greed, laziness, prejudice and obstinacy are the real enemies. The only harm that electronics will do to any of us is if we abuse them; or if we get so nervous of them that we refuse to learn about them ourselves, and leave them as weapons in the hands of a few clever enthusiasts whom we cannot necessarily trust.

They do not, in any deep sense, change the nature of childhood or adolescence, of human love or family kinship. Throughout human history, the props and backdrops change faster than the human heart. Ageing generations must be careful: it is easy to be put off by the latest set of gizmos and fail to notice that the people handling them are actually very little different to you, bowling your hoop down the dusty lanes of yesteryear. Cyberspace is only the shared mental space of conversation, which is as old as language; electronic games have no paranormal power but succeed only by stimulating the same brain cells that have challenged the ingenuity of toy-makers and entertainers for a thousand years. They are just things, bits of plastic and of glass, high- speed notes made by people far away whom we do not know. If we don't invite them to bring our children up for us, they can't. If they are made useful servants, they can never be the masters.

One often point. The phenomenon of parents not talking to children enough is not to be simplistically blamed on computer leisure. It is our own fault for being so stressed and materialistic and hellbent on having it all. It is also our own fault, not the censor's, if young children play disturbingly violent computer games or see a lot of corrupting films. It is a parent's job to know which cassette is in the slot. There is a peculiar, startling form of neglect observable in many affluent families which does not bother to check even that; but if you haven't time to watch the screen for a while and discuss why some things are sick, then why on earth have children in the first place?

And when the inevitable moment comes when the older offspring stump off alone to their rooms and positively demand the isolation we so deplore, there is nothing new or high-tech about that, either. I used to shut myself up for days with Bob Dylan and detailed fifty-point plans for running away. One of my brothers vanished into his bedroom for two whole years, and emerged having taught himself the melodeon. Adolescence is a mysterious thing. We all get through it in the end. With luck, the happy home is still there when we do.

Serious Talk:
Faith, fears and legends

This chapter, of necessity, has to fall into two parts. You do not have the same sort of conversation with a bright, opinionated child of twelve as you do with a five-year-old. Yet there is a continuum; the way you converse with a near-adult has its roots in the way you talked to the child many years earlier. In the early years you put down the root of the understanding between you, and also the root of the child's own ability to think philosophically and with emotional intelligence.

There will, on the turbulent surface of things, be times when everything you say is ignored or despised or flung back in a temper; but if the root is there from early years, the communication between you – and the channel for transmission of your values – will be open. At least for some of the time.

This talk of transmitting values and philosophical thought all sounds pretty high-flown, considering that in a moment we will be dealing with such matters as tooth fairy lies and party political broadcasts. But it is, I promise you, part of the same process.

The early years

One of the unexpected pleasures of early parenthood is the conversation. Granted, there are moments of pure torment, when inquiring minds come padding through to your bedroom at 5.30 a.m. with a query about how old the sky is; but on the whole, talking to small children is good fun. Whoever would have thought, gazing at that scrunched-up little pink creature in the maternity ward, that you would get barely four years' start to prepare an answer to every mystery of the universe? Why is the night dark? What are those doggies doing? Where do babies come from? What is a Pry Minister and why do we have to do what he says? Do guinea pigs go to heaven?

164

Even more awesome is the reflection that whatever you tell them, they will believe; and whatever they learn later on to prove you wrong, some tiny corner of the mind will retain that first, indelible lesson. If a trusted person tells a small child that policemen are pigs who lock people up and kick them, ten years later there will be a young teenager out on the streets who runs away from, rather than towards, the police when a fight starts. If you tell him God is good, the odds are that someday, in trouble, he will pray. If you tell him (or show him) that shoplifting is all right as long as you don't get caught, he will have difficulty forever with the question of personal honesty.

In theory, there should be nothing more satisfying and uplifting than conveying to your child the wisdom that you have spent twenty-five years learning. Some of it is easy. 'Yes, dear, your rabbit died, and his little body will turn into earth and help the flowers to grow.' 'Yeast is special stuff that makes the bread rise.' Or, 'When Daddy gets home he'll explain all about how electricity works, I promise. Yes, perhaps he will buy you a potentiometer.' However, as the child gets older and more canny, equally innocent questions begin to turn into ticking time-bombs. More of those later.

And – another pitfall – what about legends? What about Father Christmas, the Tooth Fairy, the gnomes beneath the toadstools? Are you storing up trouble by passing on these tales, which will be proven untrue? Will one falsehood discovered bring down the whole edifice of trust forever? Few of us agonize for very long about such matters, since they become rapidly buried under the sordid matters of everyday life, but they are worth considering.

Talking to children is natural and personal. But there are a few universal strategies which make it smoother. To begin with the easiest of the difficult subjects:

Politics It is not too difficult to work out a general attitude to life which is kind, considerate, and socially responsible. Children see television news every day, and wonder about it; if a car bomb in the news worries your four-year-old, you will have to find a way of explaining the background, even as you reassure him that his own family is probably quite safe. But it is pretty tough, spending the whole of bathtime on the Irish question, or the politics of Saddam Hussein.

The trouble is that in a society as politically polarized, as argumentative and chippy as ours, there are several different ways of answering certain questions. You may know what you think, but exactly how much right have you to indoctrinate your child? Or at least, how far must you try to be fair and put the opposite point of view to your own? Try these for size:

'Why are they building a road across the marshes?' 'Well, so that people can get to the new power station faster. You see, the local council is in charge of deciding whether to allow anyone to build a new road or house or factory, and making sure it doesn't spoil anybody else's home. And they decided to build the road. Well, yes, it does spoil our house a bit, and it is a shame about the wild ducks having to go away, but it's very important to have electricity here. Well, Daddy doesn't actually agree, and I know he did say the government is a load of wallies who ought to be pushed off a cliff . . . well, yes, we did sort of choose them, at least not us, but most people . . . well, not exactly most people, but –' (diversion into structure of parliamentary elections and theory of proportional representation; child yawns). 'Well, anyway, they're building a road because the law says they can. Yes, it's funny that the law says we can't disturb the wild ducks or shoot them, but the roadmen are . . . well, that's how it goes . . .'

Or:

'Well, no, there isn't a war right now. It's just that our country has decided to drop bombs on another country because their government is being nasty to some people there. Well, no, the government people haven't been hit, and yes, some others did get hit who hadn't done anything but . . .'

Or:

'Well, you see, some people don't have jobs. They want jobs, but there aren't any. So they get given some money called unemployment benefit so they don't actually starve. Yes, it might be better if they had jobs, but there just aren't any . . .'

The anxiously liberal parent ties himself in knots, bending

over backwards to be fair and let the child see the complexity of the problem. The angrily committed leftist abandons the attempt, takes his child on demonstrations and encourages him to throw a squeaky rubber Blair puppet to the dog. The staunch Conservative tells her own version. None is doing a perfect job but at least all these people – the right, the left, and the woolly – are trying to explain, and putting a bit of thought into it. I have stood at the kitchen sink myself trying to explain why children starve in the Third World while we are throwing out half a stale cake; it wasn't me, I promise, who brought up the subject, it was them, confronted by an Oxfam advertisement. Being able to tell them about aid workers helped. You need, with children, always to find some kind of bright side to look on.

But the moments that are really worrying are the ones when – tired or cross or thoughtless – we convey to our children not sincere and well-thought-out beliefs, but appalling, half-conscious prejudices. Everyone has them. The children who taunt black children at school are not doing it out of blind natural instinct: someone has given them a cue that ethnic minorities are fair game. That is an extreme, but have you honestly never said in your children's hearing that, say, the Irish are all mad? Or that you can't trust the French? Have you let them go out for walks with a friendly babysitter who – excellent though she may be – firmly believes that you will get leukaemia if you buy ice lollies from the Asian corner shop because dusky hands are dirty hands? (A true example, vintage 1986.) Or do your children perhaps boast one of those lovable grannies who reckons that playing with children from the council estate will invariably give you nits? Watch all this. Listen, casually, for signals.

Religion It should not be too difficult to communicate your own religion, or lack of it (though it is surprising the number of fashionably agnostic parents who are so afraid of discussing death with their children that they resort, rather shamefacedly, to talking about heaven after all). If your faith is strong and explicit, and supported by a powerful sense of community like Judaism or Sikhism, you need no help from me. However, if you have no more than a vague, generalized, woolly Christianity, the sort of knit-your-own-nativity, white-wedding faith so endemic in Britain, you need to think it over before you start answering questions from small people who trust you.

To reduce it to rock bottom: culturally, it is of considerable importance that children should know the basic Bible stories, the Creation myth, the Nativity and Crucifixion and Resurrection, and the Ten Commandments. If they do not know what these things are, and what they have meant down the centuries, they lack the basic grammar of Western culture; the vast majority of our plays, novels, poems and paintings will mean very little to them. However, it is up to you whether you teach these things on exact parity with Hinduism, Buddhism and Islam; or even with the legends of Greece and Rome and Ancient Egypt. Even a determined agnostic often decides that it is wise, in Britain, to give the Christian stories a bit of extra consideration; after all, the churches on the landscape and the bishops in the House of Lords are more relevant to your children's life than Isis and Anubis. In a multiracial area, Diwali and Eid and Chanukkah may be vastly important, but it is curious and rather sad to find – as you do in some British schools – children who have been made able to reel off every detail of these festivals but allowed to remain hazy about Easter. In the early seventies I interviewed some schoolchildren of eight and nine in a highly progressive state primary in Oxfordshire, and discovered that they had no idea who the characters were in the Christmas crib. The deprivation was intellectual, as much as religious; great swathes of Western art and literature would mean nothing to them until they learnt such basics.

It is also important that children pick up the idea of religious tolerance very, very early. My own son was lectured by a six-year-old Jehovah's Witness in his first year at primary school, and informed that the God of school assemblies was actually the Bad Serpent who tempted Eve, and that we were all devil-worshippers. Luckily, he told me instead of letting it fester, and with a deep breath I sprang into a rambling but determined

168

tour of comparative religions, with the emphasis on the idea that different people have seen God differently through the ages, the many names He has been given (from Jehovah to Gitchi Manitou), and the strong suggestion that if there is one thing God cannot abide, it is people fighting over him. With a final coda on the subject of Mr Rushdie having to hide from the Islamic fatwa, I let the poor child go back to his Lego bricks.

Legends We have a very useful phrase in our family, dating back to the summer we sailed round Britain recounting every improbable bit of local folklore to the children to pass the time in rain and gales: there were giant codfish washed down chimneys by waves; the Muckle Mester Stoor Worm of Orkney whose liver caught fire and turned into the Iceland volcanoes (his teeth are the Faeroes, Shetlands and Orkneys); the giant buried beneath St Michael's Mount in Cornwall; and so forth. The phrase is this: 'It's a legend. A legend is a story that is so old that nobody knows whether it is true or not.'

This, I find, maintains delicious possibilities of giants, enchanters and fairies, without giving them too solid and historical a presence.

However, there are family legends too. Take the Tooth Fairy. We never intended to be bothered with the Tooth Fairy, but when your child comes to you with shining eyes and a bloody little chip of ivory, having learned in the playground what riches may come from the said pixie, it is hard to resist it. So we began: teeth in tinfoil under the pillow, replaced, by morning, with money. Then he began writing notes to the TF, and naturally the TF had to reply (in curly writing). Then, reaching a slightly more sceptical stage (we thought), he and his friends began sprinkling talcum powder on the windowsill to catch the footprints; sure enough, the TF left the little bootprints (pad of finger and pad of thumb: try it).

There was a certain advantage to be got from the legend, in that the TF only likes clean teeth, and knows if they've been cleaned after falling out, which doesn't count. Tooth after tooth fell, from child after child, and always the money came under the pillow. I rather liked the TF, just as I like Father Christmas.

There is something soothing for children in the idea that their own parents are not the sole source of all gifts because the universe is peopled with benevolent beings. It is a primitive sort of religion, and all primitive human beings – like children – need some kind of folk religion.

But when do you stop? When do you admit the benevolent deception? Note the cautionary tale of the seven-year-old whose mother thought he knew, and made a conspiratorial little joke about it; disaster, trembling lip, he hadn't been sure at all. Mother racked with guilt, realizing that she had caused the magic to fade to dull daylight, and rung up the curtain early on the hard adult world in which there are no fairies. Soon after, he drew his own conclusions about Santa, and that was that.

I have to admit that in our house Father Christmas has never actually been allowed to retire. In the early days he came down our big wide chimney, and had carrots left out for his reindeer. They are dirty beasts, and used to scandalize us all by biting the tops off the carrots and spitting them down the chimney onto the hearthrug. FC himself, we find, eats a mince pie, kicks over his whisky glass and leaves strange things: mysterious, wooden, foreign, odd sorts of presents that you don't find in the local newsagent. (You do, however, find them in the Tridias, Hawkin and Oxfam catalogues, which is just as well.) I have to admit that he has been a bit upset of recent years, finding himself popping in such little extras as the CD single of 'Smack My Bitch Up' by The Prodigy, but no damaging admissions of non-existence have ever been made. Not even to teenagers. I got the perfect formula from the astute writer Christina Hardyment, who has raised four daughters: 'Some children at school tell you there is no Father Christmas, do they? What a shame. You see, once children don't believe in Father Christmas any more, he can't come to them. What usually happens is that the parents take over, and fill the stockings instead so nobody is too disappointed. But of course it's never quite as good.'

This is extraordinarily clever. It gives scope for a child to half-believe, or to cling to belief and give it up at his own private pace; and yet not to feel cheated if he spots some wrapping paper that Santa used, or something turns up in his stocking which he saw sticking out of a box under the stairs, or if he actually catches Santa in the act. It keeps the cosmic mystery, and lets it fade without violence into ordinary, parental, loving kindness, and eventually to an ironic joke between adults.

And does all this Santa-tooth-fairy nonsense – as some earnest types try to claim – cause children to feel betrayed, and cease to trust their parents ever again?

No. It doesn't. If the love and the jokes and the presents keep on coming, children on finding out seem to accept it as a kind of dramatic production, a game you play together. Why else do they so much enjoy keeping up the pretence, in cahoots with you, for younger siblings or cousins? Children are very sophisticated about suspended disbelief, because they spend so much of their own lives announcing that they are princesses, or tigers, while knowing perfectly well that they are not.

Fears You or anyone else may set them off. Here are some sample fears, from different families:

That pit bull terriers may hide under the bed and tear your throat out as you sleep (origin: news on television. Cure: nightly check under bed, possibly by firing water pistol at invisible dog until whole thing becomes a riotous joke).

That the Angel of Death will come for the First Born again (origin: school bible study. Cure: quiet word with RE teacher, and lots of calm reassuring chat).

That the Tooth Fairy will strangle you (origin: Lord knows. Cure: leave tooth in locked room downstairs).

That Father Christmas won't come (cure: ring or fax him to check, or claim that you have e-mailed his website).

That Father Christmas will come and be a strange hairy man in the bedroom (origin: fearful department store Santas with bad breath. Cure: stockings hung downstairs).

That wishes will come true. This sounds silly, but there was once a fearful moment when a child burst in weeping. 'Do wishes come true?' he asked. There was a bit of havering about how they sometimes do, sometimes not; but after some time, the dread was extracted from him. He was terrified of his own imagination. 'I just wished that I were a elephant, but now I don't want to be!'

That the hole in the ozone layer will drown us or frizzle us all up (cure: talk of scientists working on the problem, the whole world aware of it and working on it, and so on).

That there will be a New-Kill-ee-ar War (again, speak of goodwill and political work, summit conferences and the universal desire for peace).

That Mummy and Daddy will die (cure: hugs and reassurance and permission to sleep in your bed till the fear passes).

That child will die (same cure).

That sibling will die (same, assisted by pointing out aggressively rude health of sibling. Also worth pointing out in a casual sort of way that just wishing someone was dead never ever works. Fear probably has its origin in just such a wish).

That burglars will get in (show off locks, bolts, and such with great gravitas).

That witches, goblins, ghosts and devils will get in through the walls. A tricky one. Merely saying they don't exist may not work. Once I had a visiting child who terrified mine with tales of witches that came in to Get You. Unable to calm any of them down, and getting desperate for some sleep myself, I reverted to my Catholic childhood and showed them a crucifix which happened to be on the wall, and a picture of St Brendan in his boat, explaining that no evil thing could come where a holy picture was. It worked instantly. The only problem was that the visiting child went home and told his mummy – and the whole neighbourhood – that at my house we went to sleep holding a crucifix to keep vampires off.

I could go on forever. Any mother could. A few children have no such fears, or at least not many; some have a new one every night. The important thing is to keep the lines of communication open: always listen to them however daft and repetitive. If they are sad universal fears (like being homeless, or unloved, or orphaned, or caught in a war) it is curiously helpful to tell the child that everyone gets these feelings sometimes, even grown-ups, and that you get used to chasing them away. This creates a comradeship, and a healthy sense that it is not the disaster which is the real enemy but the feeling of impending disaster.

If they are wildly improbable fears, you shouldn't laugh, or go all psychological and automatically relate them to the birth of a sibling, a house move, or any of the other reliable old chestnuts. These may have a bearing too, but the fears themselves are worth respecting. Try to trace them back to their source. One small boy was depressed for days about his father's impending six-week business trip. It turned out that he had misheard it as a six-year trip, poor little devil. My own daughter developed a fear of sleeping in her own bedroom, and we alternately raged and coaxed her in vain. After she had taken to sleeping in various rooms in rotation, dragging her white teddy and duvet with her on a restless royal progress like a small Queen Elizabeth, I went one night into her own bedroom. Downstairs, my husband was watching television, and a trailer came on for some tawdry thriller. 'I'll kill you – I swear it,' hissed a voice, curiously amplified through the floor. My poor little child had been suffering night after night from a sinister approximation to the techniques of sleep-learning. The tacky, violent, sensational television culture had been invading her rest. No wonder she went walkabout.

Later years: talking with teenagers

Nothing turns round overnight, but gradually the conversations between you and your child change in nature.

In the early years parents are the fount of all wisdom, and their ideas are accepted more or less without question. It would be grotesque if this were to continue. As you grow up you have to think for yourself, and make connections for yourself. You learn to evaluate other people and their behaviour in a more objective way than when you were a newcomer to the world. The nearest adult people to practise this evaluation on are usually your own parents. Hence Oscar Wilde's line: 'Children begin by loving their parents; after a time they judge them; rarely, if ever, do they forgive them.'

Well, it is not always that bad. But we cannot fossilize our authority, or demand uncritical respect for all we say. Maybe parents once could, though I doubt it was ever a wise move. But today, with our children open to a thousand other influences from media, and encouraged in school to think for themselves, we have to be persuaded to argue our corner good-humouredly, without taking offence at the very idea that they might disagree.

It may be galling to a lifelong socialist to produce a cartoon Tory Boy, and shocking to a pillar of the establishment when his daughter spits revolution at him. It may be a source of despair when your children turn their back on your favourite good causes, or embrace others which you despise; it may be an embarrassment when you are on the local Highways Committee and open the evening paper to the horrid sight of your children peering defiantly from a protest tepee on the new bypass and informing the world they are called Earthsister and Badgerfriend.

But your role is not to huff and puff and order them to think differently. Argue your case, stick by your guns if you feel it is right, ask for moderate behaviour and reasoned debate; but don't pull rank. It won't work. Try to remember your own teens, and the way you thought of your parents' views. And be cheered by Mark Twain's observation that when he was eighteen his old Dad was hopelessly ignorant and knew nothing, but five years later he was amazed by how much the old man had learnt . . .

It is important, though, not to confuse this kind of free debate with an abdication of all adult responsibility. A fifteen-year-old has a right to think you are wrong about the legalization of cannabis, or the age of gay consent, and to say so; but you have the responsibility to keep that fifteen-year-old clear of crime, and of personal damage, as far as you possibly can. Strangely enough, making this clear can often improve the situation between you. Yes to free thought, yes to debate; but *no* to staying out all night at a crack 'n' bondage club. The yes and the no are not irreconcilable. Keep that in your mind, however unnerving everything gets. One of the exasperating things in the modern age is the way that even the most competent seeming families are prone to say, 'Well, kids today, what can you do?' All that this means is, 'I have no will, and no leftover energy to confront this monster. I give up.'

You would need a heart of stone not to sympathize with this line of thought, given the stressed lives that many parents lead in an age of long hours and job insecurity; but if you do completely give up, the message to the teenager will not be a happy affirmation of his or her adulthood. It will be that you do not care.

However, your tolerance and good nature with teenage tantrums and rebellions should not be a one-way street. Oscar Wilde was right about children needing to forgive their parents. Given the complexity of modern lives, most of them have a few real things to forgive us for (being away too much, being snappy, putting other things before them, getting divorced, whatever). But that does not mean that they have a right to carp and criticize and make you feel lousy *all* the time. Although the teenage years are notably self-absorbed ones – they can't help it, it's the hormones – it is reasonable to expect that they should cut you a bit of slack.

Don't put up with shrill criticism and constant nagging if you don't dole it out; assert your right to the occasional quiet drink or access to the comfortable chair during the television news, and do not accept it meekly when your clothes, music, TV favourites, reading matter and friends are derided in an unpleasant way. A bit of ribbing is fine – and you are better equipped to take it than a nervy teenager is – but I have heard parents putting up with rudeness from their teens which fairly takes my breath away. I had a lift once from a mild, nice, man in his forties whose daughter, in the back, kept on at him all the way about being a 'spastic' driver, having a crap car, going bald and being generally 'sad'. I wanted to box her ears. When we had dropped her off he just simpered and said, 'Ah well, kids. You get used to it.'

Why should you? Unless there is a real excuse – an unhappiness at school or in love that you are aware of – feel perfectly free to stand up for yourself, not as some ogre of authority but as a human being. Parents have feelings too, and a right not to be bullied. This should not need saying, but alas, it does.

Falling Over, Feeling Poorly

If you want to be convinced of the frailty of the human body, try sitting in a casualty department for an hour on a fine Sunday evening. Kids hobble by on crutches, still wearing the Day-Glo shorts and elbow pads which indicate that half an hour ago they were kings of the world on their roller blades. Glum-looking toddlers sit on their mothers' knees, one wrist suspiciously chubbier than the other. Adults sit clutching various wounds inflicted by lawnmowers, dogs, and other acts of God. There may be a teenager in a netball skirt, hopping around explaining to her father how she only just missed the equalizer; and at least one child with its finger stuck in some treacherous domestic utensil, or wrapped hastily and bloodily in something that looks very like its baby brother's vest. They all sit there, obedient and unnerved, waiting to be given a hospital number and turned into patients with neat white proper bandages on; the adults occasionally prowl hopelessly in search of something to read other than the usual hospital issue of a ten-year-old copy of *Reveille* and half a knitting pattern. Sometimes – not nearly often enough – a brisk nurse whisks out and calls somebody's name.

The casualty waiting room is a unique place, even within the hospital. Medical clinics have a completely different feeling because most of their customers have had an appointment for weeks, and known about their problem for longer. They are acclimatized. They have brought magazines to read, or knitting; the children have been carefully prepared for the experience with cosy little books called *Mary's Happy Hospital Visit*, or *Percy Pig Gets His Hernia Done*. Everyone has had time to practise having a bright, sensible attitude to it all. There have been 'counselling', and family conferences.

176

In real emergencies, where life and death are at stake and will be decided in moments, everything is different again: dramatic and desperate, with trolleys and rushing and fears of the worst. When you are fearing the worst you don't feel boredom or embarrassment; it is only in Accident and Emergency waiting rooms that adults and children alike have this curiously forlorn look, like a row of landed and stunned codfish. Minutes ago they were larking around in the sun, now here they are feeling let down and foolish, facing up to the fact that a split-second misjudgement may mean weeks in itchy plaster. Above all, the parents of injured children are either pointlessly blaming themselves in silence, or else tearfully assuring everyone else in the waiting room that it was a very well-built tree house really, who could ever have known he'd try handstands on the safety rail . . .

It can happen to any of us. It *has* happened to most of us. You may be next. In order that you may face the experience with more dignity, calm and efficiency than I managed, here are some hard-won lessons. They are gleaned from bitter experience and muttered questions to other parents.

Casualty life

Kit yourself out Never approach a hospital, if you can help it, without a personal comforts bag. Unless it is a desperate matter of unconsciousness or haemorrhage, allow yourself five minutes to think and pack a few things. Do not be a wally like I was, and dash off on a forty-minute drive with the child shoeless and coatless, no handbag, money, tissues, drinks of water or reading matter. You will have plenty of time to ponder your shortcomings as you sit on a vinyl bench in casualty awaiting your turn. By great good luck, my car is an ambulant rubbish tip, so there was an ancient copy of *Alice Through the Looking-Glass* stuck behind one of the seats. Without it, things would have been pretty unbearable for Rose (and me) during the two hours' wait, the fifteen minutes outside X-ray, another twenty minutes waiting for the doctor to see the X-ray, and sundry other waits. In the end we got all the way to the White

Knight before actually finding out what was wrong with her arm (broken).

I was deeply admiring of a woman who had come in with a black-eyed, blood-caked, limping nine-year-old but had somehow managed also to bring a carton of apple juice, a pile of comics, her knitting, and his Sony Walkman with a supply of story tapes. 'Well, it's our third time in casualty,' she said. 'Or is it our fourth? He's ever so brave on his BMX bike. Just like his dad. His dad's broken both legs, on the speedway. We like this hospital, they're ever so nice.' Experience tells.

Watch your tongue Once you are in a hospital, do not promise anything except that 'the doctor will try to help you get better' and 'Mummy/Daddy won't leave you'. The second promise is more or less safe to make: few hospital procedures involving a conscious child now exclude parents. It has been a hard-won right, as any sixties mother will tell you. There was a time when you handed your child over at the door of the X-ray unit, into a world of strangers with strange machines; and a time even more recently when children's ward sisters actually discouraged visitors for in-patients because it 'unsettled' them. Today you can say 'Mummy will stay close' and mean it. However, do not start making rash promises like, 'Of course the doctor won't hurt your sore place, he'll just look at it, (he might hurt it; he might have to), or, 'No, I'm sure you won't have to have a horrid plaster on.' Above all, don't say, 'I'm sure we'll be home in time for the *Teletubbies*.' You won't.

Never assume you're just an out-patient You may be whisked through rubber-shielded doors to a new world of wheelchairs and ward signs, either because they want to operate or because they are keeping a damn good eye on you in case it is a 'non-accidental injury' (don't be insulted. They have to. It is in your child's interest that they allow themselves to suspect even a fine upstanding citizen like you. Calm down). Use some of that waiting time in thinking out contingency plans in case you have to stay away for the night. It is a useful mental exercise, even though rarely needed. (Do not, however, emulate my

178

friend Victoria who plans out in detail an entire lifetime of support for a permanent invalid every time one of the family sneezes. She reads the Health Pages too closely, I always think.)

Explain only what the child actually asks In the broken-arm unpleasantness, Rose's only crisis of confidence occurred when a sister came to explain the procedures for the operating theatre with the help of a book about Herbie the Hedgehog who lost his spines and put on some Magic Ointment provided by the fairies. Rose took one look at the book and began to weep. 'I'm not up to strange hedgehogs,' she said, quite understandably.

Older children will probably want to discuss their case with the doctor, and have a perfect right to do so. Don't keep interrupting or answer for a child who is just about to speak.

If it is a longer-term problem, be calm, be competent, talk the case over privately with the doctors, interpret it your own way to the child, and – if at all possible – always be there. However, if you can't, be content with your best. I once spent twenty-four hours on a children's ward for a journalistic assignment, and grew furious about one little boy of seven with a leg in traction, who cried for his Mummy and stared sadly at every new visitor to the ward. From 7 a.m. to 11 a.m. I cursed this heartless bitch who couldn't even be bothered to stay with her own child.

At eleven she arrived, and I spent the next four hours silently cursing myself instead. She had, so she told me in a brief moment in the Ladies, come via three different buses, leaving children of one, two, and four at home with a neighbour; her husband had left her the year before, and the boy's road accident had forced her to give up her job and go on social security which barely paid for food. But she had arrived with a cheerful little picnic, homemade toys, and pictures from the small siblings, and sat chattering and singing to her little boy for several hours, as if she hadn't a care in the world. She taught me the other rule: that your best is good enough, and guilty weeping over your child won't help.

But there is one more hospital rule: even if you stay all day and night, get out of it sometimes. Children do sleep; nurses can be trusted to be kind to them if they wake. It is hot and enervating in hospital, overlit and undomestic. It makes you feel unreal and institutionalized and helpless to control your own life. In order to bring a breath of fresh normal air in to your child, you have to get outside the building once a day, even if only to walk round the block in the rain and buy a magazine from a corner newsagent and discuss something bland with him, like the weather.

Childhood illnesses

Most childhood illness, of course, does not involve a hospital at all. It involves a box of tissues, a jar of Vick, and a lot of endurance. Turn to your medical dictionary for advice (and a quite unnecessary fright or two), but take my word for it that children's illnesses generally follow a set pattern:

Act I Appalling behaviour Suddenly he or she is two years younger, six times whinier, and not at all nice to know. You get irritated, threaten to dock pocket money and send him to bed. Suddenly the child says he wouldn't mind, actually, going to bed. He develops a symptom: under six or seven it almost inevitably takes the form of vomiting all over the place; over that age it presents itself as 'a headache'. So, you are precipitated, anxious and loving, into:

Act II Nursing Apart from your dreadful guilt at having been so cross with him earlier, this is the easy bit. You get the doctor, or go to the surgery, and the doctor does the usual checks for meningitis or inflamed ears, then looks reassuring and tells you it is 'a virus that's going round'. Either you get an antibiotic syrup or you don't. The child has some mild painkiller and goes to sleep, waking four or five times in a sweat but otherwise improving slowly. Sometimes the most sensible thing is to share a big bed with him by yourself, with bucket and towel at hand. Maybe some vivid spots come out and it is chickenpox; maybe bits swell, and it is mumps. Then comes the very worst bit:

Act III Convalescence School or playgroup is still out of the question, but so is bed. No diversion lasts more than five minutes. Television or videos help immensely, especially for a child who is normally rationed; but your patience is tried as at no other time. Especially as you have now caught the bug yourself and feel like death.

This last disaster is worth examining. The nursing of children is a subject covered in many books, but nobody gives much thought to the problem of what, precisely, is supposed to happen in the well-regulated household when Mummy Gets the Mumps. Yet looking after small children, especially once they mix freely with other small children, is like trekking across some fever-laden swamp. The bugs they bring home often turn out to be mild for them, but extremely nasty for adults. The little ones sniffle and recover; we are left reeling with flu for days. They get a briefly swollen face, and sit around eating ice cream and watching *Popeye*; we catch mumps and go around feeling as if we had been sandbagged and left for dead. They get mild chickenpox, we get appalling shingles. And so on. They, after all, are new and strong. We are old and extremely battered. Well, I am, anyway.

Working – or part-time working – mothers get a particularly raw deal. There is an all too familiar cycle of family illness in which first the children get ill (one by one, naturally), thus disrupting the household; then Mummy gets ill, and when she recovers the nanny or babysitter has got it. Everyone sits around gloomy, convalescent, and in their boss's bad books, brooding on the inevitable fact that by this time next week Daddy in turn will be swollen up like the Phantom of the Opera, and will spend several days living from one dose of Panadol to the next and evading his responsibilities.

Children, quite rightly, get looked after when they are ill. If they want to sleep all day, they can. Drinks of water are available day and night for no more effort than a feeble cry. Diet is supervised. Gentle cooling baths are given. No wonder they get better so fast. But parents have nobody to tend them, especially Mummy. Her illness follows a far less satisfying pattern than her children's. She goes to the doctor croaking, 'I

181

think I've got this . . . aah, no, darling, don't break the doctor's stethoscope – this virus thing the children had . . . my head is splitting, I think I've got a temperature, only the dog ate the digital thermometer thing – no, sweetheart, we'll get an ice cream when we go home . . . don't hit the baby . . .' The doctor replies, 'Ah, hmmm, yes, nothing too serious here, Mrs Ah . . . couple of days' rest should do the trick. Just stay indoors and take things easy.'

Easy? The doctor clearly suspects that, left to herself, the poor woman would whip up a gross of jam tarts for the local bazaar and swim forty lengths of the swimming baths. He reckons she could ease up her schedule nicely just by putting off the jobs of hand-starching the pelmets and running up a set of new duvet covers. He does not realize that with a houseful of children, some probably pre-school, time is not something you have much choice about. Very few of the routine jobs are unnecessary. Mummy has probably spent the last eighteen months trying to finish the same paperback novel.

Even if she 'takes it easy' to the maximum degree, children still need dressing, washing, feeding, amusing, taking to school or supervising, and preventing from climbing out of the windows. They want their questions answered. They want to know how space rockets fly. They need walks in the fresh air or they get fractious – what does the doctor mean 'stay indoors'? Suppose you live in a flat and can't send the children safely into the garden?

Then they need a bath, and something clean to wear in bed. And something else to wear in the morning. And your head hurts, and the only glimmer of light on the horizon is the possibility of half an hour lying on the sofa during a particularly absorbing edition of *Sooty*. As a regime, it is not exactly what you might call total bedrest.

So what do you do, if you are not ill enough to precipitate a crisis and bring your husband home from work, or merit a home help? The kind of minor illnesses which in your childless days meant a day or two in bed with a comforting hot whisky and lemon have turned into a nightmare. Nobody cares about you. If a mother is sufficiently robust to stagger through the day, driven by altruism and necessity, nobody will step in.

Unless you ask. The key lies in asking, and it is no disgrace. I remember one morning when I was alone, being sick for the fourth time in an hour at 8 a.m. with food poisoning, and realizing that the children were starting to get worried. My gay little remarks through the lavatory door – 'Out in a minute – don't worry – has Teddy had his brekky yet?' – were starting to lack conviction. So I staggered out, rang the next-door neighbour and said, 'Can't cope. Can you chat to the children while they have breakfast?' and went straight to bed. I was lucky to have the neighbour: no mother should ever allow herself to be on bad terms with the people who live, physically, closest to her. Dear and reliable friends five miles away are not always enough. Apart from neighbours, friends and family and grannies and favourite babysitters will also play their part. With luck. Only *ask*, shamelessly.

Some young children are capable of real sympathy and help to sick parents. But, again, you have to explain that you are poorly. I know a single mother who went through a terrible bout of flu without ever admitting to her son of four that she felt ill. She didn't want to frighten him. The only result was that the child found her short-tempered and odd and unwilling to hug him, and never knew why. On the third day he burst into tears and said, 'Mummy, don't you love me these days?' and when she said yes, she did, only she felt ill with a bad cold, he was so relieved that he nursed her with dogged enthusiasm and slopped drinks of water all afternoon. Girls, even more, seem to like the idea of a Mummy curled on the sofa being looked after, even if you do have to spring to your feet occasionally to avert some disaster. It is definitely worth exhibiting your weakness.

The only other strategy is to have a little reserve of something exciting, new, and quiet to do in case of illness. I always have had, although I thought erroneously that it was in case of the children being ill. I kept a box of special easy press-out models to make, transfers, puzzles, new felt-tip colouring pens and so forth. In fact, small poorly children do not usually want such things at all. They want good old mangy Mister Rabbit, their revolting old muslin dusters to suck, and to watch a video of Noddy or Paddington, worn thin by endless replaying. It is when *you* are ill that the box of surprises comes into its own. You can lie on the sofa in a light delirious doze, watching them out of the corner of your eye and hoping for better days.

Keep taking the vitamins. There's a lot of it about.

Older children's illnesses If a life-threatening, prolonged or chronic illness strikes a child, you may need more help than a general book like this can offer. You are likely to want contact with other sufferers, support groups, helplines, all the comfort and inspiration that comes from a truly shared perspective. Above all, you need the wider family and real friends.

But most of us have one or two scares as our children grow up, periods which go beyond the common round of colds and 'flu and limps and arms in slings. Some of us end up sitting beside hospital beds with drip-stands up. This experience brings both practical and emotional surprises.

Older children and teenagers seem, at first sight, like adult invalids. They sleep willingly, see the point of accepting medicine and treatment, and make a conscious attempt to be brave. It is easier to look after them than when they were small and fractious.

So it may take some effort to keep remembering that they are not adults, and that their experience of illness is probably very slight. They watch melodramatic TV hospital programmes in which every twinge heralds a life-threatening disease; they read the papers and magazines full of organ donor stories and headlines like 'Tragic Lucy's last brave letter'. They know that young people die, or are permanently crippled. Behind that brave facade, they may be unrealistically scared. On the other hand, inexperience may make them equally unrealistically optimistic, and confident of getting to next week's party or school trip. Some doctors are excellent communicators to the young, but others are not. It is up to you, as the parent, to understand all you can and pass on the information with as much optimism as is accurate. There is no point flannelling, or

184

pretending things are not serious; but there are ways of delivering the news which are more tactful than others. For instance, you don't start talking about long-term after effects to someone who is still feeling lousy. Help them to live for the day, and to deal with disappointment when they miss treats.

School work may be a worry if they are off for long. Most schools will co-operate, but need parental help. Go in, get the work, talk it through with the teacher; if necessary ask about local freelance teachers who will give some one-to-one help for a few hours during the convalescent period. This will reassure a conscientious patient or one who has exams looming.

If the child is not worried, and the school isn't either, then it is probably best to leave well alone.

As for nursing, remember that however big and gruff the child is, he may be lonely up there in his bed, or wrapped up on the sofa, and with loneliness comes depression and fearful imaginings. Make sure there is company, lots of little drinks and chats. There will probably be tape cassettes and music on tap in most teenage pits, but if you offer to read aloud for half an hour, you may find to your amazement that even huge louts enjoy a bit of Harry Potter, read to them by someone who loves them. Likewise teenage girls (however much they appear to despise you most of the time) may enjoy having their hair brushed and make-up brought, and all may curiously welcome cuddly toys resurrected from babyhood. Illness makes children younger.

But all through the crisis, remember that it does not affect only the patient and the chief nurse. The rest of the family suffers too. There may be a sibling feeling scared or left out, a father who doesn't feel able to show his terror, grandparents fretting alone without news. When there is real illness in a house you can see that even the dog gets depressed and nervous (not the cat. Cats just selfishly lie on the fevered one, for the warmth). During this time, whoever is the strongest member of the family is going to have everyone else leaning on them. Watch your own health.

The Ever Younger Teenager

Gepetto the carpenter got along just fine with Pinocchio at first. He had, after all, known the little puppet ever since he was a lump of two-by-four on the workbench. He had shaped his little head, kept his evolving body straight and graceful, and pulled the strings with discreet pride and paternal care. He knew all about Pinocchio, and no doubt sank into a pleasant complacency about his perfectly formed puppet.

Then what happens? Pinocchio falls in with low company, starts throwing money around, tells lies, grows his nose long, develops an unsettling ambition to turn into a real person, turns stroppy, runs away, and ends up hanging out in low-down dives (like the inside of whales) with guttering candlelight and dangerous substances. Poor old Gepetto hardly knows what to do. Kids today, what do they know?

But in the end it all comes right, and Pinocchio, after his wild rite of passage and uncomfortable nights inside the fetid whale, emerges to become a Real Boy, a full human being who can be a good son and a credit to the old woodbanger at last.

And they call that a fairytale. An everyday story of teenage life, more likely. Just when you think that you know your child well, have an intelligent and loving relation based on trust, have passed on fine ethics and old values, etc., etc., some surge of hormones makes you the bewildered recipient of abuse, stamped feet, volatile mood swings and unreasonable demands. Just when your son gets big and bright enough to keep his own room tidy, he loses the will to do any such thing; just as your daughter grows into a swan, she wrecks the effect with an unauthorized nose stud and purple hair. Just when your kids are mature enough to have adult discussions about current events with you, they suddenly decide that you are wrong about everything.

It is a familiar picture, a timeworn joke; so worn, indeed, that it is actually a slight shock when your own teens get merely a mild dose of it, like a passing rash, or prove to be balanced and humorous enough to make a joke of it with you (many find relief in sending up their own feelings by impersonating Harry Enfield's creation Kevin the Teenager, hyperventilating 'uh – uh 'uh' and bawling, 'You are NOT my PARENTS.' God bless Harry, I say). Some teenagers, indeed, remain still recognizably the nice little children they were the day before yesterday; some, I am told, make it right through to twenty-one with hardly more than a pair of pursed lips and a sotto voce imprecation against the iron rule of unreasonable parents. There is really no way you can tell whether your own teens will be a) very troublesome b) normally awkward or c) no bother whatsoever. Expect nothing either way, and you won't be disappointed. Roll with the punches.

A great deal depends on where they are at school, whether they are happy there, and what other influences are bearing on the pressure-cooker of their transition into adulthood. One central truth, however, makes the contemplation of all teenage problems a lot simpler. This is it: *everything goes better if teenagers are happy.*

Obvious? Yes, but how often do you hear parents talking about wanting their big sons and daughters to be happier? We fret about their schoolwork, their exams, their friends, their behaviour, the risk of drugs and early sex, but we don't give a lot of thought to their happiness. If we do, it is just to say something about it being a terrible phase that has to be grown out of. We take the defeatist attitude of the headmaster in *Forty Years On* – 'Progressive heads always abolish CCF and compulsory games. They think it makes the sensitive boys happy. In my experience sensitive boys are *never* happy, so why bother?'

Yet every psychologist, every experienced teacher or youth leader agrees that the biggest problem of the teenage years, the thing which leads most surely to crime, drugs, and underage pregnancy, is unhappiness. They may call it, in psychobabble, 'alienation' or 'low self-esteem'.

187

For once, psychobabble is bang right. It may sometimes be hard to realize that the apparently arrogant, rude, snarling, contemptuous monster teenager in your life is actually suffering from a deficit of self-confidence, not an excess; but it is true. It must be, otherwise why would so many problems be alleviated so miraculously by the boosting of that self-esteem, in everything from Prince's Trust projects for young prisoners to a schoolteacher's sudden unlocking of a talent?

There are other kinds of unhappiness too. There is the loneliness which is endemic to these years: the sense that nobody understands, or even cares. There is the longing to have palpable successes, and the fear that you won't. There is the dread of disappointing your parents (some really rough behaviour, I suspect, is due to a panicked sense that you are bound to disappoint them sometime, so you might as well get your nose pierced now and call them rude names so they don't get their hopes up about those GCSEs you fear you might fail). There is unrequited love, which strikes at this age with a terrible thunderbolt force which us battle-weary old lags may have forgotten about. There is plain clinical depression, which can be aggravated by disrupted sleep and a silly diet either too high in fat and sugar or anorexically low in both.

So, rather than think only about remedies to teenage problems as if they were nothing but a crowd-control problem, think instead about what contributes to their happiness. Not a spoilt, overindulged happiness, – just the plain bread-and-butter satisfaction with life that everybody needs. What makes a happy teen? Well, they need some new things, and some which are continuations from earlier childhood.

Physical health If you eat rubbish, you feel like rubbish. If ever there was a time to make sure that there is more good food than bad in the fridge, this is it. Boys in particular eat like gannets; if what they find is fruit, cheese, lean cold meat, vegetables, baked potatoes and the kind of pizza which has proper nutrition in it, that is what they will eat. Girls need to be discouraged from the binge-starve diet cycle, because they will feel miserable while they are bingeing, suffer sudden sugar 'highs' and

188

resulting lows, and then get even more miserable while they are starving. You can't enforce healthy eating, but as manager of the household food supply parents can at least make it easier than the opposite.

Exercise is part of the above. For those teens who are not committedly sporty, and who get to school by car or bus, it is amazingly easy these days to give up physical exercise entirely. Schools are sometimes supinely ready to let exam candidates do virtually nothing physical all year – just at the time when brains need a good supply of blood and oxygen. *Any* sort of exercise is good. That includes roller-disco as well as conventional sports.

Fresh air Everyone is happier if they spend some time out of doors, and in contact with nature. The slightest sign of interest in climbing, sailing, canoeing, cadet corps, etc. should be backed as enthusiastically as a request to do extra physics. If not more so. Family walks are a rare taste for teenagers, so don't expect much enthusiasm there. But remember to be extra helpful about the fresh-air activities when it comes to the next ingredient of happiness:

Interests One of the best single things you can do to make their life and yours better is to back, and (as far as you can) to support and fund any serious interest that develops. Obviously you have to be cautious; it is madness to buy all the kit for something which might be given up after a few weeks. But if the taster session of whatever it is – from scuba to competitive chess – leads on to saving up, immersion in magazines, and continued signs of obsessive enthusiasm, then get in there and back it.

It may not even be a matter of spending much money; one of the things you can do with your adult competence (and perhaps your Internet access) is to research clubs, grants, governing bodies, etc. of the sport or hobby in question. Or even tour dates of the admired band, sources of cheap electric guitars, etc.

And do not judge the interests (unless they are illegal or very wrong). They are not yours. It is galling for a soccer-mad father to find he has produced a ball-blind figure-skater for a son, and hard for a nervous mother to back her offspring in a passion for skydiving; but it is not our life, it is theirs.

Anyway, from the safety angle, your participation in the research will be reassuring. You know, at least, that you are handing your child over to a properly accredited adventure centre, an experienced skipper, a club with a good record. Ask all the safety questions, but either do it out of your embarrassed young adventurer's earshot or else involve him or her in the selection process. My son, once his basic training in the freezing Cornish waters was over, developed a very good eye indeed for the difference between a dodgy dive centre and a good one wherever we subsequently went on holiday.

Friends You cannot police a teenager's friends. Better to have some dubious ones than no mates at all. The things you can do to make friendships easier and also safer are:

Keep open house, and keep a low profile in it yourself. Do not chatter wildly or try to take over. If friends come home it has two great values: firstly, you stay in touch; and secondly, if they do make dangerous or exploitative friends, seeing these people against the familiar home background will most likely cause the scales to fall from their dazzled eyes. 'Ronnie,' said one of my friends years ago in our teens, 'was just amazing, so cool in London. When he came home for the weekend and met my parents they were terribly nice to him, but I realized what a seedy fake he was.' Clever parents, I say.

Don't make it difficult. If you can help maintain contacts with friends by helping out with transport, etc., or having great messy sleepovers in your house, then do. Particularly if the friends in question are not part of the daily school or college round. It is good to keep up with people from your past lives, because if the present gang gets cruel (or, due to unrequited

190

love, embarrassing) you always have somewhere to run to. This is as true of teenagers as of adults.

Be as tolerant as you can of the way their social life is conducted. If there is a party in your house, well, it is your house and you are entitled to defend it (going away for the weekend and allowing a party is crazy. Gatecrashers will come and your basically good child will be as mortified as you by the unsavoury result. Don't do it). But with that proviso, and a clear set of rules about sex and drugs, let them have their own kind of social life. When a new gang of friends is forming, don't crash into a roomful of drawn curtains and noisy rock music and urge the inhabitants out for a lovely picnic. Keep separate in your adult world. Unless, of course, you are actually invited to do the food.

Finally, refrain from flirting with their friends.

Avoidable friction Life is tough enough without people bitching on at you about trivia. This is what I have been told, anyway, with some force. There must be rules about rooms, clothes for public occasions, doing homework, etc., but for heaven's sake pare them down to the essential minimum. What on earth is the point of souring your relationship with your beloved child by nagging on about tucking his shirt in, for God's sake?

Sense of achievement Exam passes are good, but there are other things too: small school distinctions, being chosen to lead a group, completing a swimming marathon, raising funds for charity. However surly the teenager, however crossly grunted the reply to your praise, parental approval and pride does matter. No, trust me: it does.

Manageable freedom Things which were unthinkable for a six-year-old (like travelling alone or making your own meals all day) are routine for a sixteen-year-old. Every family, every individual child, progresses towards this sort of independence at its own pace. The trick is to pick up the cues, know when your own offspring is ready, and give as much trust and freedom as you dare.

More on this in the next chapter, but the point here is that it must be *manageable* freedom in order to contribute to happy confidence. Sometimes, even big teenagers want to be babied a bit, picked up, protected, bought their tickets, organized into things. It makes them feel secure. Some parents overdo this, sure; but you can tell if you are doing that because the victim sighs and says 'Mo-ther!' and lets you know what a bore you are. When you underdo it – impatiently assuming that your child can run its own life, and showing contempt for helplessness and incompetence – there will probably be fewer complaints. But there might be a great secret sense of loneliness.

A sense of usefulness Don't understimate this one. The subject may appear to be unspeakably self-centred (hormones, hormones, keep on saying that to yourself as you grit your teeth) but every human being needs to feel useful. In the ancient scriptures of Judaism there is an instruction that when you give charity to the poorest, you must always give more than is necessary so that the poorest can themselves give charity. Nothing is worse than feeling like a parasite. Teenagers need to be involved in something useful, whether it is being a prefect or some kind of leader at school, raising money for charity, babysitting, helping someone in the extended family, or doing a job. If it is altruistic so much the better, but even the satisfaction of doing a paid Saturday job is a great counterweight to depression. You do it well, people are pleased you are there, they don't know what they did without you – that feels good. If there is no element of being useful in your teenager's life, there should be.

But he or she may not, of course, take the first suggestion you offer. Get someone else to make the suggestion instead. What else are favourite uncles for?

Being listened to It may sometimes appear that your teenage offspring do not tell you anything at all. They just grunt, or yell in frustration and put their foul music on loud. But there are times – often rather late at night, or when you are busy doing something else – when they decide to confide something in you.

This moment, alas, will not be properly announced and flagged up with a 'Hi, Mom, I wanna share something with you in a quality moment of communication'. It is far more likely to trickle out at the far end of a very tedious account of the entire plot of a ghastly film about some man who tears his face off and turns into a cyborg from the future, or during the course of a long grumble about school.

But be alert for it. Try not to doze off during the dull bits, or say 'Yes, yes, but what point are you actually trying to make?' Pretend you have more time than you do. *Make* more time than you have. Long drives, alone in the car with the child, are good for this; so are jobs like tidying out the shed or the attic, if you are lucky enough to have the kind of family which joins in. If you work at home some of the time, try and make that time coincide with their getting back from school, or messing about at home; and if you can bear it, keep open house in the room you work in, accepting interruptions and pausing for cups of coffee with invaders. Important things will come up in these unexpected sessions. Make space for it to happen, if you possibly can.

So those are the ingredients for happiness at this stage; and happiness is the central ingredient of easiness and pleasantness to live with. It makes it less likely that your teenager will succumb to the three Ds: depression, drink, and drugs, and gives you at least a fighting chance of knowing what is happening with the big S, sex.

Depression

Everything above is part of the defence against it, but it is widely accepted that modern teenagers are dangerously prone to serious depression, partly because of weak family structures, partly because of the inexorable peer and media pressure from every side, partly because they are forever being told that there

193

is a lot of unemployment and failure out there waiting in ambush for them.

If it strikes, it should be recognized, and if necessary given the same treatment as an adult would get. True depression is not the same as moody adolescent melancholy, when your cheerful practical child suddenly turns into Lord Byron for the day. It is not just bad temper, and it is not curable by brisk instructions to Pull Yourself Together.

If you have reason to think that your child is suffering from the formless, meaningless, miserable absence-of-pleasure which is clinical depression, if he or she seems unable to enjoy anything, is silent, withdrawn, solitary and no better after a night's sleep than before – do something. Raise the subject; admit that it exists; take roundabout routes like discussing some programme or article about depression, or the latest celebrity to go public on the subject. Talk to your GP. If the GP is unsympathetic, talk to the school nurse, or the tutor – whoever. The routes to alleviation are not alarming, but should be treated with measured, sceptical caution.

Therapy I would always advise starting with a no-nonsense practitioner of what is called cognitive behavioural therapy. Rather than drawing the patient into deep analysis and searching through the past for the source of the trouble, cognitive therapists try to help the patient define the feeling, and work out strategies for coping with it. The process, especially with teenagers who do not have any heavy trauma to contend with (abandonment, rape, brutality) is brief; sometimes three or four appointments supply the necessary sense of perspective and armoury against the Black Dog of depression.

Do not be ashamed of therapy, or let your child be ashamed. Explain that people really close to you, like parents, are less able to help because they are tied up in the whole mesh of strong feelings, being upset that you are upset. An outsider can sometimes see into a muddle more clearly, just as when you watch a hamster tunnelling around in a glass tank you can see ways out that he can't. The outsider could be a relative, or a teacher or mentor; but it might be a professional therapist.

The drawback here is that there may not be nearly enough NHS provision in your area, and certainly not available fast enough. You may decide to pay privately. If you seem to hit a brick wall of impossibility, do not give up. Schools may have contact with mental health charities or voluntary counsellors.

Antidepressants No doubt about it, they've got better lately. The SSRIs, like Prozac, can act as a wonderful crutch for severe depression, taking the edge off the worst misery without turning you into a smiley (or sleepy) zombie.

However, for teenagers whose brains and intellects are still developing and changing fast, they are an *absolutely last resort*. If you suspect that your GP is a bit slap-happy with prescriptions, take other advice. If the drugs go on beyond six months, look really hard at your life, and the child's, and see if there are other changes that are crying out to be made so that you can all be happier.

Drugs Drugs are too huge and fast-changing a subject to deal with in detail here. Let me add, though, a few observations to the literature which school and surgery should be putting out.

Firstly, substance abuse is not something that happens to other families – less careful families than you, who don't bother reading books like this. It could be you, it could be me. Smugness is inappropriate. In a modern Western country, most children of sixteen have been offered a chance to take an illegal drug, and usually in pretty safe, undetectable circumstances. Some will have agreed, 'just the once', and got away with it alive and unaddicted, and therefore developed a false sense of security.

Having everything – school success, lots of hobbies, friends, loving parents, sensible drug education – gives you a better chance of avoiding becoming a user, but not a hundred per cent guarantee. Therefore all of us should be alert to the mood swings, secretiveness, bits of tinfoil, mysteriously spent money, odd-looking eyes, forgetfulness, etc., which, taken together, may mean more than ordinary adolescent weirdness.

'Soft' drugs are not a joke. Cannabis, for instance, is very much stronger now than it was in the soppy sixties; it has been selectively grown for maximum punch, and the average joint today is over twenty times stronger than the stuff the forty-something generation used to droop around with at university. In sensitive subjects it can cause real mental confusion, loss of concentration, and aggravated depression when you stop taking it: its physical effect on the brain has been scientifically mapped, and is real.

Ecstasy and other MDMAs can kill, though this is rare and usually associated with the behaviour it brings on rather than the drug itself. Sniffing glue has disastrous effects, up to and including sudden death. Children need to know these things.

They also need to know about crooked dealers who cut the stuff with poisons, and about the very important, and unfair, fact that some people can use drugs – notably cocaine – recreationally for years and not get addicted, whereas others are hooked very rapidly and suffer agonies trying to come off it. There is no way you can know which you are so it is best not to experiment.

Wearying though it is, parents should keep up to date (by educational leaflets, books, etc.) with which drugs are around, and what the packaging and support systems look like. They should also have some idea of where their offspring's income is going. Too rapid an outflow, without a corresponding inflow of overpriced designer clothes or high-speed roller blades, is suspicious.

If the drug thing begins, don't put off getting help. Again, school may be able to advise (though some schools have the short-sighted policy of suspending users, even non-dealers who are trying to come off it). Youth groups, mental health charities like Young Minds or Turning Point, or self-help groups (try Citizens Advice Bureaux for addresses) may assist. Do not be afraid or ashamed if the search for expert help leads you well outside your normal social round. It may prove very mind-broadening.

If you think your child is dealing, do not panic. The horror of the drug culture is that most dealers are not callous monsters but small-scale dupes, doing it to feed their own habit. However, it is probably in everyone's interest (though hideously uncomfortable all round) to march the culprit round to the nearest police station to confess and hand over any supply and all the information. In Britain, parents are lucky enough to have the example of the Home Secretary himself having had to do this . . .

Drink

Alcohol can be as dangerous as drugs. Teenage drinking causes accidents, falls, fights, stupid dares that end in tragedy, and no end of pregnancies (the Child Support Agency staff say that a common excuse for not knowing the father's name is that the girl was being sick out of the window at a party at the moment of conception. We must assume some of them are telling the truth . . .)

Teenagers can also become addicted alcoholics, and since their brains and bodies are still developing this is very bad news indeed. Moreover, drink is legal and you can get it anywhere including the supermarket, as long as you look eighteen; and a lot of fourteen-year-olds do. And on top of all this, a cynical drinks industry is forever bringing out lovely, sweet, lemonadey, fizzy, harmless-looking alcopops to tempt this market, even though they pretend aloud that it is really adults they are after.

So drink needs to be brought into the family circle, learned about and tamed. There need to be warnings about excess, but there also needs to be guidance about moderate drinking. Our solution was the continental approach – little sips of wine or beer with meals early on, a permitted glass of wine for older children on special occasions, and a relaxed attitude to sixteen-year-olds having a beer with their evening meal after a long active day. Some swear by this, because being allowed alcohol inside the family home makes it less of an illicit thrill outside. Others say it does no good at all, and may do harm. It probably depends on the tone of your family life.

But it certainly does no harm – if your child is lucky enough never to have seen a real adult drunk – to see the occasional film or programme which depicts the horribleness of drunks. Teenagers are quite fastidious, even boys (at least until they go into the woo-arr, laddish phase) and they hate to lose face. The idea of vomiting in public, or wetting yourself, fills them with salutary horror. It is also useful to point out that every drink makes the next drink more likely, ending up with you in a state where you will say and do things so embarrassing you will want to hide forever.

However, the time will come when your son or daughter does get stinking, rat-faced, hogwhimpering drunk, just to see what it is like. In my perhaps eccentric view, it is best if this first binge takes place close to home, preferably in it. So if the next family gathering sees your sixteen-year-old knocking back rather too much cider, it might be politic to let a few more bottles be sunk than you normally would. The resulting hangover and bad memories will be fine aversion therapy. Get the victim up nice and early to help you clean the car. But *don't* turn a blind eye to overconsumption of spirits. That can actually kill people.

Sex

Sex education has come up elsewhere (in 'Below the Belt', p.93). Sex itself is a more practical matter. How much you know about what is going on, what actually does go on, and whether you have any influence about the way it goes on – these things will all vary widely according to where you live, what sort of peers your child has, what your own teaching and relationship has been, etc.

Under sixteen Surveys suggest that two-thirds of children under sixteen in Britain are *not* having any kind of sexual relationship, although from some pruriently sensational reports you would think the opposite was true. On the other hand, factors proven to make early sex more likely are:

low achievement, and low sense of achievement, in other
fields;
uninterested parents;
a broken home and consequent desire for someone of
one's own;
a history of abuse inside or outside the family circle;
a peer group with a strongly sexualized culture.

Some of these you can do something about, some you can't.
Girls should always be made aware of their absolute right to
say no, *at any stage*, and prepared for the feeble arguments boys
will put up about it being 'dangerous' to stop, or wrong to
tease. Boys should know their duty to respect the girl's 'no'.
They should also be told that there are other ways to prove you
are a man than having sex, because sometimes it is the girls
who pressure the boys into it.

I was very struck by one thing which a fourteen-year-old girl
said to me many years ago. She had been sleeping with various
boys since she was thirteen, when her elder brother died in an
accident and her parents split up acrimoniously. She said that
the thing in her life which had helped her most was a teacher,
who presumably knew about what was going on, and saw that
she felt guilty and dirty and was treated as a 'slag' by the boys.

This teacher gently said to her one day, while pretending to
talk in general terms: 'This virginity thing is nonsense, you
know. Someone who stops sleeping around deserves just as
much respect as someone who never has.' Until the teacher said
that, the poor child was as much the victim of the old 'damaged
goods' idea as any ruined Victorian scullerymaid.

After sixteen it is legal, and the argument changes. You can
persuade – if they will listen – but not coerce. Try to be sensitive
to the fact that they may genuinely be in love; and try not to put
your big foot in it by talking heartily about condoms and the
Pill when the young lovers are not, in fact, sleeping together or
intending to. Many teenagers are mortally offended by this
kind of 'understanding'. Mother! Really! Wash your mouth out!

Remember that your house is still your house, and that if you disapprove of bed-sharing outside marriage you do not have to condone it. On the other hand, in the case of a pair of committed seventeen-year-olds, you may decide to do just that rather than have them take risks elsewhere.

If you think that your teenage son or daughter is grossly exploiting someone else – two-timing, standing them up or blowing hot and cold in an unfair way – it is as much your duty to point this out as it was, years ago, to prevent the pair of them hitting one another over the head with toy tractors. If they live in a civilized house they behave in a civilized way, and that is that.

Gay teenagers have a terrible time. Whatever your religious or political views about homosexual orientation, it is undeniably a fact. It is one of the hardest things to talk to parents about, but hiding it is even harder. Some get by by pretending to be uninterested in sex at all until they have left home. Some try really hard to have the appropriate kind of boyfriend or girlfriend, which leaves everybody a bit baffled. Some hope that the feelings for their own gender will go away (and sometimes, truth to tell, they do. There are a lot of confusion and crushes around at this age, especially in sheltered naïve children, which is why many people mistrust the idea of legalizing gay sex at sixteen).

As a parent, you have to do all the usual things: be around to listen, and let conversations wind their way slowly towards the subject without pushing. If you have the slightest suspicion, it is wise to exhibit a generally tolerant attitude about gay friends or public figures. Create a safe atmosphere. Don't go on about wanting grandchildren. With luck, one day you will be confided in.

Then however you feel, stay calm. It may be a sadness to you that your child is gay, if only because it is still harder to be gay than straight in the outside world. But it would be far, far sadder if you were to lose the love and communication you have spent years building up. Smile, though your heart is breaking. Keep on loving.

Older lovers, awful lovers, demon lovers The hardest thing in the world is to accept that your child is crazy about someone who is a) revolting b) untrustworthy and/or c) twice their age. However, furious opposition may spark off a Romeo-and-Juliet reaction in which the affair heats up over the flames of your indignation. Go very, very carefully. Let the repulsive object of love come to the house, and be contrasted with you and the normal friends and relatives your child gets on with. Hope that the whole thing withers on the vine, as most young infatuations do.

But remember that it is still your right to make rules about what cars your child goes in, how late he or she gets back, etc. This is particularly difficult if the man taking your seventeen-year-old daughter out is thirty-four and runs his own public company; but you are still the parents. If there is anything good about him, he will respect that.

If your seventeen-year-old son brings home a 39-year-old bottle blonde divorcee with a deafening laugh and a dirty wink, good luck. Perhaps this is the moment for Father to make the ultimate sacrifice and lunge at her himself. Certainly she should be lured into the kitchen at some point for Mother to ask her sternly whether her intentions are honourable. Cross fingers, it might never happen.

Kids who don't bother Some parents, in these hectically sexy days, actually get fretful when their children reach the late teens showing no interest whatsoever in having a boyfriend or girlfriend. Pull yourself together and repeat after me: *this is perfectly normal.* Fifty years ago lots of people never did any courting till they were in their twenties; some very happy marriages are made even now between first lovers well on the wrong side of thirty. Sexual drive varies according to individual nature. You don't have to spend your entire adolescence rutting after the opposite sex in discos. There are other traditional and reasonable ways of spending it, like hiding in your bedroom teaching yourself the accordion, or doting on dogs and horses, or climbing crags, or reading, or standing around giggling with a gang of your peers. Don't interfere, don't trouble trouble.

Freedom and Adventure

Before we leave off concentrating on children and move into the wider ecology of the family, a few words on the hardest thing of all for a parent to give: freedom. In the last thirty years, British children have lost a great deal of the independence that once was taken for granted. When I was nine years old I went out all day, along the coast, with lunch in a khaki gas-mask container from the army surplus shop. Thirty years on I would no sooner have let my own nine-year-old daughter wander off like that than let the baby juggle razor blades. But it is possible that I was wrong, and overprotective.

Most parents are. Numbers walking to school, alone or in groups, have decreased to under a fifth of what they were in 1978; streets are now deemed too dangerous to play in. Part of the change is entirely reasonable: traffic has become plentiful, dangerous and fast because of lousy town planning. Reassuring figures like beat policemen and park-keepers have become virtually extinct. Some fears, though, are media-driven. There is an exaggerated fear of kidnappers and paedophile molesters, and a terror of crime fed by ceaseless crime fiction on television and sensational reporting in the newspapers. We have lost the innocent 1950s sense that all adults keep an eye on all children, and that a stranger will reprove or rescue, as needed. Given the suspicious and litigious tone of our society most passers-by would be terrified to attempt either reproof or rescue, for fear of being knifed by the malefactor or accused of abducting the victim. Many children have no outdoor space close to home in which they can run free, form alliances and gangs, and lead that casual social life that children used to have as a matter of course from five or six years old upwards.

The results are all around us. Children are measurably less fit, despite good healthcare and nourishment, than at any time

202

since the second war. Indoor pursuits like television and computer-gaming flourish because parents take the option that feels safest, and encourage children to stay in the home rather than run out or ride bikes. The result is that electronic leisure takes up a disproportionate amount of children's attention, with predictable results in terms of neurosis and depression. Even sports move indoors, with an emphasis on swimming, gyms and other leisure-centre pursuits – which are fine, but which are both expensive and artificial, and do not bring the sense of freedom that comes with stretching yourself physically under the wide sky.

These are all endemic social problems. And none of them alters the fact that eventually these children will grow up and *have* to face the world, catch their own buses and make their own judgements about walking down the road in the dark. Either they will be students far from home, or else they will just get so big and frustrated that you are forced to relax all the rules at once and shruggingly let them go, unpractised and unprepared.

So to some extent we have to buck the trend, be brave, and let them venture out on small adventures, then bigger ones, then bigger ones yet. But it is hard. If there is one thing worse than having children quarrelling underfoot all day, it is not having them underfoot and wondering if they are all right. Is the lifeguard really competent at that pool? Will the young ones remember to look right, left, and right again? Will the older ones be picked on as sissy snobs by the street gang in the shopping centre? Will there be an earthquake, a fire, a bomb while you aren't there?

It is hard, but we have to do it, or we risk inflicting the subtlest and most lasting kind of harm. We have to teach independence as deliberately as we teach letters and numbers.

It begins in babyhood, long before real freedom. We have to resist the impulse to officious smother-love. I have seen playgroup mums who, when their child gets on the ride-on toy lorry back to front and can't find the steering wheel, immediately scoop him up and reverse him to face the right

203

way, without waiting to see whether he would work it out alone. Such mothers keep toddlers in baby-walkers long after they are needed, and feed them rather than let them use their newly discovered prehensile fingers. We have all, to some extent, been guilty of this.

Time goes on: the child reaches school age and we discover with a shaft of panic that we cannot solve all the problems. If he, or she, gets lost between the playground and the classroom and has to be rescued by a dinner lady, it happens out of our sight. But still in those early days we have control: we can insist on bike helmets and seat belts in alien cars and minibuses, and check out the houses the child visits. We make the main decisions.

More time passes: there are new demands. Can I go and ride my bike in the park with David? Can we go to the cinema by ourselves? Can I go on Scout camp? *Everyone* else is allowed to go clubbing . . . abseiling . . . swimming off the cliffs . . .

We have an instinct to protect; they have an instinct to explore. We can make sensible conditions (helmets, proper road training, registered adventure centres, curfews) but we cannot pad the entire world with hygienic plastic teddy-bear patterned quilting. Not any more.

Here are some of the generally accepted guidelines which sensible people like Kidscape offer, with some comments of my own.

Under seven should never be left at home alone, however competent. Even home can throw sudden crises at you: flooding taps, leaking gas, strangers at the door, broken glass. Attempts to be helpful (sweeping up the broken glass) could end in an accident; panic could make things worse. It probably won't happen but is not worth the risk.

On the roads, this age group is not yet able to judge the speed of approaching vehicles, and shouldn't have to make crossing decisions unless there are lights.

At eight or nine it is reasonable for country children to go out on bike rides with their friends, and town children on short errands to the shops (often shadowed by anxious mothers or watched down the road by a curtain-twitching chain of neighbours). Tall blocks of flats with lifts are a problem here, and in cautious families can delay independence. Very few of us would want this age out after dusk alone; and indeed, it is one of the most difficult to handle. Sometimes you have to be frank with the child and make it quite clear that it is *not* their incompetence you worry about but the intentions of strangers and the irresponsibility of drivers going too fast down dark roads.

On the subject of roads, it is worth remembering to tell children that competent and careful though they may be with their road drill, they are still shorter than adults, and therefore might be hard for a driver in a hurry to see. Having it explained that it isn't their fault salves hurt pride.

If it is possible for primary children this age to get themselves to school, that is terrific; a short, regular, routine purposeful journey is the best way to get used to a bit of independence. Ours took the train at nine and ten to a nearby small town and walked up through it to school. The opportunity to stop at a newsagent for a comic and a bar of chocolate seemed to me almost as educational as what they did at school.

However, if you do this, make it absolutely clear to the school that if *ever* your child is absent and you have not rung to explain this, they *must* call you (be on a mobile if you are not at home). There have been cases of schools idly assuming illness while children went seriously missing all day long. Make yourself quite clear to the form teacher. If they say they have no time to chase up absentees, offer to set up a rota of parents (as in many US towns) to do this task every morning.

By eleven children can be home alone for reasonable periods (though not, in sheer kindness, all evening. That is worrying). They also want to be allowed out shopping or to the cinema with their own friends. Public transport should be no mystery. Some of the misery of parental anxiety can, however, be slightly alleviated these days by giving them the use of a mobile phone (with hands-free wire to prevent the brain being fried, until

205

someone discovers otherwise). If this is excessive, or your child would be bound to lose it, at least give them a phone card and practice in using it. They should also have reliable watches, and know what time you will start worrying if they are not back. Some children (especially around thirteen and fourteen) are very lackadaisical about this; you don't have to put up with that. Make it clear that you are quite capable of ringing the police if they are more than an hour over time. The threat of this embarrassment works wonders.

If you live in a tough area, granting independence should be harder than if you are in a peaceful community where a lot of people know your children. Yet parents in leafy suburbs and small towns are often more fearful than big-city families and keep their children in or under surveillance for much longer. Evaluating risk is one of the hardest disciplines, and the one most of us are worst at (*any* risk seems outrageous where your own child is concerned). But you can bring the child into your reflections about the risk, and discuss emergencies, who to run to, how to put off pests and wolf-whistlers and drunks and gangs of bigger children. Make it clear that they can always use a taxi home, and have it paid for, if they are afraid of a situation or miss the bus.

Teenagers want their own lives. Suddenly there are strange people ringing, grunted assignations, and a wailing complaint if you try and work out who is going where, with whom, and for what. The process of your letting go has to be gradual, and the freedom has to be manageable. You know your own children, and have to try and spot when they are getting out of their depth. A curfew of midnight for fifteen-year-olds seems to me not at all unreasonable; but it would be crazy (false-teeth-by-post again) to suggest that any blanket rule would fit all cases.

There are new things coming into your ambit here – like 'clubbing'; an activity few over-forties really quite grasp, and which ranges from the wildest drug 'n' lapdance joints to grimy premises where teenagers hang around listening to music and drinking lemonade. So the best bet is to ask their friends' parents what the local place is like and whether it is all right. With luck, there will be some with older children who have been round the block before.

Adventure

Here the issue is not so much about personal freedom. Most adventure sports and expeditions will be under supervision by experts, or at least the child will be professionally prepared for the night hike before it happens. It is worth saying a few words about this here, though, because the same fears beset parents. Indeed they can be worse fears. If your child is hurt on a city street, it is part of everyday life and feels like a risk you had to take. If your child is hurt while abseiling or sailing, you fed that you will never forgive yourself for allowing this frill, this gewgaw, this unnecessary luxury to threaten him.

But physical adventure, in some kind of wilderness whether on land or sea, is not a frill or a gewgaw. It is an essential counterweight to an age of machines and virtual reality. Everybody needs some contact, sometime, with the qualities and perceptions you can only get from outdoor adventure. It might only be a long walk and a night's camping, but it is an essential part of growing up and understanding the world. Most children hanker for this kind of adventure as they grow up; I would not actually coerce a reluctant one into it, but the slightest sign of interest is to be encouraged.

Outdoor education is, in Britain, undergoing something of a crisis of confidence. You may have to look for it rather than rely on school to organize it. A few years back, there was a rescue on Dartmoor, when blizzards struck in May while 2,400 pupils between fourteen and nineteen happened to be out there on the Ten Tors race, a moorland and hill walk of fifty-odd miles in self-sufficient groups of six. The rescue went well, and everyone had sensibly bivouacked down and kept warm according to their survival training. Yet there was a lot of media chuntering about the 'danger' of having them out there in the first place; and it transpired in surveys done around that time that many schools have quietly binned the idea of outdoor education and given up adventure centre trips and school outings of this sort because of the increasing worry about litigation, the difficulty of finding leaders, and scandals about ill-run centres. Even Scout and Guide camps seem pretty often to be watered down into the experience of sleeping in a tent in the back garden of the group leader.

This is a pity. The Dartmoor parents and teachers were, in my view, absolutely right, and continue to be. We risk turning into a nation of outdoor illiterates. Every winter flimsily dressed adults are rescued in their cars from snowdrifts, without a shovel or a sack between them, because they have kidded themselves that the inside of their warm car is some sort of virtual computer game which cannot put them at risk. There are deaths on Li-los drifting out to sea, deaths from not realizing that waves on cliffs are dangerous, deaths when people set out in fishing boats with neither flares nor lifejackets and with an offshore wind. Outdoor illiteracy is dangerous; the best way to prevent it is outdoor education. Let the new teenage generation learn about the physical world, about real sea and moorland, mountain and forest. Let them get a hint of the eternal reality beneath the thin skin of civilization, beyond the shallowness of fashion and style, and learn basic truths about themselves and their capacities.

Apart from anything else, if they never get this experience then a great deal of history, literature and art will never properly touch them. Let them enjoy for a while a world where clothes are for warmth and protection and not appearance, where food is fuel, where cold and heat can kill you and where, above all, you depend on your companions and they depend on you.

There is a distinction between sport and adventure, sometimes a narrow one. Sailing a boat round the buoys on the reservoir and coming back indoors for a shower is sport; doing the Tall Ships race, or sailing a tidal river and working out where to pitch your tent on the beach so the tide won't get it, is adventure. Doing the climbing-wall at the leisure centre is sport; climbing a rock is adventure. Riding a horse round an indoor school is sport; going on a trail ride is adventure.

If you get a chance to let your child taste adventure, take it. Apart from the shared benefits, each gender gets quite specific advantages from it. Teenage girls taste the pleasure of not being fashion victims, or objects marked out of ten by boys, of letting their hair get lank and wet and not caring because they have achieved a tough goal. Boys get a sense of manhood, but also are taught stern and immutable rules about safety equipment and managing risk. Some accident-prone daredevil boys, indeed, are never so physically safe as when they are halfway down a Welsh hillside in abseiling kit.

Parents should, however, know a few basic things. There is a new accreditation system for adventure centres, not entirely in place in Britain as I write; such accreditation should always be checked. For climbing trips the instructors should have British Mountaineering Council qualifications; for sailing or boating, Royal Yachting Association (RYA) grades, and if there is canoeing involved the instructors should be experienced at that specific discipline. For riding, the instructors should have British Horse Society qualifications. For diving there should be BSAC or PADI instructors on hand. In all these cases, check that there is a reasonable proportion of senior instructors; in some activities the junior ones may be hardly older and not much wiser than your own children.

If a survival course is offered, make sure it is led by a trained survival leader and not just by a keen teacher who has read a book on it. If you are in some doubt, opt for an activity run by the Scouts or Guides, a Cadet Force, the Sail Training Association, Ocean Youth Club or other sail training organization which is approved by the RYA and whose boats guarantee to meet DoT standards.

If your child is under fifteen or so, give some consideration to whether – in addition to professional qualifications – these people have the empathy and sense to remember that these are children they are looking after, not adults on a management course. I once sent my son to a sailing centre, at only ten, where they let him do capsize drill in British seas at Easter without a wet suit on, and nobody showed any interest in making sure he warmed up enough or got his clothes dry. They had too many

209

keen nineteen-year-old instructors and nobody to see to comfort. Younger children should go to a centre where there is some kind of matron who is not expert in the sport but who *is* committed to children being warm and dry. Older teenagers, frankly, should have developed enough sense to put their own sweaters on; but pack a good few in case.

None of these things guarantees that there will never be an accident, but they do make it a lot less likely. And the experience will never leave your child, even if it is never repeated. For some it may be the beginning of a lifelong passion, for others not. Not all teenagers who do adventure training want to carry on. I always remember a school expedition in Suffolk where I went to see some twelve-year-old girls bivouacking in the woods and cooking rabbits on sharp sticks in front of their bender tent. A keen headmistress had sent them out to have their characters formed by an ex-SAS type, with women teachers hovering distractedly in the background to see fair play. I asked one beautiful creature, her unprotected hair streaming wetly like a dog's ears in the relentless downpour, what she had learnt from twenty-four hours hiking and camping. 'Not to go out when it's *waining*,' she said. Well, it was a start.

II   THE FAMILY

Becoming a Family

'Aaaah!' the old ladies say, leaning over you in the maternity ward, breathing sherry fumes from an outbreak of family celebration. 'You're a lovely little family now!' This makes couples feel rather strange, as if the only thing that anchors them as a unit in society is the whiffling baby in the transparent cot. It seems to act like a sort of scrunched-up, squidgy national identity card, an entrance ticket to the theme park called Familyland. Even stranger is the thought that you have become 'A Family' instead of a couple; and that you will never be just a couple again.

But of course in reality it does not actually happen all at once. There is no such thing as an instant family (as many step-parents can tell you, with grimaces). Why should there be? You cannot make an instant garden or an instant farm, and a family is every bit as complex, organic and prone to blight.

What we have in the twentieth-century Western world is often a very gradual transition from singlehood into family life. Now that so many couples live together unmarrried and child-less, instead of an abrupt step from maidenhood to pregnancy a curiously gentle slope has been created (though girls, beware: the old step is still there to trip you up). Generally speaking, you are no longer expected to cope with your first house, first sex, first taste of living with someone who isn't a relation, and first pregnancy all in one go. God knows how anybody ever survived it.

Instead the slope is gentler. You date, you start staying in instead of going out, one of you cooks for the other; you decide you might as well share a flat and save the bus fares. If you get on well together you may get married. Then, unless you are hellbent on an early baby, you carry on much as before. A couple, but not a family: affectionate and committed flatmates,

213

but each with your separate job and a few separate friends and interests, and the option of flouncing out after a row and staying out all night.

Of course, you each came from a family of your own. But your own families are likely to be rather shadowy at this point, and a good thing too. New husbands and wives who run home to mother for a bit of decent cooking and sympathy are not concentrating on the job in hand. It is necessary for fresh-minted couples to be separate: Adam and Eve, starting the world together. It prepares you for the responsibility of parenthood. During early couplehood, wise parents of bride and groom keep their distance, offer their support only if needed, and generally cool down their natural parental ardour. Their time will come again. As grandparents.

Because if the idea of 'family' fades away a little when you are courting, it returns in a new, bewildering, joyful and terrifying form when the first baby comes. I have written enough about the nuts and bolts of this enormous, shattering change (in *How Not to Be a Perfect Mother*) but what was not as clear to me then as it is now, sixteen years on, is that when you first have a baby you really have hardly any grasp of what is waiting for you in terms of family life. In fact, if both are back at work after maternity leave, you are quite likely to end up behaving like the bachelor couple you were, only with an obstacle course to get round. The baby becomes hardly more than yet another management problem in a crowded modern life. 'If you've got a ten o'clock meeting, you could drop James at the childminder and pick up the dry-cleaning, then I could get to my appointment early enough to nip into the shops for more nappies and some supper. If I could have the car, though, because of the dentist afterwards . . .'

This obstacle course causes much wear and tear on the parents, especially if they work in the kind of office where everyone gaily pretends that nothing much changes when you have a child. But the new baby knows no better, and as long as it is warm and fed and cuddled a lot, by someone it knows well, that baby generally puts up with the situation and thrives.

And gets bigger. Whereon it starts getting firm, outspoken

214

preferences about its minders, parents, mealtimes, and sleeping habits. By the time the first baby is two, there is no disguising the fact that you are turning into a three-cornered unit: a family. Instead of a strong adult couple protecting a weak, helpless scrap of life and making bossy decisions about every aspect of its routine, you have three strong wills all trying to inhabit the same space. Fraser Harrison, author of *A Winter's Tale*, the story of a temporary family crisis, described it beautifully as feeling as if you were all sewn into the same small suit. You struggle to find space, or indeed a sleeve hole. You forget who you were, and what you wanted.

It is not uncommon for the two-year-old to have the strongest personality in the house, and for parents to feel they are struggling feebly for survival themselves. Every parent of a toddler should give themselves an undemanding evening sometime by watching the hit Disney film *Honey I Blew Up the Kid*. I found myself riveted by this sci-fi fantasy, especially the bit early on when the toddling baby grows to seven feet tall and starts lurching around the house, ripping off doors and causing chaos. Surreal as this sequence was, it rang horribly true: there are times when the presence of a toddler is the largest thing in the house, and everything hangs from his or her whim. I spent the rest of the film – while the baby stumps around Los Angeles like a capricious King Kong – brooding on this, only to find myself nodding wisely, deeply moved, when it reached its denouement. The solution, you may remember, is that Mommy has to become even bigger than the child in order to reassert organization and peace. 'Gee,' I said, in one of those embarrassingly explicit American psycho-moments, 'that is so true. A Mommy has gotta be bigger, in every way, than her kid.'

If one parent has stayed at home full-time, the process of becoming a three-cornered family happens slightly faster, but more unevenly, usually precipitated by the mother deciding to bark a few home truths at the insouciant homecoming father along the lines of 'I don't care what sort of a day you've had, I haven't had time even to look at the paper, have you any idea how much work a baby is?'

Either way, gradually a family emerges. If more children rapidly follow the first, the mixture becomes richer and more complex, the juggling and compromising more skilled. A family is growing, a team is building up. There is not a lot you can do with the individual building blocks, but all of you somehow have to fit together into a viable structure: the egotist, the nervy one, the martyr, the short fuse, the one with special difficulties. The family becomes an organism, so that it is impossible to imagine life outside it. One day, the parents look in an old diary or photograph album and say, 'Good heavens! There really was, once long ago, a time when we had nothing to do but earn a living and keep ourselves amused! What did we do all day?' In the grip of this new job, the family job, they can hardly believe it was ever so simple.

So let the family grow, gently, at its own pace. Don't look at other families, least of all at the ones in advertisements and cheery television series, and say, 'Oh, they're so happy, they do so much together, it's all so well run and harmonious.' It probably isn't, once the front door is shut. Look instead at what is nearest: the state of mind and happiness of your own little tribe.

Not just the children: remember, at the heart of the family lies the marriage. Or, if you must, a less formal arrangement (though once there are children, there seems little sense avoiding the certificate; you're morally tied anyway). The kernel of every family is *un homme et une femme*, together because they were drawn together in the mysterious process of falling in love. It is amazing how often this gets forgotten about in the general chaos of family life – rows, meals, dilemmas about school, desperate dawn searches for Cub woggles and lost homework, confrontations with sullen teenagers and sleepless nights with sick babies. But we forget at our peril that there's still a marriage in there somewhere. If there had never been attraction, flirtation, love and passion then there would be no family. For the physical passion to cool down for a while is quite understandable (what better contraceptive could there be than a wakeful baby?) but even that will, with luck and humour, come back. It has to come back; because if the love and attraction and mutual amusement and appreciation in a marriage go sour, there will be estrangement. Estrangement may lead to separation, and thence divorce. And – let us not mince matters – unhappy children.

Divorce matters There was a period in the sixties and seventies when it was fashionable to pretend that children really didn't mind divorce and that they preferred their parents to be happy and 'fulfilled'. More recent, and more honest, investigation has confirmed what most of us knew by instinct anyway: that short of real violence, children prefer almost anything to the break-up of the familiar family. They do not like having their loyalties divided, hate the artificiality of access arrangements, and secretly blame themselves for it having happened. For a healthy normal child, its parents' 'emotional fulfilment', like their professional fulfilment, is a pretty damn low priority (when did you last hear a child say, 'Gosh, the best Christmas present I could get is for Mummy to get her promotion to Marketing Director – her career fulfilment is really important to me!' or 'I'm really pleased that Dad has found a woman who really understands him at last'?).

If they do pay lip-service to such priorities, at least under about fifteen, it is rather sad. Their childhood, their secure time for growing, has been taken from them. This is not fair. There is a new tendency around to be gung-ho about parental self-ishnesss (note the recent warm reception for an anti-mummy-ing book called *'I'm OK, You're a Brat'*) but the boring old truths and duties do not go away. These children didn't ask to be born. They didn't impose themselves on us. We invited them, either deliberately or by default. We brought them into being by our actions as free, responsible adults. We owe them the basic courtesy of a secure home and access to their parents.

If divorce is inevitable, the plain duty of both parents is to bite the bullet, swallow their pride, and behave with impec-cable good manners, fairness, and loving, generous considera-tion of the child's feelings. I drove a small boy home once to his mother's, after a weekend with his father and new girlfriend. In the car he said, 'I wish I hadn't had so much fun at the swimming pool.' Why? 'Because my mum always asks me if I've had a nice time with Dad and Wendy, and if I say I have, she cries and says I like him best. But if I tell a lie and say I haven't had much fun, then I feel I'm being bad to him.'

Dad, it must be said, had behaved pretty scummily towards this child's mother, but she had no right to pass on the pain. It was hers, part of her life's allocation of misery, not transferable. I could have throttled her. When we arrived she came to the door and hugged the boy and said, 'Did you have a nice time?' – and he said, 'Sort of,' and gave me a guilty glance. It was horrible.

Most parents behave a little better than that, and some display exemplary restraint, charity and mutual chivalry. Inevitably, doing this involves a certain amount of personal humiliation and a burning sense of unfairness in at least one party ('He's off with his girlfriend, buying them treats, I struggle through the school week, nurse them when they're ill . . .' 'She's got the house, the kids, her new man, I live in a crummy bedsit to pay the maintenance . . .'). But in the end, trust me, everybody will be happier if they have behaved well. Not like a complete doormat, just *well*. And if only one of you is even trying to behave well and the other is being an impossible bastard or a selfish bitch, the good partner has to make a superhuman effort not to retaliate, because two wrongs do not make a right. The only comfort must be that there is often a kind of justice at the last. Children are not fools. As they grow older they will know which parent behaved best, and work out what it must have cost them.

Stepfamilies are a vast, endlessly fascinating and painful subject. There are specialist books written about them, although I suspect that more useful than the instructional books are the bleakly sensitive novels, like Joanna Trollope's *Next of Kin*, and the classic warning tales like *David Copperfield* and the story of Snow White. Every family is different, and has its different problems of mutual adaptation and commitment; the hardest job, for the incoming partner to a family with children, is making a leap of generous imagination: understanding exactly

218

where the stepchildren stand in the wavering line of progress I have traced in Part I of this book, and yet never presuming that they have got it right (even natural parents don't, always). The best step-parents are the best people: generous, humorous, chivalrous to the young and the weak, tolerant, and willing to accept the need for some sacrifice of their own instincts and wishes. It is a tall order. Unfortunately, it is also morally non-negotiable. As an incoming step-parent you have to try and be as nice, and as intelligent about your behaviour, as humanly possible. Otherwise don't do it. Don't move in on your beloved's home life; be a secret, private, discreet, occasional lover instead, well off the premises.

But never mind divorce and step-parenting, not at this stage. Most marriages can be kept in good repair, and once there are children involved, they ought to be.

Marriage Maintenance

In 1837 the 28-year-old Charles Darwin scribbled out a list of pros and cons concerning marriage. In favour he found: 'Children (if it please God) – constant companion (friend in old age) who will feel interested in one, object to be beloved and played with – better than a dog anyhow – Home, and someone to take care of house – charms of music and female chit-chat. These things good for one's health. Forced to visit and receive relations but *terrible waste of time*.'

Further tormented, he moved to the advantages of not marrying. 'Not forced to visit relatives and to bend in every trifle – to have the expense and anxiety of children – perhaps quarrelling . . . less money for books etc.' He only stopped short of the brutal frankness of one relative of mine who dismisses the whole business of married life as 'harsh words by day, foul smells by night'.

It may make us gasp, but such frankness with oneself before marriage is not at all a bad thing. Younger women in particular have a dreadful tendency to blind themselves to the realities of the state, refusing to envisage the relentless daily companionship, the hairs in the washbasin, the real implications of 'in sickness and in health' and the rash promise to endow one another with all worldly goods. We allow a cloud of white tulle and rose petals to obscure such vital questions as, 'Does this man really just want someone to take care of him ("better than a dog anyhow")?' The idea of a premarital contract laying out everything from finance to childbearing is perhaps taking it a bit far, but an astonishing number of engaged couples have never even discussed the possibility of children, let alone who is going to look after them. As for talking about such matters as who would be most likely to relocate across the country to follow whose career promotion, or how the money is to be organized in the event of one partner losing their job, it is rare indeed to meet brides and grooms who admit to having thought, let alone talked, about it.

But that private Darwinian list of pros and cons might be a useful thing to concentrate one's mind. The best bit of advice about marriage is, 'Don't do it unless you can't bear not to.' And the best description of marriage is Robert Louis Stevenson's: 'Marriage is one long conversation, chequered by disputes. Two persons more and more adapt their notions one to suit the other, and in process of time, without sound of trumpet, they conduct each other into new worlds of thought.' Ergo, if you can't hold an enjoyable conversation with someone, and haven't adopted some of each other's thoughts, think twice about getting married.

Once you do marry, no question about it, you feel different. I had only been ten days wed when I fell into bad company at an office party after my early morning radio news shift. It lasted all morning and developed into a pub lunch. I got home at about three o'clock, singing, and spent some time trying to get the key into the front door of the flat. Then I fell face downward on the bed and knew no more until I woke up in the chilly dusk and remembered that it had been my turn to take the communal pillowcase round to the laundrette. A fortnight earlier, living in the same flat with the same man and the same bag of shirts, I would have shrugged philosophically and left it for the morning. In my new status as a married lady I panicked. Too drunk to do the laundry! The sure mark of a Bad Wife! The shame of it!

This was replaced later by a conviction that I was a Bad Mother (not cutting babies' nails often enough, putting them in nonmatching booties) and a Bad Housekeeper (never any lavatory paper). Until one day I saw the light, and realized that wearing a white frilly dress for a couple of hours does not convert a slob into a hausfrau, and never was going to, any more than there is a magic spell in the wedding ceremony capable of turning a frog into a prince, or a roaring rugby fullback into a man whose greatest thrill is to trail round Habitat looking for rattan bathroom stools. *Caveat emptor*: if you don't like it, don't marry it. You marry a person, not an

221

idea; the only real essential is to carry on the conversation you started.

This is harder than it sounds. There is a mysterious process by which couples who, while courting, spend hours going on and on about their innermost souls, childhood memories and deepest aspirations, often find that after marriage the conversation dwindles down to 'Have you seen my hair dryer?' and 'We're supposed to be going to the Carters in half an hour, or was it yesterday?' By the time children arrive it can be a positive struggle even to get these simple messages across. I was once asked to write a Valentine poem for a newspaper's collection, and rather to my horror found that this came out:

> Had we but world enough and time
> This note would be a Valentine
> Since married life is what we have
> It's to remind you to bring home the
> haddock and the Sanilav.

But the real conversation must go on. Couples with children have different ways of seeing that it does so. Some go on holiday together without their children once a year. This is all very well, especially if you have a good granny on duty. But if you are a working mother who feels she spends little enough time with the children anyway or a neurotic worrier who wastes the whole holiday worrying whether they are all right, holidays without children are not the answer. I have traipsed round Venice sobbing, 'Gosh, the children would love this,' and that was only a weekend.

Occasional weekends alone together (or with old friends) can be a help; it is amazing how much conversation you can fit in between Friday and Sunday evenings if you are not being constantly interrupted by shrill demands. You even have more sensible discussions of the children's needs, with the clear view of distance. Formality can help: during the busiest years my husband and I both worked mainly at home, although at very different occupations, and sometimes made an actual appointment to have lunch together while the children were at school.

During the most tumultuous years of early childrearing and keeping two careers going, we devised a habit of holding an Annual General Meeting on Boxing Day. We got in a babysitter, and walked off the Christmas festivities on an epic fifteen-mile walk lasting all day. The purpose of this walk was to discuss the past year, how life had gone, and what we both really wanted to do next. If we could not afford lunch, or a babysitter, we would just announce one television-free evening a week when the children were in bed, and talk then. It may sound astonishingly simple and obvious, but it has always been quite clear to us that when we have spent too long a period not taking these deliberate chances to talk uninterrupted, we become angry and snappish and difficult. We lose communication.

Even if the conversations themselves are difficult (i.e., too much about money, or troublesome relatives) it is essential to have them. Otherwise a marriage slowly weakens like an unwatered plant, and falls prey to the first gale (or gal, or guy). Whereon one says to the other, 'I never knew you were feeling like that! I had no idea!' and the other says, 'It's too late now!'

Through conversation, and frankness, and a willingness to admit to anger or irritation (over money, or sex, or working hours, or who gets up first, or the way you speak to one another in company), you get a better understanding of what the psychiatrist Robin Skynner calls the 'secret contracts' of marriage. Old idealisms about equality, openness, mutual respect and homemade bread give way to pragmatism and an understanding of your real needs. As that wise man once said to me, 'People marry for some very obvious reasons and for others not obvious even to themselves. The businessman who seems powerful and strong, even to himself, marries a wife with a traditional submissive role; but there may be a secret contract that she will mother and nurture him. A downtrodden wife may be, secretly, the boss; a strong, decisive woman may want to be cosseted and tucked in at night. Just look at the Valentine columns in the papers, all that baby talk about Piggy-Wiggy and Snugglebotty. People get married because they want to be babies with each other sometimes. But that's not in the formal contract, is it? Although it's just as important.'

Sex

Sex, of course, *is* in the formal contract. 'With my body I thee worship.' The arrival of children changes all that. The female body, in particular, starts worshipping the idea of a quiet night's sleep, without anything crying or kicking and wriggling in the bed or needing its nappy changed. As long as both parents are utterly flattened by night cries and daily pacing, the problem is not too serious. But if Daddy is fresh as a daisy, and has not quite grasped his new status, he can become aggrieved. Women naturally become angry at being pressed, and men get angry too.

One friend of mine, who we shall mercifully disguise under the name of Eric, expressed his resentment in startlingly primitive terms. 'It's as if she'd got what she wanted out of me, and I was a redundant breeding animal.' Well, Eric, I said in my supportive way, that is exactly what you are, really, isn't it? Or did you want another baby on the anniversary? We then came to a more reasonable conversation about it, and concluded that the problem is that since the Pill we have all separated pleasure and love too sharply from the bald biological *raison d'être* of sex. The result is that when children are born we expect the pleasure to go on operating independently, as it did before. But Nature thinks otherwise, and little as new mothers are likely to admit it, she closes down the female libido with pragmatic ruthlessness during most of the lactation period.

This is not to say that breastfeeding women don't make love; it is a matter of the kind of love they make. If a woman has dwelt upon an erotic pedestal, and sex has hitherto been associated with clean tumbling hair, fresh nighties, candlelight and a crooner on the stereo, the earthy chaos of early motherhood may be too much for both partners. If sex has been playfully and consentingly violent, things may have to change even more radically. Diana, a single girl reputed in hushed conversation to 'know all the tricks', eventually made a colourful marriage and spoke freely to her friends of vibrators, the old school gymslip and kinky whips. Years passed, and she turned up one day wild-eyed at a baby-circle coffee morning and said,

'I think I've gone frigid. Every time we try, I keep thinking "Hell, I'm not some tuppenny trollop. I'm a mother, I've got responsibilities, I'm not going to have him licking honey out of my navel!" '

Her friends who had always tended more towards cuddly, comforting couplings suddenly realized they were not such losers after all. The comforting cuddles never stop, the couplings just develop again when the time is ripe. Diana and her husband seemed, in the end, to have discovered other depths to sex than mere gymnastics; years later she said to me that whereas some of their old fun and games had re-surfaced, all the oriental postures and kinky knickers in the world couldn't match up to the extraordinary and mysterious knowledge that by doing this once before, you had created a miracle.

Even if you are doing your damnedest to stop another miracle happening just yet, that feeling remains: the marvel of Life trying to happen. And the extraordinary fact is that sex is actually better – if different – on the far side of childbirth. Men and women who understand this stay together. The ones who don't – the women who cool off entirely, or grant themselves grudgingly as a favour, the men who see no difference and grumble at the roundedness and tiredness of the maternal woman – are most likely to fall into the miserable chaos of affairs and estrangements. Take your pick. Be prepared to accept change, as spring turns to summer and later to autumn. As in so many areas of family life, you can't have everything, but you can, with patience and humour, get a great deal of it.

Fighting

I sometimes think that TV drama has had a disastrous effect on marriage. Not merely because it innocently gives the impression that all husbands and wives are attractive and have beautifully fitted kitchens, but because of the rows. Think of the last half-dozen plays (or even sitcoms) that you saw, and I bet there were at least six marital screaming matches. I also bet that five out of six of them ended in passionate embraces. The one that sticks in my mind is the 1990s infertility mini-series,

You, Me, and It, in which a yuppie couple were unspeakably nasty to one another for months and we were expected to believe that the moment she got pregnant all the vile words would be forgotten. Hmmm.

I suppose that because of the demands of drama – insults are amusing to onlookers and fun to write – writers have overdone the rows. Ever since Jimmy berated Alison for two hours in *Look Back In Anger* before starting to twitter again about bears and squirrels, there has been a dramatic convention that such rows do not damage the relationship but actually ginger it up. Parts of the therapy industry – and the feminist movement – now seem to be keenly bolstering this idea that people should 'express anger freely'. Take Dr Elizabeth Stanley, who wrote in a newspaper, 'It may be that the couples who have the more open rows – the ones who appear to outsiders to have a dreadful marriage, always yelling at each other – may have a better, stronger relationship. Because anger, constructively expressed, will clear the air. If they say "we never argue", it rings warning bells.' Or another recent claim in a magazine that 'Couples who fight aren't those who divorce the most. Lack of communication is more damaging than furious rows.'

I offer you both those quotations at face value, and you may want to agree with them. There is something in it. Occasionally a row does clear the air, and the most poisonous marriages of all are undoubtedly the tight, bitter, silent ones. Many a woman has been frustrated by a man who refuses to join in arguments at all, merely retiring behind a newspaper in lofty silence while she smashes teapots. I know one who walked out on ten years of marriage saying that whenever she raised any point he disagreed with, 'he sort of sighs, and goes on with what he's doing, and doesn't answer'. Wives have been known to pull the same trick by merely bursting into tears instead of pursuing a discussion. It is perfectly true that a marriage with no argument at all is a marriage where one partner is consistently and unhealthily giving in. So far, so good.

But arguments are one thing, and rows are another. What makes me seriously uneasy is our new, me-generation idea that all emotions ought to be expressed all the time, and that bottling up anger is always a Bad Thing. Once you add to this the romantic idea that anger is sexy, you have an excuse for any amount of insults, plate-smashing, screaming and tears, coupled with claims that the marriage is 'a strong relationship' and 'really communicating'.

I cannot go along with this. I have seen it in action, in plenty of ill-tempered marriages, and my considered view is that as a way of life, it stinks. Expressing anger is perhaps a therapy for the angry person, who can forget all about it and feel better afterwards. But if it is too intemperate, too uncontrolled, the recipient of that anger will not so easily forget. Sticks and stones may break your bones, but words go right to the heart. 'My husband,' says another young wife, Maureen,' 'once told me I was a selfish, stupid, fat frigid bitch. Admittedly I had just called him worse things, but the trouble is when he said that about being frigid, I couldn't forget it. Whenever we make love now, I keep thinking that's what he thinks about me. And I sort of stop trusting him.' She is also dieting obsessively, thin though she is, because of the 'fat' bit of the insult.

An interesting American survey recently showed that women remember the detail of rows for longer than men, but men suffer too. If you shriek at your man the information that he is an insensitive bastard, an oaf, a lousy lover and a selfish swine who is obsessed with his work, you may have forgotten all about it within half an hour and be feeling much better. But he may be stricken with unhappy, quiet insecurity about his job, his sexuality and your whole relationship. Saying 'I didn't mean it' is all very well, but in that case – broods the victim – what made you say it? The old line that angry people 'always say things they don't mean' is counterbalanced by the equally old line that *only* when you are angry do you dare say what you really mean. And most of us have pretty total recall of things said to us in anger. They are typed, for ever, in our brains. Rows do not always clear the air; sometimes rage feeds on rage, becoming a habit or even an addiction.

And what about the children of these 'strong relationships' where anger is 'constructively expressed'? Are they in earshot? If so, believe me, they do not have a sophisticated or romantic view of what is going on. They are terrified and miserable. You are abusing them, too. They will not be there to witness the passionate reconciliation later at bedtime, will they? They will be alone in their beds, thinking frightening thoughts of divorce and loss; or creeping to one another's rooms to discuss what precisely is going on and how much it threatens the home.

If you do row in the hearing of children, for God's sake explain it all afterwards, and say how sorry you are to have had a silly babyish tantrum of precisely the kind you are always telling the children not to have. How many parents remember to do that? Secretly, worriedly, children store these things up. In our house, where we have relatively few rows, and always try to make up with a hug in the children's presence, they have sometimes stunned us by citing individual ones dating back several years. The only way to defuse the memory is to turn them into family jokes. The Day Your Father Stamped On The Answering Machine. You know the sort of thing.

Of course there are going to be rows; the point is that they are nothing to be proud of. Not romantic, not sexy, rarely therapeutic, mainly destructive and silly and childish. One of the best pieces of marital advice I ever had was from a woman who had been married for fifty years. 'The main thing,' she said, 'is never to generalize. Never begin a sentence with "You always . . ." or "You never . . ." Be quite precise as to what you are shouting about.'

It is a brilliant principle. You can say, 'You fool, you forgot to get the cleaning back, now I have nothing to wear to work, you have ruined my day, if not my week!' But not 'You forgot the cleaning, you never do any simple thing for me, you are chronically selfish . . .'

It is OK to say 'I am furious that I bought theatre tickets and then you forgot and worked late', but not 'You never take me out! You only care about your bloody job!' The more you generalize, the greater the damage.

Of course, if your partner does keep on committing the same crime, this may mean that you end up having an improbably huge outburst of fury over one small incident, but at least you won't have written him off entirely in your rage. You can always explain about the background to it later, calmly, in the apology-and-discussion phase.

So tread cautiously when people start advocating 'a good row to clear the air'. Count to ten, like mother told you to. Let not the sun go down upon your wrath. Limit the damage and avoid sentences beginning 'And another thing . . .' Avoid irony and sarcasm at all costs. Make jokes. If all else fails, run round the block, cursing.

And a special note to the highly educated: however much better you express yourself in writing, *do not write little notes about your partner's failings and leave them on the kitchen table to be found late at night.*

One thing is unequivocally comforting: the longer a marriage or partnership goes on, the better chance it has of survival. If you make it to five years the statistical probability of divorce goes down; to ten years and it goes down even further. 'By then,' said one wife, 'you know what you have got. The idea of starting afresh is appalling, throwing away all those memories . . . and hell, when you've seen a man slowly grow his pot belly and lose his front hair, and he's seen you through childbirth and tummy bugs, you're sort of committed, aren't you?'

As you decline from taffeta crinoline to baby-stained maternity dungarees, so the marriage changes too. And it goes on changing, with each new phase. The silliest thing anyone ever says is, 'You're not the girl/man I married.' Of course they aren't. Neither are you. You never swim in the same river twice.

And what happened to the young Charles Darwin? Well, he made up his mind to marry, with a few pangs for lost freedom: 'Eheu! I never should know French – or see the Continent – or go to America, or go up in a Balloon, or take a solitary trip in Wales . . . never mind, my boy – cheer up – one cannot live this solitary life, with groggy old age, friendless and cold and childless, staring one in one's face . . . There is many a happy slave.'

It was a happy marriage.

Who's Who: Father

Once upon a time it was quite simple. Daddy Bear had a big chair and a big plate of porridge. Mummy Bear, a middle-sized chair and an elegantly ladylike helping of porridge. And Baby Bear knew his place. Seen and not heard.

Daddy Bear went out gathering nuts and fighting off enemies, Mummy Bear bustled round the house, Baby Bear fixed firmly to her apron strings. There was no question of Mummy Bear wanting more porridge and taking a job in order to get it, or of Daddy Bear becoming unemployed, having a mid-life crisis and moving in with Floozie Bear, twenty years younger than him. Nor of Baby Bear turning delinquent and starting to deal in illicit substances on street corners.

Was it ever really like that? And if it was, was it happy? We could argue all day about the merits and demerits of the good old Traditional Family, but there would not be any point. The only sensible thing is to start from here. Precisely where we are. And allow for the fact that none of us is starting from quite the same place.

Let us begin with Father. Few things shake a man up more comprehensively than the news that he is to become one. Even an eagerly planned embryo can floor him utterly. 'I had to sit down when she told me,' said one. 'Then I thought I ought to do something. Get on with it. Turn into a father. But I didn't know how.'

It is not surprising that he felt so lost. No important social image is so blurred and confused as that of the father. On the one hand, ancient notions of power and wisdom cling around the word: God the Father, Father Time, Paterfamilias. On the other hand, the prevailing cultural cliché which has grown up in this century is of 'Dad' as a lovable but rather inept stumblebum: anxious Mr Pooter, getting it wrong with his son Lupin in *Diary of a Nobody*, hen-pecked buffoons on comic postcards, working-class dads in TV sitcoms who skulk in the garden shed to escape domesticity. Father's Day cards depict the poor man exclusively in terms of carpet slippers, golf clubs, big macho dogs, fishing equipment and football scarves. A few gestures towards the modern age are made by the inclusion of cards showing motorcycle scrambling, TV snooker-watching and windsurfing; but otherwise the run of Father's Day cards has remained virtually unchanged in thirty years.

This must be terribly depressing for hands-on full-time thoroughly caring modern fathers; also for all those suave, sophisticated men who like to feel that they have only paused briefly in their upwardly mobile, stylish, purposeful lives in order to perpetuate their stunning genes. Just because a chap did the decent thing by posterity, it seems hard that he should be permanently stereotyped as a bluff old fogey in Prince Albert slippers, oiling his fishing rod and kicking footballs. Suppose he hates all sports? Suppose what he really likes is wearing sharp suits and eating sushi, or writing sensitive experimental novels? Hard luck. Tribal mythology has cast him otherwise: the sensible, steady, conservative and deeply boring provider, to be placated with a card on Father's Day and otherwise more or less ignored.

Or blamed. Modern father has also been bombarded by assertions that he is at worst dangerous, at best tolerable, and in any case pretty unnecessary (beyond what he can donate to a test tube or turkey baster). The very fact that nearly all divorces end up with the mother taking custody of the children implies that society does not believe a full-time father to be likely or healthy. Man, so the radicals tell us, is still an uncivilized, emotionally illiterate being stunted by his own forefathers' coldness. His only hope is to become a shiningly modern New Father, present at the birth classes (not to mention the birth), bonding with his tiny baby, bathing it, changing nappies, expressing tenderness, weeping, pushing buggies, and generally behaving like a bit of a girlie.

In the first flush of parenthood, some new men certainly do fling themselves into all this. Indeed, the divorce boom and the

New Fatherhood have formed an odd alliance to produce a uniquely modern figure: the man who leaves his first wife and teenage children (having been nowhere near the birth, thank you, and never changed a nappy) then marries a much younger woman and goes enthusiastically into the birth-bath-and-potty routine. Many a balding figure now haunts Mothercare in his lunch hour, to the secret fury of his ex-wife.

But even the New Father image fades as the children grow older. Surveys of rôle-reversed couples indicate that half the families revert to a traditional pattern within two years. Once the thrill of novelty and the good resolutions wear off, if a father is out at work all day his role can very rapidly tail off into something more like the one his own father filled. Charlie Lewis, a Reading University academic who studied fatherhood in the eighties, dispassionately observed that for all the brave talk of the New Fatherhood, 'all but a few are assistants, rather than partners, in the business of child care'. More recent research suggested that the time fathers spend interacting and conversing with their children each day can be measured in minutes, and not many of those.

But Lewis, in the same study, also exploded the naive modern belief that paternal tenderness was only invented by the Me generation and the feminist insistence upon paternal help. The truth is that not all past fathers have chosen the God-the-Father stance, remote and revered. Studies of fishermen and artisans in the Victorian era revealed that rather than being brutal, drunken and aloof like the working-class father of legend, these men were very much participant, concerned members of their household, often taking the children to work alongside them. Further back, William Cobbett moved to the country in 1829 and worked at home because he believed that a child should always have a father in sight; if friends asked him to stay without his children, he did not go.

No, we did not invent paternal tenderness, but it may be partly true that we have had to re-invent it. First the industrial revolution took away independence in the workplace from the hand-weaver or farmworker, and locked him up all day in a child-free factory; then two savage wars, with countless men condemned to constant, tough, adult male companionship for long stretches, promoted machismo and dulled the conventional man's perception of his own tenderness. Nor did Freud help much: a succession of twentieth-century babycare books have deliberately marginalized the role of the father, fearfully pointing him out as a source of future neuroses (writers before the Second World War almost universally discouraged fathers from hugging children or doing anything beyond offering a 'manly handshake'). Until political correctness began to cut in quite recently, most babycare books jokily relegated him to the status of untrustworthy nurserymaid. We mothers may complain of the images painted of us, but fathers have a case as well.

The good father

So what makes a good father? One nastily unreconstructed feminist writer scornfully said, 'One who doesn't drink all the housekeeping, and doesn't scar the children.' If you stop people in the street they will say things like, 'Well, he should be a good provider', or 'someone for the kids to have fun with', or 'an example'.

But none of these will quite do. It is dreadful to think of fathers only as financial milch cows (because what if, through no fault of their own, they stop earning?) and it is not even vital that they should be playmates. A romping, cuddling, fun Daddy is definitely an asset, yet it is hard to ignore the fact that in cultures and classes where fathers are almost godlike in their remoteness and grandeur, plenty of perfectly well-adjusted and loving citizens manage to grow up. Successful styles of fathering vary far more widely than styles of mothering (rather to the rage of us mothers). Look at the affection and inspiration with which John Mortimer writes about his father – an eccentric, self-willed and bruisingly ironic old barrister who would never admit that he was blind and told his son that sex was overrated. Not an obvious social worker's profile of perfect fatherhood, is he? But his son mourns him deeply. Or look at James Morris, whose children's love and respect survived their

233

father's sex change when he became Jan. You can even, with a pinch of salt, embrace Nancy Mitford's comforting theory about nature's own balancing mechanism: that children of roaring, raging, whacking fathers like her own 'have enough of their father in them to enable them to weather storms in which ordinary children would lose their nerve completely'.

What is it, then, that the good father does? Some say that a father is essential to a child's moral development because 'his love tends to be conditional on performance, or good behaviour, while a mother's love is all-pervading'. (Put your writing pads down, chaps. It is not me saying that, it is Trevor Berry, of *Families Need Fathers*. I toss it in only as a discussion point.) Some say that he bolsters children's self-respect, others that he energizes the family and turns it outward to conquer the world, while the mother's focus is inward, towards the hearth.

All we can be certain of is that a father is not – repeat not – a duplicate mother. When I first began writing childcare books, I was challenged by the publisher as to why I kept referring to the 'mother' instead of the 'parent'. Examining my conscience, I realized that what was happening was that I was thinking of 'mother' not so much as a sex-linked word as a job description. Like accountant. Or MP, or doctor. Some fathers do indeed carry out a lot of mothering: cuddling to sleep, listening to worries about school, physical care, sorting out socks. But hovering in the back of my mind was always a certainty that fathering was a parallel – and distinctly different – function. So distinct that when a mother has to do it for lack of a visible father, she has to change her behaviour and attitudes quite sharply.

Later, I found that much psychological theory backs up that notion. A father is not a mother. Like it or not, he stands in a different relationship to his children: less like an extension of themselves, and more like a benevolent patron. He does different things, plays rougher games, and is less ready to identify and sympathize with every bump and worry. He laughs not only with the child, but occasionally at her. He does silly things to make her laugh, not least at herself. He is a sort of advance guard of the rough, bluff, outer world which the small child will have to meet one day; a halfway house between the utter cosy commitment of nursery life, and the world of strangers which lies beyond.

It is easy to see this in action. There are always exceptions to any stereotypes, but on the whole it is true that mothers fuss about gloves and woolly hats, whereas fathers lose them. Mothers are permanently alert for dreadful diseases in their offspring, fathers only notice when actually vomited upon. Mothers empathize, fathers sympathize. A father is often the better person to take a child along to an exam, or for a vaccination (so GPs say) because he is less likely than a mother to fall into a state of tremulous nervousness and communicate it to the child. I have seen young fathers in hospital with their children, soothing them to sleep where the mothers have failed. This does not mean that they are in any way better than the mother, but that they are different in their emotional responses.

Nature had very good reasons for arranging matters the way she did: fatherhood, as distinct from motherhood, is a necessary job. Single mothers perhaps know this better than anyone, since they have to do the fathering too, splitting themselves in half at times. However much you switch and swap, there still seem to be two roles to play in a child's life: one of them reassuring, one challenging and brave and gay. Perhaps, if there is any point at all in the concept of New Fatherhood, it is that couples feel more free to take turns at both.

So what, practically, can one say to a new father?

Get involved in the physical care of babies, but if that does not suit you or your wife, don't force it. On the one hand, as Mike Rosen the poet and often full-time father observes, 'Being involved with all the poo and sick and stuff actually makes the relationship better and cuddlier. Also all the singing to sleep.' On the other hand, I know a kind, beloved, humorous, much-cherished father who only ever changed a nappy once. He was sick. His wife then had to clean up two messes instead of one, and never asked him again. Horses for courses.

Be around There is a dreadful tendency for men (and some high-powered working women) to think that unless they are doing

235

formal quality-time things with their children, or 'minding' them with no other adult in sight, there is no advantage whatever in being present, and you might as well be at work, or out. This is not so. Rosen once wrote a lovely account of the kind of domestic pottering, the background presence, which children need from both parents at times. His theory, in his wonderfully blokey book *Goodies and Daddies* (every new dad should have one), is that wiping the table, doing the school run, tidying the mantelpiece is time you use to make a relationship with your children. 'It's then that they ask the really important things – "Do buffaloes eat spaghetti?" and other vital questions. Even reading the paper, your presence is a great big affirmation that you like the company you're keeping, just as your absence creates the tiny anxiety that home isn't where you want to be and the children aren't who you want to be with. If you are around, the children will claim you.'

This is probably one of the hardest lessons for fathers to learn. Some learn it a very hard way indeed. Sir John Harvey-Jones, the industrialist, in his memoirs laid out mercilessly how he nearly let professional ambition sabotage his life. Rising through the ranks at ICI in the sixties, he starkly describes how corrupting that world was to his family life. 'I started to behave politically – not dishonourably, I hope, but deliberately seeking to demonstrate that I was better than others. I played at tycoons, threw myself into jet-set life, drinking and nightclubbing. I neglected my wife and daughter and took them for granted. In that brief period I messed up my family life badly.' He spotted it in time, and renewed it. But his description must have struck a chord with many men: caught in the dilemma of wanting to be a good provider – a top provider – and a good father.

Business and industry are only very slowly accepting that fathers need to 'be around' for their children. One headhunter brutally observed that if a man mentioned at interview that on some days he might need to be off sharp at five to get his child from nursery school, 'it would be the kiss of death'. Another man I knew, a salesman working from home, regularly spent time caring for his three children while his wife ran her own small business. 'I work out my time flexibly, and do the paperwork late at night,' he said. 'But they would be livid if they found out.' In some firms, men can successfully move into a slower lane for a while in early fatherhood, as many women do. Britain reeled with shock in the late eighties when a cabinet minister, Norman Fowler, gave up his post in order to spend more time with his young children, saying, 'I have not been the best of sharing fathers, and I want to be home more for a while.' He was back three years later, when his girls were older. There was a good deal of media sniggering about the whole manoeuvre (at one point nobody but me, in all the British press, seemed to believe in his motives), but when I polled a carriageful of rail commuters on the matter, they were unanimous.

'Lucky blighter,' said one young man. 'Good for him. I wish I could do it. I never see my kids awake except at the weekend, and I travel two weekends in three.' 'My wife,' said another, 'had to make the decision about which nursery school my son goes to. I wanted to go and see it myself, but I couldn't get the day off.' None of the men wanted to drop out, or reverse roles; they just wanted space to experience family life in the irreplaceable early years, and, as another said, 'to lay a foundation of good memories against the time he becomes a horrible teenager who despises his old Dad'. Another, interestingly, observed that since he had lost a high-powered job and taken a less good one, the time he spent with his children was better and more relaxed. 'I used to be so hyped up that I had to spend my free time blowing off violent energy, driving to the coast at ninety m.p.h. to go ocean-racing, or playing ferocious squash. I couldn't wind down, ever. Now I'm a bit of a vegetable at work, I have a more balanced kind of time with the kids. I like it, actually. For now.'

Men who slow down their careers on purpose, though, are exceptional and brave. Society still applauds the macho workaholic, and high-pressure jobs make you feel important. Children, whatever their other merits, rarely do. Any mother can tell you about that gloomy, isolated moment when the joys of family life are reduced to a kitchenful of spilt cat litter and a cross, snotty toddler. In the words of another writer, Fraser

Nature's Masterpiece

Harrison, at a certain period of his family life 'Their little ways ceased to be charming and eccentric, becoming instead infuriatingly self-centred. Their incessant noise was no longer a merry chorus to our household life, but a clamorous and grating din.' At such times a company chauffeur at the door and a sheaf of policy decisions seem like blessed freedom.

Balance is the key. And courtesy, and respect. Perhaps we should be nicer to fathers, celebrate them more. I know it seems hard, when mothers feel so chronically unappreciated; but a bit of mutual respect can work wonders – even if it does not get the lost gloves, and woolly hats, and bits of school uniform found.

Fathers and sons

Scratch the surface of the newest New Man and you find a hunter who wants his boy to go out hunting with him. A mild, sensitive chap considerably startled me once by looking at his boy-and-girl twins and saying sadly of the girl, 'She's everything one would want in a son – athletic, bold, tall, strong . . . and look at him.' The little boy cowered sweetly behind his mother, inches smaller and far more nervous than his bouncing minx of a sister.

Men have to keep a tight rein on their expectations of their sons, because sons constantly measure themselves against their fathers, and it would be a terrible strain to have both of them playing the same game. Boys easily start to feel that they have disappointed their fathers, and this makes them sad and surly. Think American-therapist-speak: the correct message for a father to project is, 'Gee, son, I am proud of you. Whatever you do.' If the son in question is actually lying on the sofa with the curtains shut at four o'clock in the afternoon, a Walkman clamped to his ears, trying to turn on the television with a horrible gnarled yellow toe protruding from a hole in his sock, this is difficult. The message may then be mutated to, 'Gee, son, I just know you've got unique gifts you could be using, is there any way I can help you to use them?' He will grunt, but it will be a pleased sort of grunt.

Re-reading the above, it sounds a bit soft-headed to me, too.

238

Blame the fact that I have just come back from a sports day where the father of an eleven-year-old who came second – *second* – in a major race was heard shouting at him for not being first. Think about it.

Fathers and daughters

I worked with a man once whom I rather disliked, most of the time; a snappy, shallow, style junkie. But his Achilles heel was his daughter, about whom he would rave incessantly. 'From the first moment she was born . . . oh God, the first little pair of buckled shoes . . . she's gorgeous, I tell you, gorgeous . . . marvellous girl, I could eat her . . .' When I saw her it was quite a shock: she was twelve, lumpen, dough-faced, lank-haired and shy. The kind of female this fashionable man would normally never be seen in the same room with. But he folded her in his arms and pushed her forwards saying, 'Isn't she gorgeous?' without a trace of irony, and she smiled happily. I really loved that annoying man, at that moment.

In order to grow up confident, daughters truly do need their fathers' approbation. This applies to physical, as well as moral, good points. It is absolutely not a father's role to point out his daughter's spots, peculiar dress sense, or rolls of puppy fat. Mothers can do this more tactfully, and friends to still better effect. A father's job is to be his daughter's first devoted and chivalrous admirer. However, when her first boyfriends appear on the scene, his role is not to grill the poor spotty youths on their employment prospects and honourable intentions. It is to retire to the potting shed and have a good weep.

One other thing. Some men are so appalled by stories of child abuse that they are afraid to hug their children, especially daughters. I know a man, call him Nick, who adores his five-year-old daughter from her gold hair to her red shoes. But ever since another little girl on his street was almost raped by a drunken stepfather, in a case which shook the neighbour-hood, Nick won't take her on his knee. 'It's better for her, in these wicked times,' he says. He is confused and upset; Emma cannot understand why her father now jumps out of bed when

239

she creeps in every morning. Time may bring them a compromise, but for the moment the situation is desperately sad. As it is in society at large. Fathers may still take their daughters swimming, but more and more of them are refusing to take their daughters' friends. Revolting and baffling though paedophilia is to most of us, cases of it send echoes of unhappiness through ordinary families.

It must not be the end of paternal tenderness. Every parent knows that children are cuddly, a physical delight. Soft cheeks against your own, heads burrowing in your shoulder, games of rubbing noses and a happy nonsense vocabulary of snuzzles and pouncies and eaty-all-uppies are part of a happy family life, sometimes until the children are enormous. A baby who is not hugged will pine or even die. Older children, suddenly finding hugs withdrawn, will feel odd and lonely. You have to hug, when it is welcome.

But when it is not welcome you have to refrain from hugging. The lesson of privacy and dignity is important too. Parents – but especially fathers, who represent strength and mastery to a child – must not pounce and hug too much when the child resists it, or is busy trying to do something else. And no child ever should have to kiss anyone unless they feel like it. But you can always plead for a hug, if you're desperate . . .

Who's Who: Mother

A little fable.

Mother 2000 fell asleep, the night before Mother's Day, having supped unwisely on chocolate mousse and the children's unfinished Marmite sandwiches. On such nights, warning nightmares swirl around the sleeper, with ghosts appearing in threes like Ebenezer Scrooge's tormentors. And so it was. The first apparition loomed at the foot of the bed, with chains of bread dough fettering its wrinkled hands. It was a stoutish, greying figure with a fixed smile. Its hair was parted in the middle, a white apron pinned upon its broad bosom, and around it clung a homely smell of cakes and ironing.

'I,' it said chattily, 'am the ghost of Motherhood Past. That's my picture, on the Mother's Day cards.'

'What did you do?' asked the dreamer.

The ghost bridled. 'Do? I baked. I made all my own jam and pickles. I rose in the dawn to cook proper hot breakfasts. I sang as I scrubbed the front step. I sewed little shirts for my babies, taught them their letters and never failed to read a Bible story aloud each evening. For twelve years I was always there at the school gate, and when my treasures left home,' she sniffed, 'I gave them stamps to post their laundry home. I was the heart of the family.' She paused, and sniffed.

The dreamer waited, then timidly asked, 'Um, what happened to you in the end?'

The ghost sniffed again, louder. 'When the children grew up, my husband ran off with a bimbo,' it said morosely. 'He said I had no conversation. And I was forty-five and I couldn't get a job because they said I had no skills. Bah!'

It vanished abruptly, leaving only a faint smell of scorching linen in the air.

A second ghost appeared, fidgeting nervously as it spoke.

241

The thing wore a neat business suit and laddered tights, at which it plucked distressfully. It carried a briefcase, a season ticket and three plastic carrier bags out of which protruded rolls of toilet paper, a length of track for a model railway, a cabbage, a packet of spaghetti and a paperback on Stress. Glancing at its watch, it spoke rapidly.

'I am the ghost of Motherhood Present, OK? I took minimum maternity leave because in my job you don't risk stepping off that ladder. I've found a wonderful nursery, honestly; the only thing is it likes the children out at five thirty sharp, and the school comes out even sooner, so Damien has to have a key, and I have to dash like mad if the departmental meeting overruns. And I do believe in Quality Time with children, don't you? So we're reading *The Lion, the Witch and the Wardrobe* and making cardboard sundials and learning Italian together in the evenings, and of course on Thursday it's tai chi, but the trouble is if I have to stay late at the office we miss the beginning of the class. I mainly shop at Marks for food but on Saturdays I do cooking for the freezer, because I do believe in homemade food, don't you? Only there's the office paper-work, and I have to do a lot of the washing by hand because the machine goes funny and plumbers won't come at weekends . . . but I've bought this new palmtop Time Manager and it's all a matter of efficiency—'

'What happened to you in the end?' the dreamer interrupted.

'Well, I'm still at work,' twitched the ghost. 'My son Damien became a Buddhist monk, said he liked the quiet, and Jocasta lives in a squat and writes poetry, and says my lifestyle is really gross and materialistic. But they always got their Quality Time. And I've kept my full pension entitlement.'

The dreamer, half waking from the nightmare, thought dimly to herself that nothing could be worse. But in an un-earthly glare, a new and dreadful figure was slumping towards her. Indescribable, it was. Whether human or robot she could hardly tell, with its mass of wires and arms and doors, knobs and levers and loudspeakers and shrink-wrapped Mini Kiev dispensers. But from its centre came a human voice.

'I am the ghost of Motherhood Yet To Come,' it said resolutely. 'I rejected the mistakes of the past. I refused to be a cosy domestic slave, nor yet a workaholic, guilt-ridden wreck. The new Britain Community directed me to go back to the workplace where my skills were needed. And the magazine writers told me not to be guilty about delegating. So I delegated.'

'What?' asked the dreamer, fascinated.

'Everything!' replied the ghost proudly. 'I have Nanny and a cleaner and an au pair for nights, and we buy microwave food, and there's a marvellous mail-order toy shop which chooses all the presents according to psychological profiles, and wraps them in time for the birthdays. Last year they both got Walkmans and story tapes, so that takes care of bedtime. As a treat they are allowed to Dial-a-Parent and these marvellous professionals, therapists and things, talk over their problems.'

'Do they like all this delegating?' asked the dreamer.

'Naturally,' said the echoing voice in the creature's empty centre. 'Any problems with their behaviour, the school generally sends me a fax to let me know that the computer has booked them in with the educational psychologist, and bleep Nanny to programme their favourite supper into the microwave and have a pre-assessed video biked round.' Suddenly, the voice grew distorted. 'Hang on – there's a problem – the Nanny's broken down – malfunction alert – the bleeper isn't coding in – System Failure, System Failure, Malfunction alert –' Somewhere, a child cried.

Mother 2000 was quite happy to wake up to the usual sight of piles of ironing, wonky school-made cards, cold toast and stewed tea on a loving tray with a daffodil, and the feeling of warm little bodies creeping into the bed. She resolved to give up all attempts at perfection, overachievement and time-and-motion efficiency, and put up with life more or less as it was. As we all do.

Real mothers

Since everything one writes about children and family life is also about mothers, it seems superfluous to consider them separately. But there are things about the mother in the family which are worth saying.

Nature's Masterpiece

The first thing which must be admitted is that motherhood is a powerful mind-altering drug. You only have to talk to people who have overdosed on it (say, by having ten children) to discover how high it is possible to get. Motherhood makes you bossy and self-assured, yet if you take it on full time, it leaves you oddly unconfident in your role in the outside world (offices are full of middle-aged women returners who allow themselves to be patronized by short-skirted kids twenty years younger and a lot dimmer). Motherhood makes you as fierce and bold as a tigress defending her young, and yet racked with guilt that you are not doing better. It makes you secure in your children's unconditional love, and yet quiveringly vulnerable to every passing worry about them. Motherhood can make you, for a while, unrecognizable to your oldest friends. The single, child-less ones may actually shun you for a few years, so odd have you become.

Relax. All this is quite natural. You get over it. You will never be quite the same again, true; but everyone grows up, and it just happens that motherhood has turned out to be part of your personal growing process. The effects of the drug weaken as children grow older. By the time the baby is three, you can sometimes think about other things; by the time it is at school you might start fancying a career again (even if you have had one all the time, you may well have been on autopilot – I certainly was). Who knows, by the time your youngest child is eight or nine, you might even feel like some late nights out dancing. And when your children reach their teens, it is more than possible that you will be looking around wildly for more interesting work, old friends, and adventure of every kind. The trick, at that point, is finding where they have all disappeared to.

For if the problem for fathers lies in realizing that they are fathers, and knuckling down to it, the problem for most (not quite all) mothers is the opposite. It can be hard to prevent yourself from getting lost in the role. If you do lose your own identity, the risk is that you start trying to find it through the children, projecting your own ambitions on to them. 'Samantha so loves her music, of course I was going to be a professional violinist myself, but she's really so dedicated . . .' trills a mother whose daughter, it is plain to any onlooker, only moderately enjoys playing the violin and has no intention of making it a life work.

Or even worse, you might start making a career out of improving your children with arcane accomplishments and certificates, to make them better than you ever were, and definitely better than the substandard children next door. There are few statements more chilling than, 'We really feel that the school fees and the tennis coaching and dancing tuition have been an investment.' No harm spending the money, or organizing the music lessons, of course; they may be just the ticket. The harm comes when you start colonizing your children, taking over their individuality and trying to shape them to your own ends. All parents feel the temptation sometimes; mothers, I think, are especially prone to it today because we feel deep down that we gave up our own individuality and ambitions to have them, and are therefore, in some sinister way, *owed* a bit of basking in their success.

Bossing

Another worrying effect of motherhood as a mind-bending drug is the way it can lead you to start inflicting the fiercest kind of mothering on people who don't need it, or want it. Such as husbands.

While a few men enjoy being bossed around by women, and told to put their warm vests on or go on a diet, many do not like it one little bit. Sometimes they absent-mindedly put up with it, because in the general maelstrom of family life this mother-person seems to be issuing orders to everyone in the same tone: 'Ronnie, get your Cub uniform ready! Janey, help him with the drawer if it's stuck! Marie-Christine, have you got the baby dressed? Down, Bonzo! Get your mucky paws off the sofa! Someone put the cat out! Darling, tuck your shirt in, and you can't wear that jacket with that tie.'

Sometimes, after many years of this, men surprise everybody by slinking off with a much younger woman, like their secretary, and everybody assumes that it's all about sex. My private theory is that it is just as likely to be because the poor sap just fancied having someone look up to him and admire him, after years of being snapped at like a recalcitrant labrador or two-year-old with none of the corresponding advantages of being able to lie around all day panting, or getting birthday cakes with candles. No, of course it is no excuse. Just a thought.

So crack the whip by all means, keep the show on the road, but in being a mother do not lose the art of being a good companion, a grown-up, fun to be with and with a mind of your own capable of soaring above the circus ring of family life. Stage a token walk-out occasionally: to the cinema, for a weekend away with a girlfriend, or to see a play that only you are interested in. When I became badly stressed and ratty one winter, I quite coincidentally started getting into a routine which meant that, instead of one night per week away from home and the rest at my desk here, I had to spend two nights away, one of them staying with a woman friend in her quiet, tidy, child-free London house.

After ten years of assuming that if I vanished for more than twenty-four hours family life would collapse entirely in ruins, I was nervous and tearful about this and assumed that it would be an extra strain. But – surprise! I found I adored my extra night, slacker routine, less frantic travelling; relished the different company, the odd party, and the quiet adult start to the next day. The family was fine under the command of whoever was in charge. When father was at home running the show they did all become addicted to some seriously trashy Monday night television programmes, and lose a good few items of gym kit; but that was a small price to pay for the resident wife and mother coming home relaxed, beaming and glad to be around.

I also came back with a different angle on their problems: more able to get a reasonable perspective on a school difficulty, for instance, or someone's row with a friend, or my husband's professional dilemmas. Everybody benefited, in the same way as they benefit when I have been reading something stimulating, or surprising, or challenging in a new field. Stressed, overworked modern mothers – possibly with an outside job

246

– tend to feel dreadfully guilty about reading, say, *A Brief History of Time*, or watching a documentary about Chinese medicine, or wandering around the house with a particularly gripping novel, but the odds are that the input from these things will contribute rapidly, and directly, to the way they talk to their families and the wisdom they bring to managing them.

The more we see or read of the world outside, and the more confident we are in other rôles than mother, the more certain we will feel of our own judgement and vision at home. The mothers who fall for every foible and fashion of childcare are the ones who get too utterly immersed in it, to the exclusion of the rest of life. Look up, look around, and be sceptical.

Smother love

Don't do it. Fathers need telling this too. It is really about children, but I deliberately raise it under the heading of Mothers because mothers do it most. We are famous for it. Overprotection of children, even rather large tough children, is a modern epidemic. For one thing, mass communication makes us daily more neurotically aware of the vile things that happen – most often at the extremes of society – to children who are not protected enough. Less laudably, I suspect that we have become extra-passionately protective of our own children simply because we don't have as many as we used to: birth control has reduced the average family to just over two, with an ever-growing number of only children. Remember that old expression, 'As fussy as a hen with one chick?'

Irrespective of the actual risk on the streets, society has seen a steadily growing belief in street violence and public lawlessness, which has coincided with the rise of television and video. The result is that huge numbers of us have frankly lost the habit of going out much, expecially in Britain. Surveys of our habits suggest that for over eighty per cent of us, a recreational evening is not a visit to the cinema or the town centre or a football match, but staying in with a curry and a video.

Our children and teenagers, on the other hand, do want to go out. So we choke on our curry and listen for the telephone while

247

they roam at large in the terrible Outside World. Every time a dreadful thing befalls a child or teenager, we scan the news for some comforting evidence that he was out at a time, or in a place where ours would not have been. If we don't find it, we tighten the house rules further.

Yet, when they are eighteen, our children will get an inalienable legal right to set out on their own into a world full of fast-running rivers, heavy traffic, drug dealers, deviants, muggers, rapists and misleading signposts. They will probably live alone, and will not always have the money for a taxi fare home.

However much it hurts, our duty to protect them is diluted by an equal duty to prepare them for the real world. Telling them about it is not enough: they have to get in the midst of it and dodge the missiles themselves. To provide a safe bolt hole for them is not only the least we can do; perhaps as they get older it is also the most we should do.

But when are you overprotecting, and when merely being a responsible parent? How long is a piece of string? Take new babies. In the eighteenth century the followers of philosophers Locke and Rousseau preached the doctrine of 'hardening' children in the Spartan style, rather like hardening off pot plants, by laying them on planks to sleep, underdressing them in cold weather and plunging them in icy baths. In the 1920s a popular babycare guru in the US called John B. Watson advised parents to put the baby out in a fenced yard and to 'be sure to dig some holes in the yard so it has to crawl in and out of them. Let it learn to overcome difficulties almost from the moment of birth, away from your watchful eye.' You could, he conceded, install a periscope to watch the baby if you absolutely had to.

Both authorities were mildly nutty, to be sure (most of us childcare writers are; never believe all of what anyone says in books like this). But have you ever watched a mother with her first adored child, officiously helping it over every small obstacle, never letting it discover the limits of its own stretching or lifting power? Our hands shoot out to stop babies toppling, toddlers falling in the fire – but they often shoot out too readily, merely to prevent smaller frustrations, knocks and setbacks. I once in fascinated horror watched a surgeon allowing his child

248

to play with a door hinge. He had, he said, calculated exactly how much damage the child could cause with the hinge that way round, and that it wasn't severe; he had warned the child repeatedly, and now it was time to allow a minor accident. I am not sure I could be that chilly about it, but he had a point.

When the child grows up a little, a new stage comes. He can pour out his own apple juice into the mug, but he spills a bit. Next time he might not spill it, because he has worked out how it happened; but the question is whether there will be a next time, because you might fussily take over again, having 'proved' he can't be trusted. He goes to playgroup, a big girl pushes him. Do you have the nerve to wait and see if he pushes back? Or do you sweep down and sort out the quarrel before it has a chance to develop any further?

Time goes on. At school, there is a test. Your daughter does badly, and your instinct is to protect her from knowing, or at least from caring. But her best friend then goes off with another girl to make snide remarks in a corner, and suddenly – panickingly – you realize that you can't protect her. More and more perils crowd in: there are no seat belts on the school bus, the maths teacher has a bitter and sarcastic tongue, the big boys call the little ones rude names in the playground. None of the perils is quite big enough to tackle forthrightly, but it still hurts to watch fate's assaults upon your child, your treasured one who has never ridden a bike without a crash helmet, never walked home alone or missed a dental check-up. Grimly, you realize the narrow limits of what you can actually do.

Teenage years loom. You see ever more clearly that although you long to be a strong protecting wall, the only way to do it is to become a jailer. It may be painfully obvious to you that the boy or girl your baby has brought home is a nasty, flashy cruel piece of work, but dare you say it? You know the kind of unpleasant men who accost fourteen-year-old girls in cinemas, but are you really going to insist on chaperoning three competent teenagers through some Kevin Costnerama when they know you're bored stiff by it? All your sons' friends catch the bus on their own to the football ground on Saturday: are you really going to drive him there in the Volvo and see him safely in? To weigh a theoretical danger against an overwhelming love is the hardest thing in the world.

Or perhaps the hardest thing is to give up your own judgement in favour of someone else's. Suppose your child wants to go on an adventure survival course, and he's never lasted more than a three-mile family stroll without getting blisters; how are you going to protect him? Not, I hope, in the way one family of my acquaintance once did: they bribed their fourteen-year-old to give up the idea of a youth club hiking holiday by giving him a video recorder of his own. They thought the walking would be too much for him (his youth leader disagreed) and that he wouldn't manage to keep his own kit dry and organized (his youth leader disagreed, again). Such parents are of the sad type who seem to pop up at their children's drug trials later saying, 'We gave him the best of everything!' in an aggrieved tone of voice, as if shelling out for a personal TV and a private education ought to provide insurance against human frailty for ever.

Mothers – and a few fathers – will always want to protect their children a little too much; the saving, balancing factor is that the children themselves resist it so fiercely. The glory of children is that they are not blasé. They want to do new things, risk failure, meet different people who don't share the family consensus. It isn't just the quest for the opposite sex; my best times as a teenager were chatting to strangers on buses, doing the ironing down at the local Cyrenian shelter for down-and-outs and being lectured on life by the tramps and dossers, or trying to get some sense out of the spaced-out cult smiles down at the Hare Krishna temple. My brothers took up gliding and parachuting, brushing off all objections from their tremulous elders with the words, 'Look, we want to survive too, you know.' My parents no doubt didn't like any of these activities, and I am a bag of nerves myself. But I pray for strength and cool judgement. I hold in my mind, as a talisman, the memory of a millionaire's daughter I once met. Her father's bodyguard drove her to and from school and her only recreation in the outer world was being driven to horse shows with her prize ponies, accompanied by grooms and her mother. From fortune-hunters, kidnappers, rapists and other perils of the modern world this child was indeed safe – safe as in a harem, safe as a bird in a gilded cage. It has not, noticeably, made her a happy adult.

Another child I shall think of is a slightly mentally handicapped boy, brought up by his parents with close protective care, allowed to do odd menial jobs for pocket money but waited on and pitied and protected at every turn. He became seventeen; the old couple died. Those of us who knew the boy were terrified of what might happen. But he bore himself with dignity through the funerals, and was soon living in a sheltered flat and holding down a regular handyman job. The pity of it is that his parents would have been proud to see it; but while they were there, it couldn't have happened. We must warn, we must prepare, we must protect; but we must let go.

A silversmith was once begged by his wife to make his daughter a simple pendant for her fifteenth birthday. Inside it the parents put three tightly rolled and folded fifty-pound notes, representing a taxi fare home from almost anywhere. He arranged the pendant so that it could be unscrewed to release the emergency money – but only once, after which he would need to repair it. That way, he reasoned, she couldn't spend the money on clothes or shoes as a silly impulse, but would always be able to get home at any hour, or book into a hotel alone if the company she fell into seemed threatening. Both parents are dead now, and their daughter is nearly fifty. But she still wears the pendant. It symbolizes at once her freedom and her parents' protection.

Mothers and sons

A boy's best friend is his mother. Um, perhaps. But it does not hurt to brood a little on the darker side of all this, if only to get a line on whatever is going on between one's mother-in-law and one's husband. And what may start going on, as he grows up, between you and your own best boy.

Write this down in letters of fire: *boys have to get away from their mothers*. They come back, of course. But they need, as

251

psychologists put it, to 'cross the river' – to prove that they are male and leave the womenfolk behind. The struggle to do this can make them dreadfully rude and ungrateful, and some stay that way. Bernard Shaw said, 'Of all human struggles, there is none so treacherous and remorseless as that between the artist man and the mother woman.' Other writers have written about mothers in terms so intemperate that one gasps. Somerset Maugham said that 'few misfortunes can befall a boy which bring worse consequences than to have a really affectionate mother', and D.H. Lawrence, melodramatic old number that he was, lamented that 'Nobody can have the soul of me. My mother had it, and nobody can come into my very self again.' A whole boarding-school culture grew up among the British upper classes to ensure the early divorce of a boy from the dreadful, unwholesome, cloying, retarding company of Mummy.

In ordinary family life even the nicest boys turn strangely surly towards their mothers at certain points. 'Look, Mum, I'm ten,' they say, 'I can look after myself.' Mummies daft enough to continue invading the bathroom and peering in ears once their sons object to it are riding for a bad fall. And yet boys need their mothers' affection desperately, even while they reject it. The only way round it which seems to work is humour, from early on: ham it up, pose as a daft old Mummy, allow them their feelings of power and supremacy. When your attentions are rejected, turn it into a long-running fantasy joke about how he becomes an astronaut, Prime Minister or whatever, and you burst into his spaceship or cabinet room in worried Jewish-Momma style, quavering, 'My boy! Are you wearing your warm vest! I brought you a hot-water bottle for your poor kidneys!'

The extreme absurdity of this seems to cheer them up. If he can see that you understand the absurdity of bursting in mumsily on a Prime Minister, it gives him some hope that you will not kiss the Captain of Football in front of his school-friends.

Although, of course, when the boy requires you to mutate back into a protective, all-wise Rock of Ages, you still have to do so.

Mothers and daughters

The trouble with girl babies, as any conclave of mothers will guiltily agree, is that you find yourself being harder on them from the start. A boy is a strange alien miracle, sprung from your body. A girl is yourself, over again. Therefore, being hard on yourself, you expect more of the girl. It is observable that toddler girls (unless they have over-doting daddies, q.v.) tend to fuss, cry, and create less than their allegedly macho, tough, masculine brothers. Probably because their mothers don't put up with it.

Girls also tend to help more around the house than boys. Yes, yes, I know; it is reprehensible typecasting. It worries me no end. But I begin to see how it happens. The cruel fact is that in the pre-teen years at least, it is just less trouble to get girls to clear the table and run errands than to make boys do it. Exhausted mothers with a child of each sex have a choice between asking once, and asking fifteen times with threats; they often take the line of least resistance. In our house when this happens everyone is prone to raise the cry, 'No Islamic Practices!' which may be a shameful caricature of Islam but makes the point succinctly. Girls should not be made to wait on boys.

As little girls grow up, it is every day more vital for their mothers to give them plenty of space to grow. Despite those treacherous feelings of identification, your daughter is not you, grown miraculously young again. You may have been a beauty and a coquette, but it is her right to turn out to be a solid, serious, aspiring veterinary surgeon with thick legs. You may have been academically brilliant and the head girl, she may be a minxy little party girl or a mumsy thing who longs to become a nursery nurse. Leave her be. Enjoy her differences from you. And do not be jealous of her. It is perfectly true that the new generation have a lot more fun and far more options than we did. That is our achievement, as a generation of women. It is not something to get resentful about, however ungrateful the little beasts seem to be.

Who's Who: Children

All through history, the worst excesses of parental cruelty have come from the tendency of adults to think of children as being property rather than people. Granted, this has resulted in them being carefully guarded; but all power tends to corrupt. We may smile, or groan, at some of the wider effects of modern legislation on children – like the warning given by a leading British teachers union that if a teacher shouts at a difficult child in class he risks a lawsuit for 'emotional abuse' – but anything is better than a situation where adults may, at their whim and with the implicit blessing of their society, impose almost any cruelty on their offspring.

If you want salutary proof that parental kindness and common sense are fragile plants, look at the evidence of history. Parents have been all too easily persuaded by society to do dreadful things to children 'for their own good'. From the Middle Ages onwards, plenty of good Christian parents beat small children violently because of the fear that they would die young and go to hell unless the sin was well beaten out of them. One eighteenth-century mother wrote plaintively in her diary, 'I have got a pain in my back with whipping Susan today, who struggled so that I have got a wrench.' They swaddled babies tightly to stop their limbs growing crooked, not knowing that it was rickets which caused the crookedness and that the swaddling itself almost guaranteed dislocated hips. John Evelyn, the seventeenth-century diarist, told how his niece was crushed to death at two years old by a restraining garment, an iron bodice. Because crawling was considered by Victorian divines to be 'bestial' and undignified, early baby-walker devices tormented infants into the upright position whether they liked it or not. If children masturbated, their fingers would be fastened behind their backs with finger stocks; if they slouched, a board was lashed to their spines. Collectors of such things can show you poisonous laxatives, lethal opiates like 'Mother Bailey's Quieting Syrup', and terrifying books like *Joyful Deaths of Young Children*.

One such collector, Sally Kevill-Davies, a rector's wife from Hertfordshire, showed me her assembly of such terrible things once and drew a conclusion I have never forgotten. 'I do not believe there is a maternal instinct,' she said sadly. 'One of the most ironic and depressing facts about childcare is the way in which ignorance, superstition and imperfectly applied reasoning appear to have triumphed over instinct and sense.'

Even today, in what we fatuously think of as an age of individualism and freedom, we often obey science and received wisdom over instinct (well, how else could you bring yourself to hand over a healthy baby for a vaccination that will make it, however briefly, unwell? I am not suggesting that vaccination is wrong, just demonstrating how easy it is for outsiders to persuade parents to behave a certain way). How can we be haughty about the medical horrors of past ages (opium grains put under babies' fingernails as a soother, solid food forced into newborn mouths to cure diarrhoea) when it is not so long since parents insisted that doctors remove adenoids and tonsils as a routine, and sometimes whipped out appendices before they sent the child to boarding school or as a precaution against having their holidays disrupted? How can we be smug about laudanum syrups of the nineteenth century, when question marks still hang over such things as the chemicals used in cot mattresses, or the effect of household cleaners on allergy? We may laugh, now, at such social foibles as the way earlier generations used wet nurses, or banned bananas because they might overstimulate sexual appetite, or placed little girls' noses in an iron press to correct their shape; but what will future generations make of such modern eccentricities as 'educating' newborn babies with constant stimulation, or 'in-womb education' through tapes? What will the future make of the British upper-class fetish for boarding school at seven, or the American one for teeth braces worn throughout adolescence in the quest for the perfect, dazzling, all-white smile? Cruelties have always been practised on children in the name of sanctity or science or social graces, and probably always will be.

So the governance of children should probably be reduced to the bare minimum. Minimalist parenting could well be the coming thing. Not quite, perhaps, to the extent that Rousseau advocated, of letting them survive in a wild state and never teaching table manners; but certainly we could do with a step back from the degree of interference which has become fashionable in recent years. It sometimes seems, from the media, that half the Western world is living in a depressed underclass which lets its children roam the streets unchecked, ram-raiding and mugging old ladies, while the other half drives them frantically around in cars from educational psychologist to violin lesson, pausing only to buy more videos and computer games lest the offspring become bored.

The image is, of course, exaggerated. I see, in all kinds of homes, a remarkable amount of pragmatic good sense being applied to parenting. And a lot of minimalism, too. One good effect of economic uncertainty is that when a family has less money to spend on nonsense, it has to concentrate on the essentials, and some of the least affluent families show the most healthy set of priorities. So do some middle-class down-shifters, who weary of the rat race of two powerful careers and give one of them up in favour of getting a family life. Where it comes to children, they pare it all down to the basic needs. Children have to be fed, clothed against the elements, conversed with a great deal, protected from evildoers and poisons, and given the chance to play and read and observe the adult world. They have to be educated, to take in the skeleton of whatever knowledge and wisdom their society has developed, and encouraged to take it further as they grow up. They have to be loved and valued, and allowed to bestow their own love on family and friends. And that is enough for anyone to take on, without any better-baby routines, hothousing, social drilling, fussy dressing or general competitive nastiness. Children are not feathers in their parents' hats. Most parents know this perfectly well.

256

But neither are they miniature adults, with precisely the same rights and freedoms as adults. They have different rights, like the ones I have just mentioned; and there are some areas where their rights are as limited as their abilities. A baby does not have the right to crawl unhampered into the fire, and a teenage girl does not have the right to stay out all night hitch-hiking along the bypass in a tight leather skirt. Parents are – temporarily – in charge of defining children's freedom.

Sometimes parents forget to do this job, for one of several reasons. Maybe they want to be the child's 'best friend' instead; this happens at times with kind and devoted single parents, lonely for adult company, who with the best of intentions give at once too much responsibility and too much freedom to their child (it is usually a lone child who gets this treatment). Sometimes parents won't be parents because they have never quite stopped being children themselves. Who has not seen a father sulking because his son won't play with him? Or a mother jealous of her daughter's carefree nights out at teenage parties? Sometimes they can't be bothered. Sometimes they throw their hands up in despair and say, 'Kids today, what can you do?' Sometimes they pretend that their own child is exceptionally mature and needs no rules or guidance. None of these attitudes, in the long run, is conducive to a happy family or a secure child.

What do they think they need from us?

I once conducted an interview with my own six- and eight-year-olds on what exactly they expected of family life. It was quite revealing. I was testing a tape recorder at the time, and lately found the old tape.

Me: What do you think mothers and fathers are for?

Eight-year-old: Looking after children. And training them.

Me: Well, I don't like the word training. You can't train people like you train dogs, can you? You can try, but they only end up shouting a lot. You have to keep children safe and give them things to do and think about, and show them how to be nice . . .

257

Six-year-old: And feed them properly. It's teatime.

Me: No it isn't. Anyway—

Six-year-old: And you have to stop them doing too much bum talk. And naughty poems. I think naughty poems are very bad. There's one VERY BAD one, it goes, 'Old King Cole was a merry old soul—'

Me (interrupting hastily): Yes, yes. Some parents get far too worried about smutty talk—

Six-year-old: (continuing regardless): 'The WC was engaged, and so was the kitchen sink –' (finishes rhyme, unfit for respectable publisher to print). Anyway, that's a very bad one. I don't think it should be allowed. I know an even worse one—

Eight-year-old: Parents ought to stop brothers and sisters fighting. It's a Mummy's job to calm them down.

Me: How, exactly?

Eight-year-old: I don't know. Shout at them, I suppose. Do you ever worry about bossing people too much in your books and your family?

Me: Yes, all the time. But mothers tend to get bossy.

Six-year-old: So do school dinner ladies. They're far too strict with children at playtime. There ought to be a law against it.

Eight-year-old: I don't think it's fair for parents to read books so they can sneakily improve their child, like a cactus in a pot. If children want to be violent and watch videos all day, it's half their choice. If they want to grow up sensible and dignified, they can. Children have their own choice about being perfect and nice or not, haven't they?

Six-year-old: But they really ought to be fed properly. And on time.

So I did. But my son, eight at the time, had hit on the nub of the matter. How children grow up is, indeed, partly their own choice. 'Sensible and dignified' – an interesting choice of words, not mine but his, picked up somehow – implies, however, that they have had a chance to watch other people – teachers, relatives, heroes of storybooks – being sensible and dignified. And kind, and forgiving, and relaxed. The main thing children

258

need from a family is that example. It is also one of the main things they need from a school, a childminder, a neighbourhood, and a whole society as reflected in the television screen. It is not always what they get.

And the Rest: Relatives

Remember Charles Darwin brooding on marriage, and how worried he was about the extended family? 'Forced to visit and receive relations but terrible waste of time . . .' Poor old Darwin, worried that the breakthrough theory of the origin of species would be clattered out of his head by the teacups of vapid in-laws. He has a lot of sympathizers. Although some are lucky enough to fall for a whole family, others find the beloved's family one of the most daunting aspects of matrimony.

Sometimes new couples blindly, unkindly, but rather bravely discard the tribes they came from. Sometimes they have to, because on religious, racial or class grounds the tribe is being so foully bigoted about the marriage. More often, I suspect, they do it out of sheer thoughtlessness: moving away, striking out into the wider world together, starting anew. As the Bible says, they leave father and mother, sisters and brothers to cleave to one another and start a new family altogether.

I notice that I have already, in musing about coupledom, rather praised this attitude and advised in-laws to keep out of the way for a while in early marriage. But with the birth of children comes a time when it is healthy, even pleasant, to let the tribe creep forward again and surround the new family with its old echoes. In other words, however decrepit your family tree looks to you, don't be too cavalier about chopping off the branch you sit on. When you start to be a family, the one which is there already turns out to have all sorts of unsuspected advantages. As well as only-too-well-suspected problems.

Mothers-in-law

Now my mother-in-law, I'm not saying she's a difficult woman, but when she comes round our house, the mice start to throw

260

themselves on the traps. Mind you, she always comes to us for Christmas. Every year for thirty years. This year we're doing something different – we're going to let her in. I'm not saying she's fat, mind, but her knickers . . .

Stop, stop. We all know about mother-in-law jokes. Men have been sounding off for years about the wife's mother: the tyrannical bat with her huge bloomers and invincible authority. Yet if you look at real life, what is the truth of the matter? Very few husbands are really at loggerheads with their mothers-in-law, and many of them actually get on insultingly well with their brides' mother, flirting outrageously and praising the home cooking to the skies (much to the annoyance of their own, working, wives).

It may wear a bit thin at times, this relationship, but on the whole men don't seem to suffer as much as the jokes suggest. Whereas women – who really *are* quite likely to suffer persecution for their temerity in carrying off Mummy's best baby boy – never seem to tell mother-in-law jokes at all. Perhaps because it is all too serious. Extended family life is a delicate thing at the best of times; the relationship between a girl and her man's mother can be as fragile as spun sugar. It is made even harder to maintain if the mother does not, and never did, work outside the home, and the young wife does. One of the most accurately deadly cartoons by Posy Simmonds shows a mother-in-law on Christmas Day, poking round her harassed daughter-in-law's kitchen and saying, 'Oh, packet stuffing – how amusing!'

The most dangerous situation comes when the man's mother does not think much of the wife, regarding her as a wimp, a slut, a silly little piece, or whatever; yet disguises it beneath bright brittle patronage whenever the family meet. Men are notoriously slow to catch nuances between their womenfolk, and the curious thing about relationships like this is how often the sons concerned entirely fail to notice that their wife has been written off. Even when she tells them. I once spent a weekend at the home of a boyfriend whose mother clearly could not stand the sight of me and was crushingly and consistently rude. When I pointed this out to him, he actually smiled and said, 'Oh yes, Mother's such a marvellous character, everyone loves her for it, she's a real individual, speaks her mind.' End of romance, not before time.

In fact, men can be their own family's worst enemy when it comes to spotting the danger signs in relationships like this. Here is a true story. Eric, who is now divorced, admits that when his young wife was grappling with a four-year-old, a baby, a part-time job and a big and chilly house in a strange neighbourhood, he regularly used to stop off at his parents' cottage, near his work, for a drink and a chat on the way home.

There, with a deep-pile carpet beneath him and a bowlful of homemade cheese straws at his elbow, he would relate the triumphs and trials of his day to his Mum. She was an interested, intelligent, stimulating listener. As we all will be one day, when we can get some sleep and not be responsible for anyone's socks but our own. When he went home to a wife physically exhausted by the babies' bathtime and still staring hopelessly at the contents of the fridge, he could not help comparing the two homes and the two women. Aloud. It was his father who eventually blew the whistle on him by coming in on one of his evening sessions with Mother and remarking (with great vision for his generation) that perhaps his own wife might like some help with getting the babies to bed. But it was too late by then. Eileen and the children went home to her own mother.

You have to accept that it is hard for mothers to give up custody, especially when their sons marry young. One moment it is a Mum's job to worry about whether he is eating, whether he should see a doctor about that cold, and whether he is truly happy at work. The next thing she knows she is the Bridegroom's Mother, handing over to some fluttery little madam who never made a bed properly in her life and probably buys packet stuffing. One experienced Groom's Mother – three sons down, one to go – tells me that the moment when you stand in church watching him wed is like walking for the last time around a house you have lived in, looking at the places where your furniture used to stand and wondering what the new owner will do. The difference, of course, is that when a human being is handed on, the first woman's furniture stays put. If

Mum trained him to throw his clothes on the floor and expect thick gravy on the dot of seven, he will remain programmed. And, unlike a previous houseowner, Mum will still be around to flit through the rooms of his life and see how marriage has changed them. 'She's such a foodie, you know, won't let him ever have beans on toast,' moans Mother. Or, 'He used to be such a generous boy, but since he married Anita he keeps his cash in a purse.'

On the other hand, mothers do want their children to be happy. And one of the best ways of deflecting criticism, interference and general mischief-making from anybody's mother is to be happy: visibly, lightheartedly, flippantly happy. So if the marriage has problems, chaps (and indeed girls) take my advice: your mother is not the person to consult until things really couldn't be worse. She may be fatally disposed to take your side, even to the point of hindering reconciliation or reform of the marriage. And if she doesn't take your side, you will be outraged, and that won't help either.

The good granny guide

Given that you are reading this book, Mother and Mother-in-Law are both grannies by now. The word, which used to conjure up a sweet grey-haired old lady rocking quietly in her corner, is now as likely to apply to a slinky blonde of forty-five going on fifteen with a tousled perm and the kind of energy that makes an exhausted new mother feel a hundred years old. She may not feel ready to pass on the wisdom of generations and the tranquillity of age, nor even to perch on the sofa drinking gin and explaining what you are doing wrong. She may not even knit.

A new Spotter's Guide is called for. On the one hand we have these very young energetic grannies with hardly time to spare from their career for babysitting duties; on the other hand, after two generations of late motherhood you get the opposite: a woman who is pushing seventy when she holds her first grandchild, and who may well bring a curious, inflexible set of attitudes from her own distant youth. 'You shouldn't pick

263

him up when he cries. You're making a rod for your own back, dear. Strict four-hourly feeding is healthiest. You'll overstimulate him with all that cuddling. Why haven't you got a nice, coach-built pram instead of that flimsy buggy? Don't hold him upright, you'll strain his back.'

Of course there are gallant exceptions. There are brisk evergreen grannies who take over children for whole fortnights. There are cosy old bodies who never criticize but provide rock-like security for mother and child alike; and there are grandfathers who let little ones play by their workbench or waggle the tiller of their boat, hour after patient hour. Family life at its best is a self-renewing idyll, with happiness and good sense passing down the generations. Never mind what it is like at its worst; optimism is the keynote. However, in the interest of family harmony and a gentle release of steam, here is the official Good Granny Guide:

Mk I: Poor Old Granny She may be only sixty-two, but has decided to retire from the more strenuous side of life. Delighted though she is with the presence of a new or growing grandchild, changing nappies is quite out of the question. So are baths, floor-level romps, lifting, or learning to cope with those new-fangled OshKosh dungaree fastenings.

POG may well have driven you out of your mind during the first three hectic years, when most of the jobs of child-rearing are practical ones, but take heart. With her almost uncanny talent for sitting absolutely still and letting people bring her things, she will provide a useful focus for busy children. Above all, she should prove madly useful as an audience for those who wish to perform incomprehensible plays with a toy theatre, do a fairy dance over and over again, demonstrate somersaults or tell a very, very long and boring story about what teacher said in school.

Mk II: Retro-Granny She wants to help. Well, no, what she actually wants to do is to re-live every moment of her own enchanted motherhood, all those years ago. Your baby is her baby all over again, every line of its pudgy little face painfully,

264

ecstatically reminiscent of her own darling's. Therefore it fol-lows that if you fail to use the identical brand of zinc and castor-oil cream, the same gigantic pram and the precise type of kite-folded nappy and soggy woollen leggings as she did, you are cruelly betraying the family. Backpacks, slings, tracksuits and Velcro-fastened mini-trainers will be greeted with shrill cries of alarm.

The only cure for this is to smile a lot and do your own thing. And remember that in thirty years' time you will probably be driving your daughter mad with critiques of her solar-powered hovering pushchair and self-destruct nuclear nappies. It would be kind to pander to Retro-Granny with, at the very least, a few pairs of long grey shorts for boys and a bit of smocking for girls.

Mk III: Scatty Granny She is not at all sure about this business of grandmotherhood. Nobody down at the singles club could believe it when she told them. She can't remember a thing about children because she was such a child herself when she had you, so she brazens it out with a lot of giggling and tickling. In fact, she fills more of the functions of a bachelor uncle or aunt than of a granny. Just pick up after her, sigh, and remember that children adore feckless adults. And be prepared for her to flirt with her teenage grandson, and display a certain degree of alarm when her granddaughter starts looking too grown- up for comfort.

Mk IV: Dodgy Granny A few – very few – middle-aged people have so utterly forgotten their own years of motherhood that they are frankly not safe around babies. They drop fag ash in the carrycot, administer scalding hot drinks, refuse to believe that a bit of healthy dog dirt could harm anybody, and watch the telly instead of the moving toddler. Alas, in the early years you must be realistic and prudent without being overfussy: better an offended in-law than an injured child. But as your own children grow into the older age range, Dodgy Granny can become quite a good friend. It is possible to intimate, tactfully, to a six-year-old that Granny is a bit forgetful about safety, so needs help. She is not one to call in an emergency.

Nature's Masterpiece

Mk V: Hostile Granny-in-law You were not good enough to marry her son (or daughter). You can tell this by the way she always addresses the child as 'poor little poppet'. On no account try to prove to her that you are a good mother/father. That way lies madness, because she won't have it. Just encourage her disapproving devotion, because it could lead to faultless babysitting: she will be keen to prove she is better than you, and will never mind how late you are back because it will simply prove her point. Call her in any time you feel the children need a bit of starching.

Mk VI: Stern Granny One of these once greeted her own daughter's fourth pregnancy with the words, 'I can't think why you're having another, dear, since the ones you've got don't seem to be under any proper control or discipline whatsoever.' Investigate her more closely: it may turn out that she went in for twenty-four-hour nannies and housekeepers, and boarding school at seven, in which case you can subtly let her know that you are well aware of the fact. But if she is a genuine martinet, prepared to administer reproofs and withhold pudding from small people who commit crimes like putting their elbows on the table, you should look on the bright side. Either the children will adore her and incidentally pick up some wonderful manners or, failing that, she will come in very handy as a threat.

Mk VII: Spoiling Granny 'Isn't Mummy strict with 'oo, poppet? Aaaah, it seems a shame. They're only young once. Come on, sweetums, let Granny buy you the sweety-weeties. Oh, aren't they the right kind? No, no throwums, my poppet! Ooops! Aaaah, never mind. Granny will pay for the broken bottles on the silly old shelf. Let Granny find you a little treat . . .'
   The Spoiler is bearable as long as she is prepared to take the consequences. The crunch comes when she fails to pull up a wild child until he or she becomes really appalling – rude, ungrateful, foul-mouthed and thoroughly nasty in her house – and then she hands it over with pursed lips and mutterings about 'bad blood coming into the family'. No known cure.

Mk VIII: Perfect Granny She cooks wonderful meals, is never cross, cuts out dollies' clothes by the hour, tells wonderful stories of the old days, reads for hours and can do everything much better than you can. Babies go to sleep in her arms instantly, bigger children never give her a moment's trouble. With luck, she also remembers to keep saying what a super mother you are and how well-reared are your children. If she forgets this little detail, you may well feel inclined to jump off the nearest bridge.

But, all in all, grannies are a Good Thing. God bless them. Also bless grandfathers, who curiously seem less prone to fall into the above categories, having a healthy helping of male selfishness and laissez-faire to keep them nicely detached. One day, God willing, our own baby will produce a baby and we will be struck with awe at the sheer miraculousness of it, the continuing chain of creation springing from our own fast-fading flesh. The joy of it all may well make us a bit peculiar in our turn. Meanwhile we are grateful for small blessings. No, honestly, we are. Really grateful. It must have taken hours to make, and it's a beautiful colour. What is it? A ballet cardigan? Marvellous . . . yes, she is a bit of a tomboy. Do her good, a peach cross-over cardigan . . .

Fathers-in-law

Rarely cause any trouble to their daughters-in-law, since if they dislike them they generally, and most sensibly, take the option of avoiding them entirely and wandering off into the garden (perhaps, like Nancy Mitford's Uncle Matthew, muttering, 'Pah! meaningless piece of flesh!').

But the relations between fathers and their sons-in-law can get not unlike the parallel female problem. Except that mothers-in-law have plenty of domestic and childcare ammunition to throw, and by tradition all a man can accuse his son-in-law of is not being a good provider. And it is money which tends to spark off masculine family disputes. It makes a man feel small when his wife's doting father keeps buying expensive presents for the family – a car, a dishwasher, a holiday, private school fees. Wives, however much they like paternal pampering, should be careful about this.

Aunts, uncles and honoraries

Whether genuine blood relations or honorary title holders, aunties and uncles are extremely good news in any family. Lone children, on giving birth, should recruit as many god-parents and close family friends as they can to be pseudo-unks in the family. Cousins, of course, are always nice (if only as a salutary lesson to your own children that there are some people in this world you damn well have to be nice to, whether you like it or not). But feckless, fancy-free bachelor uncles and aunts are particularly valuable. Remember that children's view of the world is very closely bounded by their social circle. If you live in 'couple country', forever mixing with other couples (or harassed single parents), and they have no brothers or sisters out in the world, children have no way of knowing that there is any other way to live than as a busy, scrambling, domestically obsessed parent of young children.

So the presence of a hungover uncle in the kitchen, an elderly bohemian friend playing the violin rather badly in the back bedroom or a tarty auntie spraying herself with Fracas in the bathroom, is – even if slightly fraying to the temper of whoever is making the lunch – in fact a huge contribution to family life. You can get wonderful friendships springing up between children of all ages and single people. Childless people have few preconceptions about the new generation, and are generally intrigued and charmed that these little creatures actually speak. Your infuriating teenager may seem quite reasonable to them; they, too, quite like sleeping till noon and dancing till three. It is you, even if you are ten years younger than the bachelor uncle or auntie, who are tedious old wrinklies, obsessed with rules.

Also, not having children of their own to boast to, your single friends will be full of interesting stories about how they once knew a man who rode the wall of death with a lion cub on his shoulders, or how they nearly got run over by a rhinoceros on their wildly expensive safari holiday.

The home lives of these bachelor uncles and aunties are also fascinating to nicely brought up children. We have a cherished friend, a sculptor in his late fifties, who lives in splendid eccentricity, in a house full of works of art and bits of things which might one day be works of art. But what my children loved best was to see him whisk open a kitchen drawer to reveal onion peelings, apple cores, potato skins and every kind of vegetable detritus lying there mixed up. 'The soup drawer,' he explains tranquilly. 'Next week's food.'

Bachelor uncles and aunts and godparents may offer, as years go by, recherché sports, peculiar outings, shocking political ideas and – most of all – an audience willing to listen to a teenager's disgraceful ideas and plans for a university-free future. Or for life with a horrifically undesirable boyfriend.

These spare adults are vital; they represent the adult world, but an impartial adult world which has not invested emotional energy in you, and therefore is willing to watch you make your own mistakes. They are wonderful confidantes. If I had not had my Aunt Dorothy at some stages of my teens, life would have been a lot bleaker.

And with a bit of luck, if you as parent have played your cards right, the aunt or uncle will give you some pretty good advice. Especially about the horrific boyfriends and girlfriends. One I know always advises the parents that the only way to get rid of a dreadful suitor is to welcome him or her with open arms, keep saying, 'How lovely to see you, Killer! Do tell me what the gang's been up to this week!' or 'Amanda! You must tell me where you got that skirt! I wish I had the figure for neoprene!' Your children will drop them like a hot brick if you do this. Apparently.

Squeaky wheels and hereditary pests

One of the great unsung advantages of contact with the extended family and with outsiders is that it makes life much easier for misfits. You know what I mean: misfit children,

269

squeaky wheels, black sheep, the ones you sigh over. Every large family has one, and in the days when large families were common, everyone knew that fact of life and accepted it. 'Oh, it's just Adrian, never mind him, you know what he's like.'

If the family was really lucky, its members took turns to be the difficult one, with each younger member emerging from a Bad Phase just in time for the next one to go into it. There might even be a brief lull, during which Dad or Mum could afford to run off the rails a bit themselves. But as often as not, the same squeaky wheel went on squeaking, and everyone else went on putting up with it. 'Ah well, she's never been easy, from a baby. I'm sure she'll start speaking to us again/bring back the family silver/leave the Moonies when she's done a bit of growing up.'

The trouble today is that, with so many tidy little two-child families, we have lost the knack of accommodating the less sociable and more chippy members. You have your two children and stop; and especially if they are a pigeon pair, boy and girl, everyone says, 'Aaaah! You've got your little family now!' and expects you to be marvellously symmetrical, united and tidy and loving and generally similar.

Life, however, is not like that. Whether you have ten children or two, the possibility of one turning out to be a really difficult personality – not disturbed, you understand, not abused or unloved or furnished with any particular excuse, but nonetheless bloody difficult – remains. It is one of the reasons I hesitated long and hard before writing this book. It is fatally easy, in offering advice and sympathy about family life, to give people the impression that if you do everything correctly and wisely from the start, if you are relaxed enough, loving enough, well organized enough, then all the family will be model citizens and get on well together.

Which is rubbish. Babies are born with quite a lot of their personalities already in position. We can certainly, by extreme cruelty or neglect, warp them into being suspicious and sad and unloving and eventually delinquent; but we cannot conversely guarantee that they will be easy to get on with. Some perfectly good, well-brought-up, basically sound people I know are incredibly difficult to be with: vague, or eccentric,

270

or inordinately self-centred, or distant to the point of rudeness, or so clever in one direction, like computers or creative writing, that they are almost imbecile in others. Bad parents are certainly responsible for some bad behaviour, but not for all of it. You may do everything right, insofar as there is a 'right way' to do it, and still end up with a squeaky wheel in the family.

The reason extended families help in coping with these oddballs is that being an oddball might actually be hereditary. Some women report the unnerving experience of lying on the delivery table, awash with emotion, only to find their husband's appalling Uncle Reggie staring up at them from the depths of a white cellular blanket. A smaller Uncle Reggie, perhaps, but unmistakably him: the eyes, the nose, the mouth turned down with a slight, knowing leer. For a moment, they gasp. Then the little pink mouth opens and bawls, and everything falls back into place: this is not Uncle Reggie. It is not even a boy. It is your new baby girl and you love her. And, with luck, the resemblance to Uncle Reggie will pass.

One of the most fascinating things about new babies is the way that such family likenesses keep flitting across their little faces. The genetic kaleidoscope has been shaken, two tribes have united, and for the first days, with some babies, you find yourself spotting a second cousin here, an ancestor there, a grandparent's grimace there; a half-forgotten aunt from childhood reappearing for a moment, a lost parent reborn in an early smile. The baby is, however, an individual. Different. Unique. But at the same time it has got Mummy's big eyes and Daddy's temper, and Granny's sense of humour and—

Yes, quite probably. Uncle Reggie's wild and antisocial streak, too. A little souvenir of the black sheep of the last generation. If you come of a happy tribe, this will simply be part of the fun. It will be delightful to brush your little boy's hair back one day and suddenly rediscover your own favourite brother's features at the age of five. If you are proud of your artist sister, or your husband's cousin being a soloist in the Berlin Philharmonic, you will be happy to meet these gifts again in your scribbling and drum-banging children. It is especially useful to have a friendly extended family when you have a child who is nothing like either of you in character. Suppose you are both home-loving and steady, and the child longs only for adventure, the odds are that as she or he grows up, somewhere among the grandparents or uncles or cousins there will be a person who understands. Perhaps one who has actually been and had the adventures.

Suppose you are wildly sociable, and the child is shy and bookish: you may try to be sympathetic, but there may be someone in the family who can go one better, and actually empathize, understanding from the depths of their own self what he wants and how he feels. At large family gatherings you sometimes see cousins, of widely different ages, who rarely meet, recognizing one another almost with a start of joy: I am not like my parents, I am not like my brother – but I am like you, they think. Not alone.

But this is a description of a happy tribe. What do you do if your child reminds you of a mortal enemy? It is not an idle question. One woman I know was happy with her first daughter, but when her second was born saw with horror that the baby looked very like her grandmother, the husband's mother, a cold and maliciously bitter woman who had done her best to break up their courtship, refused to attend the wedding, and disowned her son for marrying outside his class. Already exhausted, she was plunged into a postnatal depression which took months to clear. She found it hard not to shake the baby fiercely when she looked at her pursing her lips with just that sour refined expression from which she had suffered so much in the past. The baby's appearance changed, but the mother was chastened for ages. 'I could have hated her. Even now I sometimes catch a gesture that is old Celia's, and I gulp.'

Some children bring down unwarranted wrath on their heads for small offences, merely because of a chance physical resemblance or an old memory which has nothing to do with them. For instance, if your wife was a vain and selfish woman who dumped her daughter at birth and ran off with a man who said he could get her a modelling contract, well, you are not going to be too thrilled when your little girl starts staring into the mirror and saying 'Pwetty me', are you? Or if your own father was a drunkard who wrecked his family, you might overreact rather sharply to your teenage son's first adventure with a bottle of cider.

You have to recognize this, and laugh it off, and not allow any child to become the official Black Sheep merely because of family legend. The nature/nurture debate swings to and fro in every generation: forty years ago nature ruled, and the families of convicted murderers often changed their names so that the children should not be stigmatized, while women adopting orphans were given awful warnings by their friends that 'you don't know the heredity . . .' Today the pendulum has swung right in the other direction, and it is fashionable to blame upbringing (mothers, usually) for every beer can hurled off the terraces and stolen car driven into a jeweller's shop. No doubt there is something to be said on both sides. Every parent knows perfectly well that their child has had certain characteristics from birth which are shared with their progenitors, and certain quite baffling ones. All you can do is tone down the antisocial ones and encourage the better impulses.

Remember, the kaleidoscope does shake out a new pattern every time, rearranging the garish chips off various old blocks. As you lie on that delivery table, staring in horror at Uncle Reggie's leer, you can take heart. Perhaps all that misdirected energy, that devious cunning and shallow charm which led Reggie into a career of fraud, larceny, and conning rich widows will merely turn your daughter into something relatively harmless and acceptable. A journalist, perhaps?

He Ain't Tolerable, He's
My Brother: Quibbling siblings

Victoria Gillick, that doughty and controversial campaigner for
moral and family values, is a mother of ten and a gold mine of
useful information about sibling politics. I grilled her on the
subject once and she came up with several interesting – and
rare – fruits of experience. Her concept of family life is an
uncommon one today, and rather invigorating; she speaks of it
as a sort of great rolling party, where anyone who happens
along is welcome however many are already sprawling round
the table. Families like this exude a sort of cheery fatalism: there
you all are, and you might as well make the best of it. Big
families have drawbacks, but also a certain troopship camar-
aderie.

Anyway, Mrs Gillick reckons that the most difficult bit –
worse than being pregnant for the eighth time, worse than
twins, worse than having five under five and no inside lavatory, worse than mixing bread dough in a baby bath or
stretching half a pound of mince to feed ten – was the bit near
the beginning when she only had two children.

'They bicker all the time,' she says. 'And if you've quarrelled
with one sibling, you've quarrelled with all your generation.
It's lonely and claustrophobic, at once.' When the family starts
to grow, she reckons, there is always one sibling to gang up
with, always someone you are on good enough terms with to
talk secrets. Relationships wax and wane, flourish and vary
between the different ages: sub-teenagers can be very tender
with toddlers, then grow away from the babies for while, then
return as old friends.

This scene is worth bearing in mind, although few of us have
the stamina, or can bear the financial terrors, of a vast family. It

reminds us that two children – which is starting to be the norm – is a very awkward number. They fit easily into a small car with both parents in front, but that is the best you can say of the arrangement. All siblings bicker at times, but a pigeon pair, born within a couple of years of each other, can be atrocious company.

The first rule is never to be surprised, or shocked, or disappointed by how furious siblings can get with one another. Think how much married couples get on one another's nerves – and they chose each other, for heaven's sake. Siblings didn't. Nor can children defuse the tension by going to bed together, or getting drunk. They are stuck under the same roof, sometimes in the same bedroom; they know one another's annoying habits far too well. They know there is no chance whatsoever of divorce. They have not yet finished developing their ability to empathize with other people's feelings. So when they fight, they can really let rip and there is precious little to stop them.

Except you. At the point of greatest heat you can cry, 'Se-pa-rate! Now! Glass wall!' or some such code to indicate that they must no longer touch one another or listen to a word the other says until they have cooled down. But that is only first aid. A better cure is only won by sitting down, and making each child state his or her case clearly, in turn, without hyperbole or abuse. Courtroom procedures have been tried, with some success, by legally minded parents: each child stating its grievance uninterrupted and accepting the decision of the court. Others resort to mere separation, and a withdrawal of all treats and sympathy until the protagonists have come to a reasonable settlement by themselves. The first system is probably better with siblings of unequal power and personality, and the second where they are genuinely well-matched.

But you have to do something. In our own children's most warlike phase, I did wonder whether I was not making it worse by intervening in these dogfights. Perhaps I should just walk away, or push them into a soundproof room and let nature take its course. In a calm moment, I once asked them. They unanimously agreed that it was a parent's job to stop fights. 'Otherwise it would get worse, and worse, and someone would end up in hospital' they said, quite seriously. 'And if you weren't ever stopped from fighting and made to be at least polite to each other when you were small, I think you'd fight madly with everyone for all your life.' He also, after more thought, said that he thinks that is probably 'how bullies start, like the ones you get at school, by practising on their brothers and sisters at home'.

I think he is probably right. Tempting though it is to embrace minimalist parenting and let nature take its course out of your hearing, intervention is a duty. It is also a safeguard of the wider peace of the family, for bickering amongst themselves is more infuriating than anything else children do, worse than destructiveness, untidiness, cheek, defiance, lying. It is worse than whining or grumbling, because it is redoubled. It brings you to a state of near-despair that after all your efforts, these children you have borne sound bratty, spoiled, ungrateful, spiteful and petty. I now know why my own childhood was punctuated by cries of 'I'll bang your heads together!' (not that they did, much). I, too, have wanted to bang heads together. We all have.

Small children

One of the first traps that parents of the modern small family fall into, by cruel irony, is through trying to be fair and even-handed. In the days of big families, children grew up knowing from an early age that life is unfair. It was clear to the merest toddler that some people are bigger than others, get their clothes brand new instead of handed down, and are allowed penknives. In a family of four or more children, the laws of probability dictate that at least one other child seems to have had a better birthday than you, and that someone else is, in turn, furiously jealous of yours. The laws of common sense and economics prevent every child having precisely the same present at the same time as all the others. A certain competitive spirit grows up, curiously combined with fraternal warmth. It is noticeable in later life that the sons and daughters of big families make friends easily, and often have a wider area of tolerance for human foibles than lone children do; but it is also noticeable that they fight their corner, and even eat measurably faster than only children. This is because they spent their formative years desperate to get to the second helpings first before the food ran out. It is the singletons who fuss.

But in the prevailing modern two-or three-child family, life is different. It is perfectly possible for the parents of two children close in age to treat them almost exactly the same from the day the youngest reaches three. If one gets a small present, the other can have an identical one. They can both go to the film, or the swimming pool, or the shops with you. They can be given equal pocket money from quite early on, bought clothes and shoes simultaneously and even given small presents on the other one's birthday. Father Christmas generally brings them stockings with the exact same number and quality of presents in each.

But as you go on like this, you get to a point when it is absurd. One child becomes furious at the discovery that she can't share the other one's godmother; the other gets irritated when she gets a plaster on her arm and he doesn't, and is deaf to reason when you point out that his isn't broken. If it goes on like this, you can reach a point where children are so confused at the idea of identical fairness that they get jealous of one another's friends, voices, bodies, temperaments ('It's not fair that she's not afraid of the dark and I am!'). One friend recalls that when her older one was starting to learn the recorder at school, the girl was naturally bought a recorder. Her sister, too young to learn, took it very personally, and in vain did her mother protest that she had had a leotard and ballet shoes for the dancing class which her sister didn't want to go to. The habit of absolute equality was there, ingrained, and every small breach of it was an outrage, 'It's not fai-yur!' Well, you know what happened. The recorder got split in half and rammed into a flower bed to rot, and meanwhile the elder sister developed a dark, barmy paranoia about never having had a ballet leotard, even though she never did ballet.

It is not so hard to reach negotiated settlements over different treatment ('If he has fish and chips on the way home from his maths lesson, you can have them on Thursday while he's at Matthew's . . . If I buy him the rails for his railway, I'll take you to the Disney film he doesn't want to see . . .'). But you have to start early.

Fights

It helps to think of these as educational. It is difficult to take a positive attitude when the sound effects around you are reminiscent of the chimp house, but reflect that sooner or later, all children have to learn about conflicts of interest. Direct conflicts with parents are not the best way to learn: parents, after all, hold too many trump cards and children are emotionally too dependent upon them. Fights with outside friends are also problematical: opponents may diffuse the situation by going away completely, and ending the fight with no product but cold mutual dislike. But in sibling battles you are competing on fairly level terms with someone who will never go away. A sib can never utterly defeat you, yet will never entirely give in either. So these sibling battles are the perfect parable of the wider world: of border warfare, professional rivalry, marriage itself. They have to end in reconciliation, because otherwise neither of you can carry on a decent existence, and the lesson of how to end them smoothly is one which stays with you for life.

A parent's role here is to represent the universal spirit of Justice, Mercy, and Peace. You are a Kofi Anan, a Solomon. Bring sense and calm to this backseat wrangle, and you are producing peacemakers and arbitrators for the world's stormy future. If the very idea makes you crash the gears and clip a traffic bollard, I should stop if I were you and do some deep breathing. In fact, that is what I generally did when the car was the scene of the row. I opted to find a turn-off or a safe lay-by, pull up, switch off the engine and any music tape that might be running, fold my arms and refuse to move until the cursing and kicking abates. This may require a bit of prompting as to how they shall best end it, but it is worth the trouble: 'Look, if you can't agree on whether to listen to Postman Pat or the music, we shan't have either.

Would one of you like to do a swap, and have their choice tomorrow?' Or 'If it's actually her book, let's accept that. But if you're reading it, it won't do either of you any good to rip it in half, will it?' Stopping the car also enables you to fulfil the essential role of every arbitrator, which is to listen. Terry Waite once told me that the essence of his job – which was for years successful before he was kidnapped – was to sit nodding sympathetically while even the most deluded, fanatical terrorists expounded their world view. Same with you. Something may underlie this silly fight over a plastic dinosaur, and it is something you should probably know about.

I set the sample fight in a car because in a car you cannot use the classic parental cure for quarrels, which is to shout, 'Now SEPARATE! Tom upstairs, Lucy downstairs, but separate!' This has some usefulness, especially if the children need one another to play with, because in the end they will learn the vital lesson that if you want human company, you have to stop kicking it on the shins. But the more intense approach – the family conference to analyse and solve the actual quarrel – is more educational. If you can face it. And in a car (or a holiday flat), believe me, you have to.

Here are some of the things siblings fight about:

Possessions You can avert a lot of these fights by having a clear and steady policy about ownership. Every child has a right to certain things of her very own, an inner core of sacrosanct objects. She should be defended to the hilt if her private drawer or cupboard is invaded. If she knows that this will happen, she is less likely to abuse the privilege by pinching someone else's things and putting them in her private drawer.

Some possessions, however, are of dubious ownership. The stone looking like an owl which one of them found on the beach, but you can't remember which; the jointly-owned box of Lego; the construction kits they both got and mixed the pieces up. If there really is no way of knowing for sure which one is claiming correctly, the Solomon solution may work – that is, take it away completely and see which one is most outraged. But it is better to persuade the children, in a rather calm, bored

279

way, that neither of them can enjoy it while they are fighting, so they'd better work out a compromise. If you notice that one child is giving in all the time, or always producing a peace formula that costs him or her the advantage in these fights, then note it, and later lavish private praise and understanding, explaining that you know how difficult it is and that you're proud of the sensibleness being shown.

If you are preaching the message that there is no disgrace in giving some ground, don't forget to demonstrate it too. Show occasionally that even parents are susceptible to calm, sensible arguments. If you are doctrinaire and inflexible about, say, an exact bedtime even on holiday, what is there to suggest to a child that he shouldn't be equally doctrinaire about not letting his sister play gently with his train?

Dignity Young children have a lot of personal dignity. A great many fights arise because the other child, at a loss for something to do with the morning, has jeered 'fatty', or 'bum-face' or 'crybaby'. Unfortunately, by the time the decibel level rises high enough to bring you to the scene, the accused child is also letting off a flood of invective, and both sides may well be claiming, 'He started it.'

If one of them says something revealing like, 'Well, she started it by being a bum-face,' then you know where you are. Mention to the offender that you can see who started it, and do no more. If it remains doubtful who is persecuting whom, then you have two choices. Either deliver your message about how peace and harmony is more fun than fighting, warn that the first one to escalate into violence will be severely dealt with, and retire. Or, if things are really miserable, work out a way of separating the children. Siblings, like spouses, can get seriously on one another's nerves through too much proximity.

You This is the tricky one. Sometimes your attention and time are rationed by work pressures, or social whirls, or illness, or general depression. (All mothers and a lot of fathers get depressed at times. It is no disgrace.) When this happens, the children almost invariably make it worse by fighting over you, with wailing cries of 'It's not fai-yur!' whenever you do anything at all for one child. In this mood, children grill you as to which one you love best. The answer is, I suppose, 'Which of your eyes do you love best? Which of your ears? Which foot?' If there is a real problem, then you do have to be careful, temporarily, about being even-handed about material things (despite the negative side of this policy already mentioned). But you know the real answer: try to clear the pressures, drop the commitments, let down the outsiders, and be kinder to your own beleaguered self. Only then will you have enough left at the end of the day to give to your children, both or all of them.

Teenage quarrels

As children get larger, there seems ever less space for them in the house, both physically and psychologically. As they pass through stages approaching adulthood, differences between them may suddenly yawn wider. Fights spring up over completely new issues, like privacy and bathrooms and making one another look silly in front of outside friends. Bitterness may arise between children who were close playmates when one develops a girlfriend, boyfriend, or overwhelming outside hobby. Incomprehensible tensions get brought home from school to poison the family atmosphere.

Parents, at this stage, have to stand back a little more, and merely try to enforce courtesy and rational debate rather than abuse. Where there is a genuine dispute, the older children I have canvassed generally said that the idea of a family court hearing, or at least a tribunal round the kitchen table with their parents actually listening to their case, would be the best solution. 'Because at least you'd know they were taking your feelings seriously, as if they mattered.' Some said it would be good if someone took notes. One member of a family of five, whose parents do hold tribunals, said that they generally end up in gales of laughter with the original grievance forgotten.

At all ages, through all levels of pacification and negotiation, the essential lessons to get over are:

Quarrelling is unproductive. Arguments only work if both sides listen.

If a fight becomes more significant than the object fought over, it is time to wind it down. Real matters of principle are rare.

Very few objects are worth destroying a happy relationship for.

Peace with honour is always possible.

Deeper tensions Prolonged animosity between the same pair of siblings is worth thinking about. Is one child jealous of another? If so, is there a hidden reason for this? Do you habitually take a different attitude over the same behaviour, depending which child it comes from? Is a daughter being short-changed compared to a son, her interests belittled and less supported than his? Or a son being made to feel a loutish outsider in a very feminine household? Is a pretty daughter, or sporty son, outshining a less conventionally gifted sibling of the same sex?

An aggrieved sense of difference can build up from the most absurd beginnings, even in young children. I hated my elder brother for ages because he had been taken on a long train journey which I had missed. What nobody realized (to this day . . .) was that it was not the actual treat that went on rankling, but the fact that during the brief transient outbreak about it, everyone, including him, laughed at me for being jealous. You get over missing a treat, but it takes longer to get over the sense of having your feelings belittled.

Sometimes parents show apparent favouritism for reasons which are logical to them but illogical to the child because they have never been explained properly. This happens when one child is physically delicate, or has had a bad experience that nobody talks about openly. It also happens when parental memories are longer than children's. My own six-year-old daughter became seriously miffed at one stage because whenever she came down after bedtime, we abruptly chased her back to bed, whereas her brother got a more sympathetic reception. The reason for this was not that we are monsters, but that when she was smaller she had driven us bananas with endless, mischievous, debilitating appearances up to five times every evening, so that any sight of her after eight-thirty made us terrified it would start again, wrecking our only moments of peace in the day. Whereas the boy had never cried wolf but only come down with serious problems, so we were kinder. What had changed was that the girl had forgotten her old annoying habit and now did have real nightmares, but we were rejecting them for historic reasons. She raised the matter, being a forceful child; we saw her point, explained what had been bugging us, laughed about how pesty her earlier self used to be, and evened out our responses again. A small, stupid episode, embarrassing to relate, but entirely typical of the way jealousy can be fuelled by weary parents who fail to keep their eye on the ball and notice that a child has moved on to a new phase.

The good bit

Talking of problems always sounds depressingly negative, and I would hate this chapter to have made anybody decide that an only child is the only answer. The pleasure of having a brother or sister should never be underrated. Even the most stroppy, combative children are more often than not playing together, inventing private games, hauling one another outside and generally interacting. Parents can further this process by artfully introducing games which need two players at least, birthday presents of walkie-talkies, ping-pong tables and so forth; also by reading books aloud in the evening to all the children so that they have more and more common ground and common fantasy games to play.

Kindness between siblings is something you can positively promote, too, by encouraging it and praising it. You can insist on certain ground rules over matters like private sweets and Easter eggs (to wit, *chez nous*, that nobody ate a private treat in front of someone else without offering it round politely). You can send one child with good news for another (that you are all going to the cinema, or swimming), and generally work on their relationship with one another as much as you work on yours with them. All right, it takes time and thought, but so does breaking up fights.

Curiously, the most encouraging thing I ever encountered among siblings involved handicapped children. Linda Scotson, who recovered her son Doran from severe brain injury by intensive therapy, was helped by his elder sister Lili to an extent she thought remarkable – but discovered was quite common. In *The Other Child* – well worth reading for any family, whether it has a handicapped member or not – she describes Lili's ferocious determination to dress this stiff, hopeless baby, to play with him, drag him around and generally pull him into life. It is a pattern recognizable from the lives of handicapped children like the writer Christy Brown, who was trundled round Dublin in a handcart by a mob of brothers and sisters.

Linda Scotson lauds the sibling contribution: 'Unrecognized, unsung, generally unrewarded,' she says, 'sibs do their best to bring hope and humanity into operation in a desperate situation. They hate deathliness and morbidity. They know you can never go back, you have to push on.'

The cases she writes about are extreme, but strangely, looking at families of healthy siblings, the same principle applies. They push one another, goad one another, keep things moving; they counteract depression and isolation, and they know a great deal about one another (even if most of it annoys them). Even my own small warring pair surprised me on occasion: the eldest as a toddler yelling at the crying baby to 'shut up, stupid, you'll get your dinner in a minute!' and her stopping, glaring at him, before they burst together into companionable laughter. There is no better sight than a brother or sister stretching out a rough, grudging hand to defend or help another; unsentimental but partisan, they display a mute tough tribal loyalty which is deeply reassuring to the weaker and a source of silent pride to the elder. The most quarrelsome sibling will often, on being given a small treat, demand equal treatment for the others; or unexpectedly put real thought into a birthday present and the keeping of the secret.

Brothers and sisters are magic; the magic can go sour, but if you practise careful family politics to ensure it does not go too sour, they have one another as a gift for life. For the years after you are gone.

Family Rules and Customs

One of the surest signs that you – a couple and some babies – are mutating into a genuine, full-grown family is that you start to develop family rules and miniature traditions.

A family rule is not one merely imposed on the children by the parents, such as 'No TV until after homework', but one the parents also obey. Such as 'No Wellington boots in the kitchen', 'No swearing worse than "bloody" ', or 'Anything left lying around on work surfaces after five p.m. on Sunday gets binned'.

Naturally, some apply more rigorously to children, particularly where the phone bill is concerned, but essentially they apply to everyone. And there is nothing children enjoy more than seeing their father made to wash his hands before a meal, or their mother reprimanded for breaking the rule about no-reading-at-table-except-the-breakfast-table.

Family rules are not oppressive, or dictatorial, they are just an affirmation of common standards (pretty low ones, in our case) and of the fact that we all have to live together. Myself, I don't mind mess, but there comes a point when mess gets in other people's way, preventing them from sitting down, doing homework, or finding a clean coffee cup. So there have to be rules and customs to keep mess in order. Again, we do not eat very formally: side plates and saucers are virtually unknown at our table. But we have a liking for conversation, and archaic ideas about family meals, so if a family meal is happening, a special dispensation is still required for anyone, even a parent, to put the television or radio on. This includes the TV farming weather forecast. And, alas, *The Archers*. If it so happens that we are all sitting down to supper at *Archers* time, either I have to crawl to the rest of them to be let off the rule just this once, or do without my daily fix of soap opera. It may sound silly, but it reaffirms the civilized idea that decent social behaviour is not

286

something imposed by authority on the weakest, but something arrived at by consensus in a community.

I straw-polled a collection of different families for typical family rules. The healthiest families seemed to have more of these communal rules than the tense, uptight ones, which was interesting. Perhaps tense families are tense because nobody knows what the rules are until someone barks at them. The rules I collected wouldn't all appeal to us, but then ours wouldn't all appeal to you. The false-teeth-by-post principle applies again. Pay no attention to what doesn't fit. Here are a few examples:

All outdoor shoes to be left at the back door when coming in from the garden.

All personal plates and cutlery to be cleared from the table when leaving it.

All trunk calls to be written on the pad, with appropriate timings (a houseful of teenagers, here).

Bedtime is bedtime. Moreover, adult time begins at 7.30, after which large children may read quietly or play cards elsewhere, but disturb adults only for sensible reasons, or to kiss goodnight.

Everyone shall clean their teeth and sometimes wash.

And feed their own pet. Every time Mummy has to do it because they forgot, they are fined 10p pocket money.

No hamsters in the bathroom, ever. Not since the plughole incident.

No toys at the table.

No personal criticisms before 9 a.m. However well justified.

287

Everyone shall apologize to everyone else if appropriate, and be friends again, before bedtime. Let not the sun go down on your wrath.

There is a cardboard box under the kitchen table. Things which should not be lying around will be thrown into it each evening during *The Archers*. On Friday night at 7.15 precisely it will be emptied into the nearest skip, with no right of appeal (this woman has thrown a remarkable variety of things away but only, she says, one precious item per person before the message sunk in).

No item of clothing will be washed unless it is in the wash-basket. Clean clothes will be fetched by each person from the clean basket. Anyone failing to grasp this can go to school without socks, right?

No visitors to stay, of any age, without consulting or at least informing the rest of the family members in time for them to plan a getaway night of their own. This includes everyone, particularly in-laws, long-forgotten aunts, old schoolfriends, ex-boyfriends with their unknown new wives, and teenage cronies with personality problems.

You see what I mean? Some of these rules I think are quite good, some quite impracticable. It depends on your family. Do not fall into the common mistake of governments and set up unenforceable laws. This only leads to chaos. Few rules and reasonable ones work best.

Democracy

It creeps in gradually. There is no point asking a baby under three what he thinks the family should do for their annual holiday (not all that much point asking whether he wants pink or white ice cream, frankly). But as children get older they start to like the idea of having a say in family decisions. And by the time they reach their teens, if they have not been in the habit of getting such a say – or at least a voice in the family Parliament – they will be so fed up with being pushed around that they will rebel in pointless and antisocial ways.

Actually, they might anyway. But I am all for a bit of democracy. Start with the decisions which could go either way, and don't matter overwhelmingly to you as Chairman of the Board (i.e. don't start with, 'Darlings, do you think Mummy should get a part-time job?' when you know you've got to or the electricity will be cut off). And let them list the pros and cons of a situation, because it is good practice for life.

You can sit down, even with a six-year-old, put on a serious expression and say, 'Look, what do you think we should do? We could go swimming on the way to Granny's, but that would make us too late to watch *Star Trek* with her. Or we could go straight there and fit in swimming tomorrow by having an early lunch.' Children really like to be asked. It teaches them how to plan, how to decide between alternatives and make the best of a bad job.

They also, by the time they are eight or nine, often have better ideas than you do because your managerial brain has become overtaxed. They might say, 'It doesn't matter missing *Star Trek* because we could video it, and Granny doesn't like it anyway. Let's go swimming.'

The same principle applies to holidays – if there is a real choice – and even, a few years on, to schools. Though in this case, the choice is too vast and important for a child to be held to it, or blamed for it, if the chosen school turns out to be horrible.

Some parents become terrified that a modicum of family democracy will somehow 'spoil' children, but having too many rigid decisions taken for them will spoil them worse. It will encourage them to start disobeying and dodging round the rules because they are reasoning creatures and the rules seem unreasonable. Pre-empt this. Involve them in as much deciding as possible, birthday by birthday. It will pay.

Customs

This is a more flexible, and fascinating, area. Everyone remembers the first time they stayed with a schoolfriend's family, and how weird everything seemed ('They say grace!' or 'They all eat supper off trays' or 'Nobody is allowed even to say "bum".' Or 'They all play music together in the evenings!'). Family jokes, family slang, even small details like the children being served first or last at table make a deep impression and create a new, often rather exciting, atmosphere. Indeed sometimes children fall hopelessly in love with other families, and as teenagers virtually live round at their friend's house because – for the moment – the way of life suits them better.

Manners

Mind your manners. 'Don't talk when you're eating. Don't eat with your mouth open. Don't interrupt. Especially with your mouth full. Sit up straight. Show some respect for your elders, don't contradict, don't stare, don't make personal remarks. Or pick your nose. Or burp. Oh well, all right, you couldn't help the burp, but beg our pardon for it. What? Why beg? No, it isn't the same as begging on the street. It's – oh, hell, it's traditional! Go on, say it. But not with your mouth full . . .'

Oh dear, oh dear. Is it any wonder surveys suggest that the family meal is said to be on the way out, replaced by serial 'grazing' in which assorted gangling louts shamble into the kitchen at intervals during the day, stuffing lumps of frozen cholesterol into the microwave and spooning it into their vacant faces as they watch Australian TV soaps? Remember what a battleground the family meal used to be, and you can see quite easily what is killing it off.

It was, and in stalwart traditional families still is, the training ground for good manners. It is the place where the new generation learns the code of behaviour which will take them through life as acceptable companions, colleagues and spouses. We do it ourselves whenever we can. Don't eat with your fingers, darling. At least, not the ice cream. Don't put your face into it, either. However, the family meal is also a time to confide, exchange ideas, refine good family jokes and generally be together and build a family identity.

The other traditional training ground for manners is public transport (unless like us you live where there is none, and tend to go everywhere in the car, behaving like a cartful of pigs). On buses and trains the thoughtful parent may attempt to teach more lessons: don't jostle, dear. Don't get in that lady's way. Offer her your seat. Why? Because she's older than you and you should show respect. Gentlemen do offer seats to ladies (we are on dodgy ground here: the lady in question has a Walkman, two-metre hair extensions, and a T-shirt saying MEN SUCK. She is edging away from your bourgeois awfulness, not wishing to be classified as a poor old dear who needs a seat. Never mind.)

Why – after the first obvious training of infancy, (see p. 63), do we bother with manners? We live, after all, in an era when public life – press, politics, business, salesmanship – is constantly and horribly rude. Tabloid headlines scream abuse, politicians sneer. Reviewers revel in insult, style writers jeer at whole sections of the population ('Essex men', 'Anoraks', etc.). Newspaper columnists are cheerfully prepared to bring in their victims' stammers, halitosis, big bums and failed marriages as factors in quite unconnected arguments. Advertisers ask, 'Are you sure your laundry isn't full of telltale odours?' and enjoy reminding you that you might die tomorrow, uninsured.

It is a dreadfully rude age. So why not throw in the sponge, train our children in grabbing and abuse and devil-take-the-hindmost, and let them grow up throwing bones across the table and expressing their innermost feelings?

Because it would be cruel, that's why. Next time you get sick of listening to yourself nagging about manners, think of the fate of those who have none. People think unmannerly children and teenagers are ghastly. They write them off. Human beings have to learn to be acceptable, not embarrassing or annoying to be with. Children have to learn, full stop.

But you can take a minimalist approach to manners. The days

are gone when people got drummed out of polite society for drinking out of the finger-bowls. As long as children know that in company they had better use knives and forks properly, they can occasionally eat with their fingers at home. A few habits have to be kept up, such as eating with your mouth shut; but it is remarkably easy to convince a child of any age to do this simply by sitting opposite them yourself and masticating horribly with your mouth open. Or putting a mirror up while they do it. It also helps to borrow a really unpleasant, grabby, whining, rude child from another family (don't tell the parents or your family why, of course) in order to subtly impress on your own children that taking turns, passing things politely, listening to other people and sharing the last roast potato are aspects of human behaviour which are missed when they are absent.

And the family circle, the daily life of home, is the best place to learn. School dinner-ladies can drill children in using forks properly, but only home can teach true courtesy. If you as parents are not polite to one another, and to your children, any manners you teach them by rote will not sink in very far, nor survive moments of stress. If you keep barking 'hurry up, hurry up' when they are doing something unhurryable, like going to the lavatory; if you criticize their clothes all the time, are abrupt with their friends, and snatch things off them; if you never say 'good morning' or ask how they slept, or how their day was – then why should they? If parents snap at one another constantly, belittle each other's efforts in public and let slip remarks like 'Your father is a selfish moron', more than their emotional security will be undermined. Their manners will, too.

On the other hand, if you do let your own manners slip occasionally under stress, that is another valuable lesson for the young, interested onlookers. Because you can apologize, and thus teach the art of apology. As in: 'Alice, I am terribly sorry I called you a revolting child. I now realize it was not your roller skate I fell over on the stairs but Daddy's sailing boots. It was dark, and Daddy had forgotten to change the light bulb when I asked him. Daddy is a careless berk. No, I didn't mean that. I'm sorry. It was rude and vulgar. It's just that my knee really hurts. Sorry. Sorry, everyone.'

With luck, they will make Daddy apologize properly too, when he gets back from the pub.

Family modesty When I was a child, I would occasionally spend the night with another family. They were the progressive sort, always having very upfront conversations about vaginas and answering the children's casual questions with a fearful direct- ness. Modesty was unheard of; not only did the children throw off their clothes at random all over the house, right up to the late teen years, but the middle-aged parents roamed stark naked between bedroom and bathroom and joined us to watch *Z Cars* with their dressing gowns hanging negligently open and various unspeakable bits reflecting, I remember, rather eerily in the screen.

I was very impressed, but possibly not for the reason they would have liked. It was just that we never had central heating in our house during that Suffolk phase. So one got dressed either under the bedclothes or in the airing cupboard. Nudity was possible in the bathroom, but only if you switched on the overhead bar heater for about forty-five minutes first. Taking your clothes off was a major decision for eight months of the year at least, so if our parents had read the post-Freudian, progressive childrearing books of the time, and decided that it was necessary for us to see them naked in order to dispel castration anxieties, it would have been quite a performance: 'Now, children, we are all going to be spontaneous and un- ashamed. Nip upstairs and turn on the bathroom heater for half an hour.'

Times move on. I suppose that the reticence of my parents and the bum-flashing of my friend's family represented the two factions which have been at war this century over the issue of family modesty. There was an era when most children's only glimpse of adult physiology was on the washing line: 'Cor, Mum! Do they really fill up those big hammocks?' 'Shush, child, or you'll end up like your Uncle Arthur, who we never mention!' Modesty extended to oneself: convent girls of an earlier generation had to bathe in long white robes; and convent girls of mine were told not to play the radio in the bathroom because it was unseemly for a man's voice to be heard in a room in which a pure young girl was stripped. (I have told many veteran male radio hosts this fact to cheer them up, and they are genuinely thrilled to have been considered such a menace.)

Then came the gurus of utter openness, like my friend's parents in the sixties, who wanted to share everything about their physique with their children, discussed homosexuality at breakfast time, and who also, come to think of it, put their thirteen-year-old daughters on the early high-oestrogen contraceptive pill, complete with side effects, 'just in case'. Then there were compromisers who felt that before the age of six (when children are deemed to go through their early sexual phase) family nudity was vital to ensure their future uninhibitedness, but that after six (when they enter every parent's favourite phase, of not giving a damn about any of it) one could pull one's wrapper shut again with a thankful sigh of relief. So, gradually, we have all devised codes of common sense and expediency.

Instinct probably gets it right. Once the glorious immodesties of birth and breastfeeding are over, and when the penultimate toddler has had a last listen to Mummy's Amazing Kicking Bellybutton, most of us are only too thankful to retire behind a stout winceyette nightdress, permitting our offspring only casual and fortuitous glimpses of breast and bum. Dear old Dr Spock caused many sighs of relief when he discarded the extreme post-Freudian view and observed that, actually, the sight of great big naked hairy parents could upset children, and that adults should keep reasonably covered up and have 'some privacy in the bathroom or toilet'. Purists may scoff at that, citing the meaningful conversations they have had with their little sons over the Tampax applicator. If you don't believe such purists exist, just read the relevant chapter in *Talking to Children about Things that Matter* by Sheila and Celia Kitzinger, and find out how the other half raps. My principal feeling after reading it was that, unlike thoroughly modern mothers, I would not be thrilled by the sight of any infant of mine running round waving a dear little white cotton-wool mousie like Mum sticks in her bum. I would probably be furious because, the odds are, it is the last one in the house.

There is actually a serious lesson to be conveyed by a modicum of parental modesty. Few would argue in favour of strict, prudish concealment in front of children but at the same time, it does no harm to point out that whereas there is nothing intrinsically bad about the bit between waist and knees, it is a bit which you are entitled to keep private if you want to. Parents, nurses and doctors should not rudely invade this area without explaining and asking permission, even to wash or examine it. Other children have no right to pull your shorts down for fun. Tickling under the arms is OK in a wrestling match, but under the legs probably isn't. And so forth.

It follows that if your own small bum is private, then it is fair enough if Mummy does not want you bursting in when she is on the lavatory, or if Daddy hauls a flannel modestly over his floating bits when you come into the bathroom for a chat. The odd glimpse, followed by a fair answer to the question 'Why are you so hairy?' is one thing. Being constantly available as a life-size teaching aid for your children is quite another.

Besides, not all of us are as perfect as the diagrams in sex education books. One father sums up his attitude by saying that his children are allowed to see him naked until the first time they say, 'Yuck! Look at your flabby bum!' Whereon he starts hiding for fear of further ridicule. I suppose you could be very hip and New Age, and argue that Dad ought to show them even more flabby bits, thighs, the lot, so that they learn 'to reject the hollow, shallow worship of physical perfection and accept the full human form'. But this one's eight-year-old has a particularly piercing line in scorn, and I wouldn't wish such a start to the day on anyone. Myself, I started turning my back to put on a bra when the youngest observed that my nipples looked like – no, I can't bring myself to type it.

Which brings us to the painful subject of teenagers. Teenagers, as everyone knows, are extremely modest. Prior to leaving the house in skin-tight leggings and tattered shirts tied under the bosom to reveal as much midriff as possible, a girl will hide in the bathroom for hours with the door locked, trying to will away her spots. Girls over eleven are not amused by siblings' attempts to ping their bra straps or make comments on their very personal development. Nor are strapping great boys willing to let their misguided Mummies supervise bathtime or chat gaily while they take a shower.

Wise parents respect this modesty, and impose it firmly on younger brothers and sisters – who should not, it goes without saying, be included either in those confidential conversations about the Pill, the sleepover at Brian's parents' house while they are away, or the fact that the latest busty little hussy brought home by the son of the house is not sixteen at all, indeed not a day over fifteen to your certain knowledge because you personally lent her Mum the family carrycot to bring her home from hospital in . . .

But however tolerant parents are of teenage modesty codes, they are not rewarded by equal toleration. A certain loathing of parental physicality is perfectly natural. Far from wanting to accept their parents as sexual beings, a lot of teenagers would very much rather the wrinklies kept buttoned up, day and night, never laying a finger on one another except, perhaps, to knock off a wasp.

Teenage children of divorced parents are notoriously re-pelled and disgusted by the canoodling of a parent who has suddenly turned into a lover. Many a novel and memoir includes furious recollections of such things. Even natural parents do well to stick to chaste hugs and pecks on the cheek rather than lasciviously putting their hands on one another's thighs, or kissing passionately on the lips in front of their children. I suppose it is because sex, in the adolescent, is such an ungovernable and terrifying force that it is difficult for them to accept just how comfortably routine, how undramatic, a long-married couple can get. And that if your Dad puts his hand on your mother's bum for a moment, he is not actually feeling the same wild surge of adrenaline and testosterone as you did when you brushed past buxom Suzy in the science cupboard yesterday.

This revulsion at parental sexuality was never more graphi-cally expressed than by good old Hamlet himself: 'Frailty, thy name is woman! . . . Oh God, a beast, that wants discourse of reason/Would have mourn'd longer . . .' Giggling, newly-wooed mothers, however much they deserve some happiness after widowhood or divorce, would do well to remember Hamlet and be very, very discreet.

But it is not just sex which makes teenagers so dislike parental exposure. It is what Anna Ford used to call 'Body Fascism'. One teenage girl said frankly, 'I would honestly die if my friends ever saw the way my Mum's midriff hangs over her skirt before she puts her sweater on.' A boy says, 'My Dad's beer belly is just gross. It's as if that's where he keeps all his backward ideas about everything, all wrapped up in flab.' So can you blame Dad if he keeps it pulled in and buttoned up, and waits patiently for his son to grow old enough to realize that flat muscular tummies are not everything? If I were him, I would turn the heating down until the children leave home. This would have the added advantage to his peace of mind of stopping the son's disturbingly pneumatic girlfriends from ever taking off their woolly sweaters in his presence.

One magnificent family I know sometimes take revenge against these scornful, skinny, beloved creatures who moan at them every holiday in their imperfect flesh and revealing swimsuits. They have a bohemian granny in the mould of the elderly Bardot, and also have a little swimming pool. Granny turns up at their house in summer and strips off to her wrinkled dugs to plunge nude into the pool and then stretch topless beside it, dreaming of bygone days with toyboys at the Venice Lido. The parents, themselves cautiously concealed against their children's contempt inside maximum-control Lycra swimwear and thick towelling gowns, know what to do. They bide their time, then send Sarah and Simon out, all unsuspecting, with Granny's cup of tea . . .

Telephones and tellies

In the chapter 'Electronic children' in Part I, I concentrated on the impact of television, computers and virtuality on growing children. There are a few more things to be said about their impact on the small community that is a family. Frankly, technology has been ruining family manners ever since the invention of the telephone first caused parents to break off in mid-conversation with their children or each other, in order to answer a bell tinkled impertinently by some total stranger. Or a tradesman. Or a wrong number. In the early days of the telephone, grandees would get their butler to answer it, and bring the resulting message to them in the usual soft-footed, apologetic manner.

Now, however, a telephone call is the equivalent of having a visitor burst in unannounced, ringing a bell, during your most private family moments. Do not expect young children to appreciate that a phone must be answered. If you don't have an answerphone device, at least apologize to them, and if the moment is fraught – for instance, if you are finally getting the story of who bullied your child at school – get rid of the caller, sharpish.

This is, of course, a counsel of perfection. As a home-worker I have often fallen short of it, to the detriment of many family moments. I would not be the same way again; for one thing, answering machine technology has made it far easier to screen calls and restrict interruptions to the really important ones. But however you do it, you have to hammer out some kind of family code about telephones before your children reach their sociable teens. Quite apart from the cost, which you must police in whatever way is appropriate to your finances, you have to decide how far it is acceptable for one member of the family to leave the table at mealtimes in order to conduct a hushed conversation with a friend, how long any individual is entitled to block up the communal line, and how much privacy the rest of you give them. Who does not remember the agonies of confidential teenage calls in the hallway, interrupted by mocking little brothers and parental clucks of irritation?

When you have worked out a code of manners – with a timer, with separate lines, a loudspeaking answerphone or even (in some large and desperate families) a kiosk – do not forget some protocol for the taking of messages. There is nothing more infuriating than someone, of any age, who picks up the phone, promises to pass on a message, and then either forgets it completely or writes it on a scrap of paper which then blows behind the radiator. Some families have four or five message-pads, in different colours, one for each member of the household.

One other matter you have to decide for yourself is at what age you let small children loose on the telephone. In homes where all the calls are personal (or from domestic utilities like the gas board) many families seem to allow phone-answering as soon as the child can talk. This can result in infuriating conversations along the lines of:

'Hal-lo?'

'Hello. Is your Mummy there?'

'Ye-eth'

'Can I speak to her?'

(Long, stressed, breathy silence. Child puts phone down on hook.)

In such families a habit also emerges of forcing callers to talk to the infant. 'Say hello to Freddie, he gets upset otherwise.'

In houses like ours, however, where both parents have frequent professional phone calls, it is wiser to try to deflect children from answering the phone at all, ever, until they are old enough to be polite and take down an intelligent message. I speak with some bitterness, as one whose infant once got to the phone first when Sir Edward Heath returned a call, and played the toot-a-floot to him. As long as the policy is clear from the start, toddlers do not seem to suffer much from being banned from touching the real telephone and confined to burbling down their Fisher-Price replicas.

As for television, more principles of courteous sharing have to be worked out. Parents, obviously, have the final say on who watches what; but a degree of fairness is necessary where a television is shared (and even in households with lots of tellies, it may be that the satellite dish only connects to one of them, or that the one in the back bedroom has permanent snow on BBC2). For what it is worth, I place a high value on genuine family viewing – comedy or documentary, quiz or drama. When everyone is on and around the sofa, cat-calling and laughing and gasping together, it bonds the family together almost like a miniature shared holiday. The conversations and jokes and arguments arising out of a good programme or favourite series can keep you all going for years. They can also provide, without undue effort or self-consciousness, what earnest therapists would call 'family co-counselling' or 'quality communication time'. Joint television watching can provide a very valuable set of clues as to what children think about human relationships, moral values, and sex.

But growing children will also want to watch certain programmes which you allow but which, with the best will in the world, you cannot face sharing with them: football, some quiz, the *X Files*. As I have said before, if the children are under sixteen you ought to know something about the programme. But beyond that, be tolerant; and, if it is a lone television set, work out clearly in advance what the pecking order is. This is made devilishly difficult in the case of sporting events which overrun and clash with *Friends*; but some judgement of Solomon must be made. It is hard to be a parent. And if bedroom space is so restricted that homework and socializing with friends have to occupy the same room as the telly, it is harder still. But you can't duck it: you have to set out your own rules, and stick to them in a good-humoured but firm way. And, at times, make it known that your own preference is being given up for the common good.

Schooldays 1: In the beginning

It was difficult to decide whether the subject of school belonged in the first part of this book – which majors on children and their needs – or the second, which is about the wider mechanics of the family. I reckon it belongs here, because for good or ill a school becomes another member of the family. It can enhance family life, complicate it, change it, in bad cases almost wreck it.

This applies most intensely in the early years. It is never easy to hand over to relative strangers, for long hours every day, a child you know very well and know to be innocent and receptive and trusting and full of quirks that only the home circle understands. Indeed the beginnings of primary school are often more traumatic for the parents than they are for the child. Some families are so reluctant about it that they toy with – or take up – the idea of teaching them at home. Sometimes they do, successfully.

But most of us overcome that moment of panic, when we are terrified of pushing our child into a group four times bigger than anything he knows, a world where terrifying-looking children kick footballs and jump on one another shouting, 'Gertcha!' We bravely tell ourselves that every one of those children is someone's sensitive little baby, and that most of the rough-housing takes place between enthusiastically consenting bigger boys. We look at our bright, original, busy little toddlers and try to stifle our memories of the endless time-wasting of school life: lining up in twenties, handing in dinner money, answering registers, waiting for permissions. We repress our own worst memories of frightening whisperers in the corner who plot against you, cruel names called, sly pinches in assembly, the burning unfairness of teachers who tell off the wrong culprit because they didn't quite see what happened. We take a deep breath, and go for it.

Yet down at the school gate we are cowed by ancient

instincts. We set out from home as confident, assertive, well-adjusted adults to grill the head teacher, but one whiff of the old school-dinnery, chalky, Plasticeny atmosphere reduces us to nervous children again. We project such fears on to our sons and daughters. Little Freddie may have spent all his life so far in family houses, or cosy playgroup Portakabins: what is he going to make of this great barn of a building, its ugliness, its echoes? We tremble in sympathy, even as we brightly try to talk our child through the first visits with syrupy praise of his Lovely Teacher and the Lovely Paints and Toys. Oh woe, oh woe, how will my baby cope?

Cheer up. Baby will probably cope better than you – if, that is, you are going through any of the above anxieties. You may not be. I deliberately began this chapter negatively, because I began my own school-mother career negatively, and got converted, and I wanted you to know that I know how you feel. Forgive me if you are an optimistic parent of a confident child on its way to a fine little school; those of us who do suffer misgivings have a need to acknowledge them.

Besides, why not begin from a standpoint of doubt? Anything is good if it sharpens your sense of responsibility in choice, of watchfulness over the school, and constructive empathy with the bewildered child now starting. It is bad to communicate your disquiet to the child, of course, but that is only one more reason to work through the fears systematically and eliminate them before the actual first days. If you put on a bright act and pretend to yourself and your spouse that you are 'looking forward to getting the days back', while secretly you are weeping for a finished babyhood, the odds are that the only person who picks up the vibrations will be the child.

So, deal with your reservations. Choose well, start well, manage the change well. Stay confident. Primary education in schools does, on the whole, work wonders.

Choosing a school

Even if your local state primary has the best reputation in the country, go to see it (without the child), and then visit another possible school, state or private. It is the best way to get a 'feel' for schools. Otherwise there is a risk of either being dazzled by the niceness of the place (not realizing that all primary school classrooms are rather nice places to be – children do furnish a room) or being horrified by aspects of it which are in fact, shared by all schools (like the racket). You should be able to approve of the school on several grounds:

Educational It is rare to find a very bad primary school in Britain except in some of the most pressurized, understaffed, low-morale areas which are currently being overhauled with reasonable vigour by the government. There are, however, a great many which are only middling. The best ones offer things which go way beyond the meagre basics of government 'attainment targets' but it is in your interests to check how the school does against these crude yardsticks, and if it does not do very well, to satisfy yourself that there is a good reason for this statistic (e.g, a high proportion of children who do not have English as a first language).

Go beyond the basics. Taste the atmosphere (should be purposeful and busy, humming and happy). Look at the work up on the walls: does it inspire, is it well-presented and lovingly pasted up by children and teachers who are proud of it? Then arrange to drop in again ten days later and see if the display has changed. If not, smell a rat.

Be wary of private schools which make great boasts about homework schedules and starting all the pupils on Latin at five (French would be handier) and beware also of state schools which talk of nothing but attainment targets and reading ages. On the other hand, be equally wary of schools which tell you that tests are meaningless. The golden truths of education lie somewhere between these extremes. The fact is that there are two possible, but opposing, disasters: if you push children too hard at an early age it will apparently work – they can parrot things and write neatly – but may turn out disastrously for them later, when they burn out and become sullen non-achieving secondary pupils.

Yet it is equally disastrous, depressing for them and gloomy for the future, if the school is so soft or so short-staffed that an averagely intelligent child reaches the age of nine hardly even reading. Try to talk about the golden mean with the head teacher. If you dislike the answers, think carefully.

Atmosphere and tone are equally important. Is it a nice school? Does it make you feel confident and friendly and interested? Are people smiling? Do the children seem relaxed? This is the moment to discard all educational considerations and trust your instinct all the way. Some schools feel dull and sour and restrictive; some feel wild and disorganized and rough. The good ones have a sort of hum about them, impossible to define but obvious when it is absent. I never step through our local primary school's ugly glass doors without feeling immediately better and more relaxed, livelier and benevolent towards the world. This tone is set by the teachers, and carried through by the non-teaching staff, secretary, dinner ladies and above all the children themselves.

When you visit, try not to waste time pouring out all your own theories and hopes in a torrent of chat. Listen to the teachers, hope that they get interrupted by other staff and children while you are talking to them, see how they speak to one another: is there respect, affection, mutual help and interest? Try to talk to friends' children who are at the school already, but casually, to see how they view it. At this age they should not yet be into the older habit of jeering at teachers and joking about them in a Beano fashion, but should refer to them as respected friends. You may also want to consider religion, and (if that way inclined) social 'tone'; but neither of these things will help unless the school has that basic, magic, ineffable Hum.

Convenience It matters more than you think. You may find two schools which are both almost ideal, except that one will involve your child in an extra hour a day – or more – travelling in a car or bus, stuck in a city traffic jam or snaking down icy rural roads. The distant school may involve a shared school run, and the possibility that you yourself will rarely be the smiling face at the school gate. Unless the nearer school is really unacceptable, think seriously before you commit yourself and your child to the distant option. Think of bringing friends home for tea, of parties and outings; think of winter mornings, think of the waste of time on hot summer afternoons in a car. Only then can you judge whether the slight edge the other school offers is worth it.

Starting school

Leaving aside the issue of schools with a built-in nursery class (which should always be judged on its own merits, and is not necessarily a better idea than a playgroup), most primary schools offer four-year-olds the chance to spend a few afternoons in class during the term before they enter. Let me tell you, however, that even if a child hugely enjoys these and seems utterly settled, the first real schoolday might turn out somewhat differently.

At our primary school, a blanket of care wrapped itself around my eldest from the first: the other children were kind and welcoming, the teachers warm, the routines unthreatening and he loved his pre-school visits. Nonetheless, when September came he cried bitterly every day for two weeks; daily his fingers had to be prised off my sleeve, and daily I went away (almost weeping myself) to catch wrong trains or put laundry away in the oven. It was hard, very hard, not to give in to his impassioned pleas to leave. I was determined to keep on at it, and even invoked the Law, explaining that he didn't have a choice and nor did we. The only thing which cheered him up was a promise that we would let him leave at sixteen instead of eighteen.

Well, it was not *quite* the only thing. What was apparent, and what helped us to keep up the torture for that terrible fortnight, was the clear fact that his mind was being exercised in a way it had not been before. In between asking to leave school he would say: 'But if the moon is all sandy and dry, how does it shine?' or 'Mummy, do you know that water has weight?' School and its ways of learning were broadening him, new

305

people were getting a chance to plant nuggets of information and ideas and different views of the world in his mind. I felt that school would work, was working already, and that he would soon realize it. Which he did. Gradually the teachers began to report the fuss becoming briefer and briefer once he got inside. One morning I said, 'Don't cry, it upsets the other children.' (Oddly enough, it didn't. They seemed to accept it as a mannerism, and still kept strolling up to show him their toys even at the height of his hysteria.) Whereon the child said an astonishing thing: 'Oh. Do they think it's serious crying, then?' I could have shaken him. The crying had somehow mutated into being nothing but a mannerism. He stopped. All went well.

This, of course, may not happen to you and it didn't happen to us with the second child. But if it does, be resolute: give it time. Discuss it with the teachers, trust them, stay calm. A lot of the panic may stem not from real dislike of school, but from dislike of change. This is, after all, a great rite of passage and some people greet such rites – even weddings – with tears.

Easing the start

Check up on the nuts and bolts of the child's new day. Try to get an idea of its shape: explain about assembly, and playtime, and school dinner, but only in general terms. Say that there is no harm in asking, however many times you have to repeat the same question; explain that nobody will mind.

Discuss in advance such things as how you ask for a lavatory (usually 'toilet' in schools). Make sure the child is good at going alone: organize a practice on some strange public lavatories to increase his sang-froid.

Make sure he can cope with his clothes. Some schools have the tiresome and silly habit of putting five-year-olds in uniform ties and shoelaces and shirts with cuff buttons. Serve them right if it takes half an hour to dress a class for PE. The ideal costume for early school, quite frankly, is a tracksuit with a floppy neck and without tight ankle cuffs. Shoes that close with Velcro are a godsend.

Talk of your own schooldays with enthusiasm, remembering only the most harmless sorts of fun. Our children's early days were made more bearable by a very dull but reassuring story of how their father spent the whole of his first day of school sitting in a wooden rocking swan.

If you can find him a friend who is starting at the same time, that is good.

Learn the ropes yourself. Find out where to wait outside at home time, and how to send in dinner money or PE kit. DO NOT BE LATE arriving, or the child will feel awkward and guilty; and DO NOT BE LATE at home time either. Remember that you are, for the moment, the only fixed star in a shifting universe.

Don't grill the poor child every day about what happened and what he did. He might just want peace and quiet and to forget it all. But if he tells you, listen.

Managing school

Like so much else in parenthood, being a schoolchild's mother is a management skill. There are things to learn.

Control the gear Not only do you have to get into the habit of remembering dinner money on Mondays, PE kit on Tuesdays, library books on Fridays, to put the reading book back in the red folder with its marker in, and so on; you also have to get into the habit of searching your child every day, satchel and pockets, for notes sent back by the ubiquitous school system of Pupil Post. These may contain absolutely vital information about end of term, parents' nights, plays, or other things you must not miss. They may be appeals for costumes, or junk for the science room, or tedious exhortations about searching your child for nits; whatever they are, you need to read them. However, some children go on forgetting to hand them over until they are seven or eight years old. No, I take that back; some don't even hand them over when they are sixteen. Search.

Adapt to the new day Working mothers, however part-time, will find to their dismay that it is actually harder to organize life around a schoolchild than it was around a toddler. If you go away for a day-trip or longer, leaving a toddler with a nanny or minder, you can get back full of enthusiasm and promise a full programme of fun and togetherness at the swimming pool the next day. A schoolchild still has to get up and go to school, even if Mummy is just home. With a young child, you can be spontaneous about shopping trips or lunch with friends. Having a schoolchild means that you are tied down to that difficult mid-afternoon time when the school doors open; moreover you will be in heavy demand for the subsequent hour or so, as the child unwinds. I know women who have actually given up jobs when primary school started because of these pressures. 'Her hours at home seem so few, now, that I need to be there,' said one. She took a part-time job instead, in the mornings.

The first two terms are not the time to take on a new job yourself unless you have to. Remember that there will be illnesses: no school. There will be half-terms and holidays: no school. There will be strange random days on which the teachers go off for the latest retraining initiative. Develop a network of friends among other mothers for emergencies. Grannies often come into their own at this stage.

Communicate with teachers Parents' evenings or the equivalent also demand new skills. There is a fine line to tread between being pushy and aggressive ('Why is Sarah Jane only on Book Three? She should be on Book Five at least, surely?') and being too obsequious with teachers. You know your child best, but they know the mechanisms of learning. It is vital that you work together. Ask the teacher if there is anything you can do to help at home such as following a particular system of reading together, or playing games that would help with maths. If you don't understand a particular teaching system, ask to have it explained (new maths is baffling, team-teaching very baffling, and phonics have to be done right). If there isn't time, ask if you can borrow a textbook for teachers, or at least get the name of some educational text which would make it clear what they are trying to do. Don't stay in the dark if you are bothered about a subject, but don't shout down methods just because you haven't heard of them. Try to find out what other friends' children are doing at different schools, but not in an aggressive or competitive way.

Help the school Getting involved in the school yourself can be wonderfully rewarding, and is quite the best way of learning something real about it, and regaining a sense of proportion by meeting other children than your own. Many schools use parent-helpers in the classroom to hear little ones read, or do craftwork. If you want to offer your time, do it on a regular basis if possible, in a decent spirit of humility and helpfulness. Never forget that you are an amateur.

Mind you, from my experience of doing it once a week for two years, I can tell you that an hour with twelve strange seven-year-olds will ensure that you never, for a moment, forget your amateur status.

But during the first year, try not to be directly involved with your own child's group at school if you can help it. It confuses them. After that they think it is quite fun, and call you 'Miss' like the other children do.

Even if classroom helping is impossible or too alarming to contemplate, you can involve yourself up to the neck in PTAs, governorships, fetes and plays and the rest. It pays to bring school friends as firmly into home life as you can.

In other words, don't let primary school be an alien place to which your children go; let it become an extension of your circle of family and friends. That way, you will have a better idea of what is going on, and what influences are in your child's life. You will also taste one of the unpublicized joys of parenthood: the way it anchors you, perhaps for the first time, firmly into a community.

Help your child Education in the widest sense has always been your business. Visiting museums, joining the library, watching good television together, learning games, taking walks have probably always been part of your family life. The dominant educational preoccupation of these early years, though, is reading. Take it seriously, but not too seriously.

You can help by having books around, reading aloud with pleasure in the evenings, and heaping praise on a child who tries to spell out the cereal packet to you; but you can't help by pushing. All children learn to read at different speeds, and the pernicious doctrine of 'reading ages' only serves to panic parents of slower developers. There is no proof whatever that the child who reads fluently at three and a half is any better, or keener, at seven than the one who has only been at it a year. Do not get yourself, or your child, into a quite unnecessary state just because the little toad next door is alleged to be reading alone. If the school tells you there is no real problem, believe them. If you don't trust them, then get a respectable educational psychologist – if you must – to have a chat with your child informally. Try not to tie your child into any tests or exams for new schools during the period when he is learning to read at his own pace: tests are very unforgiving, and rarely allow for differences between individuals.

Above all – and it is desperately hard when you are worried – do not nag. Reading is a private pleasure, sometimes a subversive one. Remember how it was? Something you did to get away from your parents nagging you. The real breakthrough will come, not when your child drones out a page of faultless school text to you, but when he slips away to his room to be peacefully alone with a book. The pushiest, most academically neurotic parents I ever met had a six-year-old who read beautifully but was never seen doing so for pleasure. He preferred videos.

Siblings

The division between pre-schooler and schoolchild is the most definite change in life since birth; it cannot be compared to any other huge step – walking, talking, even playgroup – because it is so all-encompassing and final. From the first moment at school, a child is committed day after day, week after week, for years, to a waking life mainly dominated by school and the friends made there. She is under new disciplines: lining up, waiting her turn, hanging up her coat on the right peg, carrying a project through without losing concentration. After the utter freedom of being a toddler pottering about in the kitchen or back yard, school is quite a shock – even when it is a pleasant one. The old friends and siblings left behind have no idea of what is going on in the schoolchild's life; it can create strains in their small social world.

Handle it carefully. Close-born children (two years' gap or less) are difficult to reconcile at this stage. At 3.30 p.m. daily you have an elder child who is exhausted and wants your undivided attention, and a younger one who is jealous and can't see what all the fuss is about. Real antagonisms can develop. To help resolve them, encourage the big one to 'play school' with the little one, thus assuaging her curiosity and providing useful scope for bossing (the big one needs to boss; she feels very small and insignificant at the moment).

There may be nasty moments when the eldest brings home a schoolfriend and behaves in a foully macho and exclusive manner, setting traps for the little one and making war – again, to get rid of that dreadful sense of lowliness. Grit your teeth; it settles down in the end.

Younger friends next door are also a problem. If Rosamund and Chloe have played together four times a week ever since they were babies, but Rosamund is nine months older, there may be a whole year when she is at school and Chloe isn't. Chloe is going to be bored and restless all day if she hasn't enough other friends. And, more distressing still, she will be over-keen to come round at 3.30 p.m. However, poor old Rosamund is less keen. A child who has been solitary all day is overtaxing company for one who has been struggling bravely in a crowd since 8.45 a.m. Chloe wants fun, games, running about and confidences. Rosamund just wants to sit on Mummy's knee and be very quiet. Result, misery all round.

Time is the only cure. After the first weeks, Rosamund will relax and may quite enjoy the undemanding company of her little friend after school. But you have to be prepared for the old toddler alliances to break off completely. From now on, your child will be making all sorts of decisions and friendships without your help. But never close the doors entirely: some baby friendships revive against all odds.

Troubles

There will be times of trouble at school. There may be another child who oppresses yours, even unconsciously ('I apsley hate Joanna'). There may be real bullying. More likely, there may be difficulties in making friends (see chapter on 'First Friends', p. 22), and loneliness in a playground full of gangs and alliances. There may be misunderstandings with teachers, smarts of injustice, or largely unfounded dreads and fears of a particular teacher. We had hysteria every Thursday morning for months about one teacher a child was afraid of; I have seldom met a milder, more tolerant woman. We believe it was her hairstyle, rather Cruella de Ville.

All these problems need talking about with the child, in a tone of interest and concern (but not overemphatic sympathy, not 'It's a shame! Aaah! How dare she!'). Also you have to mention them to the teachers. Few things are more embarrassing than informing a pleasant well-meaning woman that your child is terrified of her. But if you have chosen well, and your school has a good happy atmosphere and a real concern for the whole child, they will want to help you sort it out.

Whatever the problem is, try to do so calmly; if you have been up half the night with a weeping child, it will take every ounce of self-control, humour and detachment you can muster but you must listen to the teacher's viewpoint as well as putting forward your own. A story which came to you about a bigger child knocking yours over and trampling on his hat may have reached the staff quite differently: Possibly as an account of your child kicking the other one on the shins and tearing up his birthday card.

312

Remember, if your child is unhappy for some reason, the teachers should be just as concerned as you are. The mark of a good school is that its focus is always on the children. But they remain your children first and the final judgement is yours. If you think you are being fobbed off, and the problem is seriously upsetting the child, keep on persevering.

Schooldays 2:
The middle, and the end

At eleven, everything changes. At least, it is usually at eleven; some schools change at nine and a half to a middle school, and some primary schools run through to thirteen. Whenever it happens, there will be a distinct moment of transfer to 'big school'.

The question of choice is an immense one, too wide to cover here. If you find you have a choice (not everyone is so lucky) then many of the same principles apply as with primary schools: consider the buzz, the reputation on the ground, the statistical record (in its place) and the convenience for family life. The quality of your own involvement, however, is bound to change. Unless you are a teacher at the school, a governor, or a very active PTA member or pillar of a community college, it will seem a more remote world than the cosy neighbourhood primary.

This is no bad thing, certainly after the first couple of years. If there is one thing worse than a completely uninterested primary school parent who hardly knows what the school is called, it is the parent of a teenager who won't back off. I had to learn this myself, from my children, being at times forcibly reminded that they are not babies and can sort out various problems or tackle difficulties with teachers by themselves. Other teenagers concur: they tell their parents about the problem with the football team, or the unfair punishment, because they want a sounding-board. *Not* an avenging Fury. If parents keep sticking their oar in too obviously, the children will stop telling them about the problems. There is a time to sit on your hands, and bite your tongue, because it is their life and not yours. You chose the school, but you aren't the consumer; they are. Even when asked to accompany a class trip to a museum (Oh yes! Yes! Anything rather than work! I love

314

coaches, and museums, and gossiping with teachers, I do!) I learnt humbly to ask my offspring whether they minded. I am at this moment a school governor; but if my children asked me to resign, and meant it, I would.

A few parental actions, however, do help with schooldays.

Listen If there is one thing that parents of growing-up children all agree on, it is that the job is even trickier than having toddlers or primary school children. Young children are often very ready, bursting indeed, to tell you about their day. So if you are around, for a reasonable number of days in the week, straight after school you will get the full story. As they get older they wait, and brood, and choose their moment to come out with something devastating ('I think Mr Farthingale fancies me, he looks at me in a funny way in biology class' or 'Mum, do purple pills with yellow bits on count as drugs?'). And even if this moment is halfway through your favourite programme or at eleven o'clock at night, it would be rash not to listen.

Try to understand the school's ethos A school is not an efficient information filling-station; it has a strong pastoral, moral influence on your child, or else it is not much of a school. But its ideals may not be quite the same as yours, and there can be clashes. It may be more, or less, religious than you; more, or less, tolerant; more, or less, 'politically correct' about the ways in which minorities and those at a disadvantage are spoken of.

Some people are shocked when they find that sex education at their children's school is exclusively about health and the avoidance of AIDS and other diseases; others are irritated when the school PSE ('personal and social education') lessons talk up marriage and fidelity as essentials of life.

You do not have to find a school which exactly mirrors your own attitude – you'd be lucky if you did – so the important thing is to know its line, so that you can discuss such matters with your children yourself, challenge the school view if you want to, and generally broaden their outlook without confusing them. It does no harm to point out to older children that

315

being a whizz at maths does not necessarily make a teacher sound on the subject of sex. Or religion. Or race relations.

Keep the rules The uniform may seem to you to be outdated, impractical, and even a touch perverse. Why the hell must little boys wear shorts in mid-winter at certain schools? What is this curious terror that makes us quench glowing, growing girls in grey polyester? What is this obsession with pleats? But if you have committed yourself to a school for other reasons, you are stuck with it. The same goes for other things which may annoy you, as a sane person (such as Saturday morning school, or funny rules about hair). You can protest mildly, but there is no point in encouraging your child to break rules, however silly they seem. You can say that you agree they are silly but point out that in adult society we all spend half our time obeying damn silly rules, like not parking on double yellow lines in deserted market towns, or not spitting off Westminster Bridge, and that we do it for the sake of general law and order and the Greater Good of all. Perhaps you could points out that Mummy's office doesn't allow trousers. Or that Daddy has to wear a tie every day of his working life. Tell them that if they work hard and pass their exams, they can grow up to be the people who change the silly rules.

Do not get educationally neurotic Difficult, this one, in an era of education as political football, when every saloon-bar philosopher has a theory about what is wrong with our schools, and opportunist politicians trade insults, and educational psychologists are forever touting for business and setting up reading-and-maths-age tests you can do by post to check up on your child. There is a very fine line between noticing that a child is not learning much and getting obsessively pushy about it. In education, there will always be parents who don't care, parents who do, and parents who care far too much.

I once, for journalistic reasons, imposed one of the correspondence tests on my own daughter (chosen because she actually enjoyed exams very much). She sat down to the paper and batted through it in half an hour, reading from 'jam' to 'incandescent', though unaccountably failing to spell 'cham-

316

pagne' (shows the scummy household she comes from). The psychologist diagnosed her reading and maths ages, rather impressively, much as her school had done, but then shocked me by saying, 'She's a super reader, good speller, and fine on maths, but not as high. That's where she should concentrate.' At this point a philosophical difference emerged between us: why should the poor child concentrate on maths when she was well up to the average?

'Because in order to fulfill her potential,' said the psychologist sternly, 'a bright child should be ahead by the same amount in every area.'

We never agreed. It seemed to me that you should be allowed to be an Einstein in maths without being forced to read books above your age group. Or an adventurous and accomplished reader who just struggled along normally in maths, or an obsessive natural historian who knew all about the life cycle of slugs but showed little promise of distinction elsewhere. Every child needs balance, and to accomplish the basic normal standards, but being good at one thing should not lay upon you a burden to be good at everything.

Don't press the school to accelerate a bright child. This is a controversial thing to say. A lot of parents feel a bright child is bored among its age group, and are all for pushing him or her up two or three years. This happened to me – not because I was bright, but because I came from an advanced educational system, in France, to a backward one in Johannesburg for a year. When I was twelve, I was in a class of heavily pubescent fifteen-year-olds.

I have to tell you it was not a success. If a child really is too bright for their class, a freer approach to personal study could be urged on the school. Many will accommodate it. It is occasionally true that a child is mature enough to mix with others two years older on a regular basis. But most of them can't, and hate it. A contemporary of mine went to Oxford at fifteen and a half instead of eighteen, and much good it did her: out of her depth for three years socially, she eventually turned against her own gifts, married at nineteen and has hardly looked at a book since.

Changing school

It is a truism that changing schools is stressful for a child. One or two even run away at this time, or develop mysterious illnesses. They need as much support from their home base as anyone else undergoing a rite of passage: a bride, an exile, a newly and dizzily promoted executive. They are even, in a sense, bereaved. Children who leave a good primary school are losing a close and familiar family of teachers, even if they stay among their friends. And often they leave their friends as well, to go into a whole new culture, with different slang, different habits, and higher expectations.

Matters are not helped if the parents, too, are feeling bereaved. A good primary school – the first outside body to which you ever entrust your child – can creep into your family life as a very important influence. If you are active, help with parties and outings, sit on the PTA or act as a classroom volunteer, your life, too, will be changed when your child leaves. Some primaries are so beguiling that parents can't bear to leave the PTA, and stay on when their children move. A psychiatrist once told me that she sees a lot of mothers whose children have just gone to secondary school, and who find themselves plunged into unaccountable depression. If the new school is a bus or train run away, and you no longer have a daily meeting at the school gate with the other parents, you may feel even more bereft. And if – as bigger schools often do – it keeps parents at a cooler distance than your friendly little first school, you may get positively upset. Moreover, if there has been conflict between parents as to which school the child should attend, even more tension is generated.

I am not saying all this will happen to you. But watch out for it. Children pick up the moods and doubts of their parents very easily; they need to go to the new school with optimism and confidence. If the parent is tearful and fearful, it might be best if that parent kept clear of the first school runs.

Conversely, of course, if you have fought hard or made financial sacrifices to get your child into the particular school of your dreams, you want to avoid giving the impression that you value the school more than the child. If he or she absolutely hates it, at least listen to that point of view. If the child goes on hating it for a long time, consider giving up your dream and moving him or her. It may have fabulous science labs, elegant grounds and a superb academic reputation, and still be a rotten depressing hole. I remember once congratulating a new acquaintance who mentioned that her children were at a school which had topped a league in one of the proliferating 'Good Schools Guides'. She snapped, 'I'm moving them next term. It's an appalling place. They pass all their exams but they've never had a school outing or a school play, the teachers never seem to crack a smile, the children are exhausted and nervous, and the headmaster is a raging racist snob whose assemblies are somewhere to the right of a Nuremberg rally.'

If you decide – after long discussion with one another and your child – that the only solution to a problem or a running unhappiness is to find a new school, then do it. It is too important to let it slide; these are vital years. But give it a chance, and make sure that before any decision, you have talked with the head, personally and at length, and asked whether anything can be done to right the problem. Be calm, if you can; be reasonable; try to back up your complaints with evidence from other parents. If you still get nowhere, you will all have to face the anxiety and upheaval of change. If so, see the head again. You owe it to the school you are leaving, and to the other children there, to make it absolutely clear why you are doing it.

And if you can, refrain from winding up all the other parents you know whose children are still there. They may be unable to move, or not feeling the problem as you do. If you go on and on at them, justifying your own move, you will only lose friends.

The examination years

At sixteen, and again at eighteen, come public examinations. In Britain – especially in England and Wales with GCSE and A-level – the results and standards of these exams are under public media scrutiny today as never before. If pass rates are

319

down there is headshaking about low school standards, if they are up then headlines suggest – not least to the poor candidates themselves – that the exams have been made too easy.

At the same time there is immense pressure on children to get 'qualifications' or face a bleak, jobless future. But although it is true that employers (especially of those without degrees) place importance on exam results, in real life the most important qualifications for any kind of work are energy, adaptability, and the sort of creative initiative which solves problems. In most jobs it also helps to be pleasant and confident. Moreover, the predicted future of work (short contracts, advancing technology, flexiwork, portfolio careers, much of it already with us) is going to require those personal qualities more than ever before. If there ever was a time when good school grades won a good job and safety for life, it has gone.

So the things your teenagers really need – the personal qualities and the curiosity and range to use their intelligence independently – are not necessarily those which public examinations measure best. And, by a dreadful irony, the kind of stress they live under during their last four years at school may actually militate *against* the development of the real qualities that adult life will need. The best schools are alert to this danger, and make sure that exam candidates have a rounded life, take plenty of exercise, and have some pastime – whether it is drama, music, or sport – which helps them to keep the exam stress in proportion.

If the school is not too good at this, and confines itself to pushing hard and piling on work, then you, the parents, have to help. Show your children that you have confidence, but not over-inflated expectations. Show them or her a bit of the world; your own working world perhaps, or some aspect you can access through 'work experience'. If they are worried, offer them accounts of patchwork lives which succeeded despite early lack of school acclaim or grades (John Major, Greg Dyke of the BBC, Winston Churchill, etc.). Keep their vista broad and optimistic, and do not let the school or their own worries narrow it down to a stifling tunnel of academic pressure. Every year there are suicides of terrified teenage exam candidates. Be alert to any sign that your own child feels desperate.

Of course, the problem may be the opposite: the child appears not to be working at all, and teachers complain about this. When that happens, a parent's role is to stay in close contact with the school, and do what is necessary to enforce the completion of the minimum of coursework at least. This may involve grounding, removal of bedroom television, or whatever measure seems likely to work. It will undoubtedly be a great bore. But keep the lines of communication open, and if necessary leave communication on the subject to whichever parent is the least hysterical. There may be a reason your child is not doing any work. He or she may be doing quite the wrong subjects (especially at A-level), or just have got to that terrible stage we all know, when you fear you have fallen behind due to an illness or a lousy love affair, and can't bring yourself to start catching up because you dare not contemplate the acres of untouched work. This requires detailed help from the teacher, possibly through the intermediary of the parent.

If such help is not forthcoming, it may be necessary to appeal to the head of department, or the head teacher. Whatever you do, stay calm, stay loving, and don't reinforce a sense of being a useless feckless failure. It is better to have your child fail a few exams than turn his back on you for good.

Leaving school, making decisions

There comes a time when parents have to let go. Today's school leaver is, as likely as not, eighteen years old and legally an adult. He or she will have been equipped and briefed to make certain decisions: about A-level retakes, gap years, university applications. Some parents (especially when they have to keep on paying) like to keep control of these decisions. I do not think that this is a good idea. You can suggest, you can discuss, you can certainly act as a research assistant about courses and careers and universities and colleges and apprenticeships. You can even, if you must, make those appalling fraught telephone calls pleading with admission tutors to let your chick aboard even though he got AAC instead of AAB in his final grades. You can attach strings to your financial support. You can help (if you are welcomed) with flat-hunting.

But you can't live their life for them. Not once they are eighteen. So it does no harm to devolve decisions gradually, sensitively, over the years beforehand while they choose exam subjects and sort out their priorities between music and hobby, or social life and homework. Sometimes, for a parent, the most difficult and the most loving thing to do and say is precisely nothing.

Fun, Fun, Fun

Trips and treats, guests and gatherings, parties and holidays are as important to a good family life as anything. Good memories, larks, jokes and adventures bind you together. Even the holiday disasters and the misdemeanours of sozzled Christmas uncles contribute to the tapestry of shared memory and hilarious reminiscence. Telling families how to have fun is possibly the most ridiculous thing which anybody could attempt in a book – false teeth by post indeed – but there are a few observations which might be useful. Broadly, the subject falls into two halves: private family time and shared whoopee.

Family time

As a natural hippie (oh, how I long to live in a commune and only have to wipe down the kitchen table when it is my day for doing it, once a week), I used to set my face squarely against the ultra-cosiness of little nuclear families doing things together, without outsiders. Especially in matching sweaters. I wanted life to be diffuse, communard, free-flowing. 'The more the merrier!' I would cry, including hordes of other children in trips to steam fairs and seasides, filling the house with guests, idly offering the spare room to passers-by. It seemed, somehow, to dilute the fearful intensity of the early childraising years. So did the habit of taking private escapes – each parent away, with an adult friend, remembering how life used to be. I still do all these things, to some extent, but as children grow older it is increasingly borne in on me that parents and children need a ration of communal time, communal pleasures taken by all of them together and nobody else.

It is particularly true when both parents work. We have all got so efficient, so managerial about time-juggling in family life

323

that we have created the curious phenomenon of the 'weatherhouse family'. This is the household in which one parent is always out while the other minds the children. The good side of this is that children get a chance to talk to each parent properly, without the parents lapsing into some sort of gibberish adult code which excludes them. The bad side is that if you are not careful, everyone's interests diverge so much that you are hardly a family at all, more like flatmates.

We have had periods like this, and my husband is particularly good at calling a halt to them and imposing family time. I would say, 'Look, you take the children to the boat and I'll work,' and he would glare at me and say, 'We'll wait till you're finished, then we'll all go.' So we did, and another shared memory, however trivial, ties us together.

It doesn't have to be an outing, or even a walk or a visit to the swimming pool. It could be just a family meal, after you have been eating separately for a while; a television programme or film everybody enjoys together, or a game of Scrabble or Monopoly. It could even be an accident. One family I know got stranded in their boat on a mudbank for eight hours with nothing to read or play with. They are, I would say, an averagely quarrelsome and difficult bunch, like any of us, but they rose to the occasion. They had a picnic basket, plenty of beer and lemonade, and invented games like striking matches to draw charcoal pictures. They also, as the tide rose, sang their way through a whole songbook. They all agree, right down to the baby, that it was one of the best days out yet. Just being themselves, together, unable to get away, making the best of it. Every family needs a bit of this; if you don't get it, you feel the lack of it. It is worth forcing it even on your sulkiest, squeakiest wheel.

Adventures together Adventures are something which sets off this family feeling, and makes it easier to recapture when you are all together for some later, minor thing like a meal or a walk. Some families plunge into really big adventures and weld themselves together that way. Years ago, the writer Christina Hardyment suddenly decided that she was tired of being a lackey and chauffeur, servicing children's clothes and delivering them to schools to be processed into adults. So she, and her whole family, removed themselves for a summer and did a grand tour of Europe in a yellow camper van, trying to trace the origins of the great European children's stories, from Babar to Heidi.

Reading her book, *The Canary-Coloured Cart*, inspired me in turn to revive an old ambition to sail a small boat, slowly, all the way round mainland Britain (1,700 miles), and to persuade my husband that he and I and a five-year-old and a three-year-old (she had her fourth birthday on the way) would get along just fine in a small cabin together for three and a half months. And we did it, and wrote about it in *One Summer's Grace*. And these things are catching (or else families only admit their crazy intentions to other families they think will understand) because since then I have talked to one lot who bicycled across Europe with the youngest strapped to Father's bike and three other children pedalling their own; to four children and their unemployed, broke, single mother who sold the flat, bought a camper van and spent four months travelling round the UK living off odd jobs, typing and cleaning and knitting; to numerous water gypsies who decided to sell up and sail, all together; and, most strikingly, to a workaholic property developer, struck by the recession, who suddenly announced to his gobsmacked wife and children that they were all going off for the whole summer to camp in the Rockies and see America, because business couldn't possibly be worse than it was and he wanted to get to know his children before it was too late.

All these trips were successes. Even one or two which were, technically, failures and did not reach their objective. The great pleasure of adventuring together is that however maddened you get (read *One Summer's Grace* if you want to know just how nasty a Mummy I can be), is that it lays down that set of common memories, family jokes, private language and general kinship which can be too quickly diffused and lost in the everyday modern world of TV and video, cars and hobbies and distant, centralized schools. A family adventure is a pressure cooker, all right, but good nourishment comes out of it. A journey to a new place jolts you out of yourself, reinvigorates you, makes you see more clearly; if you all share this new vision, you grow closer together. The adventure can be quite small: one year after Christmas, feeling stale, we took the ferry across to France and the train to Paris, and stayed in an extremely cramped, extremely cheap hotel in Montmartre. All we did for two days was walk around, but adventures came our way. The children found gargoyles, and were spoken to kindly by a real bishop. We saw a huge tent and discovered a temporary exhibition of Polish cribs. We ate different food. We climbed the Eiffel Tower. Years later, we all still talk about it, and it is all the better because we did it together – even though there were at least five rows, numerous snapping matches, and one child was in the process of coming down with a feverish flu. I am not sure we exactly enjoyed every minute at the time, and it was certainly not relaxing (I have never been so exhausted as on the ferry back). But we have enjoyed it a lot in retrospect, and retrospect lasts longer.

Holidays Family holidays, ordinary ones, can be adventures. But the trouble is that we are all so tired by holiday time that we stop wanting adventures. So as a society we often opt for packaged relaxation: for places guaranteed to 'keep the kids busy all day long!' without parental intervention. We try to rule out adventure in the real sense.

Work is partly at fault. There was an interesting survey recently which showed that whereas junior staff in companies – the fancy-free, childless ones – show no unwillingness to slope off on holiday as often as possible, senior staff (the kind with growing-up families or teenagers) often fail to take their full holiday entitlement, even when they are dispensable at work. I suspect that part of the reason, at least, is that the executives view a fortnight's trip away with their families as far more stressful than staying at work or having a bland week's rest at home. They have a point here. We are, in the majority of cases, still talking about men, and it is an unfortunate quirk of fate and biology that just when a man gets to the stage of controlling a department full of bickering, unpredictable, back-

326

stabbing staff, his family life has matured as well, providing him with a parallel houseful of bickering, unpredictable, back-stabbing teenagers. Taking this hornet's nest on holiday may seem to him every bit as stressful as staying put and master-minding a takeover bid for Amalgamated Consolidated Food-stuffs. You cannot, after all, sack your thirteen-year-old son.

Daddy (or high-flying career Mummy), may have been working such long hours away from home, among profes-sionals, that he/she has forgotten what it is to give a crisp order and have it met with indifference, derision, or a suggestion that he/she goes to get his/her own ice cream. By the time the whizzy parent has learned to wind down, to smile, to play beach cricket and meet setbacks with a shrug, two upturned palms and a murmur of 'mañana', the fortnight is up and it is time to go back to the office in a dangerously relaxed and vulnerable state, stripped of the protective carapace.

The answer to both problems – holiday stress and lack of family adventures – is, to me, the same. Be active. More research shows that professionals who actually do something with their families – hiking, sailing, cycling, camping – are far more willing to take the time off, and that families look forward to it more, and co-operate better, than if they were merely being hauled off to a pre-digested holiday experience which never quite lives up to its promise. For one thing, it forces everyone to concentrate, and therefore to make common purpose. The former BBC Director-General, Sir Ian Trethowan, used to say that only a sailing holiday really relaxed him because when he dropped the mooring he was forced to concentrate on the wind and tide instead of fretting about the latest BBC row. Even if the rest of the family merely wants to lounge around while Mr or Ms Executive wants to chase about venting nervous energy, it can be organized. I met a very successful family boatload on a Greek flotilla once. Father had always wanted to sail, son wanted to chat up girls, and daughters and wife wanted a bikini holiday with lots of tavernas. Greek flotilla sailing being extremely undemanding, they all got what they wanted: Cap'n Bligh happy as Larry, commanded the ship, while the rest of them lay around getting brown and ignoring the commands.

Nature's Masterpiece

If you have any of the outdoor urge (and I admit, some do not, and will be reading this section with shuddering loathing. Do yourself a favour. Pass on to the cultural section, will you?), you will find that it does a lot of good to family relationships if children can watch, and help, their parents struggling against the elements. We spent one Easter break with friends living for three days in horse-drawn caravans, huddling round fires of sticks in a bracing Norfolk gale, charring sausages and trying to remember which way to strap our stocky, wall-eyed mare into the shaft of the caravan for the next leg of the journey, up hill and down dale at 2 m.p.h. In the evenings we struggled with devilishly ingenious folding bunks, tucked up the under-sevens, and drank heavily to keep out the cold. Lots would be drawn last thing for who should squelch out to the meadow with a torch and check that the horse was still there. We never did manage to put up the fiendishly ingenious lavatory tent. All in all, it was a great success. As were the horrible Norfolk Broads cruiser in the sleet, the wherry aboard which we all started drinking at 9 a.m. and the potty got kicked over, and the canal boat with ice on the windows and two lost lock windlasses.

It is logical, I suppose. Children need to see their parents facing difficulties in new environments and solving problems, so that they learn what work and life is all about. If you run your own holiday – even if that just means reading the timetable and travelling independently – they see you grappling with problems (with luck, keeping your temper, too). Even in a twenty-mile seaside tailback in the car, your Dad is more likely to tell you rude jokes from his boyhood than he is on a bench at Heathrow airport. If you take a canal boat, or a horse caravan, or hire a dinghy, children have to join in and be useful: throwing ropes ashore, holding the reins. Children are naturally busy and purposeful; it makes no sense to reduce them to beggars and drones, wheedling more money for theme park rides, hanging about waiting for the next meal or – if old enough – making sheep's eyes at Spanish waiters. Active holidays, in short, build character.

I liked to tell myself this at 2 a.m. in that appalling caravan, when I wanted a drink of water and found that although my ear was conveniently wedged against the caravan sink, the foot pump was under my bunk, and the only way to it (without lifting the bunkboard and disturbing the rest) was to climb out over the shafts, on to the mud, heave myself up, wriggle into a narrow gap, crawl under the bunkboard and operate the pump by hand. When I got down there I remembered I had not put a glass under the tap. But it really built my character when I couldn't wriggle out without waking everyone. The children talk about it still. Also about the night in the tent when Rose kicked the stopper out of the communal double Li-lo, and we all sank to the cold stony ground together. And the time she fell off the canal boat . . .

Cultural trips Oh, all right. So you aren't an outdoor type, and the above accounts make you feel ill and tired before you even start. So stay in a hotel, or a villa, and go sightseeing. Before you swoon right away and say, 'Whaddya mean, sightseeing? With children? All they want is a theme park!' let me assure you hand on heart that I know, I know. What you do is to promise them a theme park and do the other bit first. As in 'visiting Paris on the way to Eurodisney'. Or 'popping out from Center Parcs to visit the Anglo-Saxon village museum'. Believe me, keep at the sightseeing and in the end they will thank you for it. Well, they won't, not in so many words; but you will see the results, in their lives, of having been exposed to interesting things early on.

You may, however, have a few small frustrations along the way. I must have been ten years old when my mother took me to see the treasures of Tutankhamen. We were coming home by ship from South Africa, and took the option of leaving it at the southern end of the Suez Canal and rejoining it in Port Said. I remember the Pyramids, and a Sphinx with no nose, and riding a camel called Monty. I remember our tour bus tearing through the desert towards the astonishing sight of our own ship apparently rolling through unbroken sands. I remember buying a riding whip with a plastic head of Nefertiti for a handle. I do not, however, remember anything whatsoever about the treasures of Tutankhamen.

Years later, when they came to the British Museum in London, I mentioned at home that I was vaguely thinking of popping in to see them once the queues got shorter. My mother exploded. 'You've seen them! I took you! In Egypt!' It was the age-old cry of the culturally frustrated parent: you can take a child to wonders, but you can't make it think. Or even look. Some families give up, and say that you might as well stick to theme parks and paddling pools for smaller children, and disco joints and windsurf-hire beaches for teenagers. Some dump the children all day in a French-style 'Club Mickey' and go off alone to look at pictures and buildings. Sightseeing with children, they aver, is a waste of time. Venice is off, until they leave home.

But is it? Despite my total amnesia concerning the boy Pharaoh's tomb, I have perfectly clear memories of Monty the camel (his breath smelt), the Sphinx, the sand, and the crowds of Cairo. Delving into memories from years before, when I was only four years old in Thailand, I could draw you a clear picture right now of the huge toes of the Sleeping Buddha. I am not sure I ever managed the long walk to its head. I seem to remember something about wet knickers. And from almost babyhood, I remember the petrified figures of Pompeii sleeping eternally amazed in their coats of lava, even though I spent barely an hour in that museum. As for the cave in Switzerland where Saint Nicholas of Flue fled his family to lead a hermit life, well, obscure it may be, but I remember that, too. Possibly it was impressed on my mind by certain acrimonious parental discussions about men who are never there when you need them, always sloping off to the office, or cave . . . Ah well.

The moral seems to be that it is worth taking children to see the sights, wherever you are, as long as you don't expect them to see what you see. A childhood travelling the world because of my father's job has, at least, taught me that. Children, and teenagers, do not carry around the same cultural baggage as adults; they have to be allowed their own vision. They don't think, 'Ooh! The Taj Mahal!' or 'Venice! How wonderful. What was it Ruskin said . . .?' They just go round corners and see things, and say, 'Oh, look!' Often they are actually looking in what we, who have read the guidebooks, regard as an inappropriate direction. Every parent knows the experience of taking a child to the zoo and finding it prefers the plastic frog-shaped wastepaper baskets to the real animals; we put up with that. So extend the same tolerance even when you have travelled hundreds of miles to introduce them to the marvels of civilization, and they end up mesmerized by a lizard on the castle wall.

You can manage, with superhuman effort, to prevent yourself from getting annoyed when a child stands before the finest stained-glass window in Europe and refuses to raise its eyes. You can tell yourself that children often spot far more interesting things, less obvious ones, and give the whole family a new perspective. They see a carved mouse on a knight's foot on a tomb, an unexpected eagle in a ruined mosaic floor, a gargoyle with its tongue out. So play along, and enjoy it. Forget the stained glass; they can get a postcard of that on the way out. The sure way of putting a child off travelling, and art, and civilization for life is to insist in a shrill hysterical tone that it take a proper look at the marble Madonna or whatever, because it's all been paid for with good money. You can promise (and deliver) more physical, childish or teenage satisfactions later in the day or the week; you can make a game of it, as one family does, by letting everyone choose a postcard at the entrance to an art gallery, and then dash off and find the original, and scribble down all they can about it.

However, as any sweating family fighting its way through the Acropolis in August can tell you, there are ground rules. Duck out of the big crowds. There are always back streets, byways, lesser sights which are equally characteristic of a new city and – to a child – different and impressive. If St Peter's Basilica is uncomfortably crowded, well, Rome has other wonderful churches. If the most famous and intricate of the Lycian rock tombs in southern Turkey seems to have six coaches at the foot of its steps, it is not far to a miraculously silent, equally ancient and atmospheric corner where there is a lesser tomb. Remember that if children are still shorter than adults, there is not much fun looking at anything through a forest of bottoms and dangling camcorders. Use bad weather, or early mornings, to see the big attractions.

Along the Turkish coast once, caught in some violent April rain, we took a bracing walk to a 2,000-year-old ruined amphitheatre in a hillside. Nobody else was there. The rain stopped. We sat on the tiers of seats while the children, still under five, ran around at the bottom. Old pantomime aficionados that they were, they rapidly worked out that this must be a theatre. Immediately they put on an impromptu production, lasting five minutes, and ending in a spirited rendering of, 'Wheel yer perambulator, John, wheel it nice and slow!' The acoustics worked beautifully, as they always had; I like to think that they got the point of amphitheatres that day, and got it rather better than they would have done on a guided tour.

With older children you can be more structured; but the trick, I fear, is to read the guidebook yourself before you go, mug up on all the history, and then keep quiet about it until the actual questions come. If someone looks at a castle and says, 'How old is that? Who built it?' it is nice to have an answer. But nothing is more deadening than the educational parent who never lets up.

As for museums, remember only that if you don't force them on children, antiquity and natural history fascinate quite naturally. A museum does not need to be a theme-parky, interactive 'experience', filled with novelty heritage waxworks or animatronic knights. These are all good fun as far as they go, but even the most conventional museums can thrill children who are relaxed and receptive (because their companions are). I once helped escort a school trip round the Natural History Museum in London – ten- and eleven-year-olds – and while they enjoyed the obvious show-stoppers like the interactive rooms and the giant blue whale, on the bus home they talked with equal affection about the enormous Victorian cases of stuffed hummingbirds, and some rather dry-looking but ancient fossils. A skeleton, of course, is always very welcome to all ages; and so is a relief map with tiny mountains, or any kind of stuffed furry animal.

It is worth persevering, through all the low moments, the whining for ice cream in the Uffizi and lavatories on the Rialto.

When things get desperate, dive for a cafe. When children whine, don't whine back. Uplift the atmosphere. Jump on a wall. Act childish and enthusiastic yourself. Anything which sticks, any wonder of the world, is a massive investment in their mental and spiritual future. We spend spare money on travel, always, rather than on dressing respectably or furnishing the house like grown-ups should, so we have taken the children to quite a few places. After journeys round Britain, through southern Turkey and Greece and a few jaunts elsewhere in Europe, I consulted them at ten and eleven as to their best memories. 'Center Parcs,' they said, and as my face fell, 'Oh, and lovely carved holes in Turkey where they used to put dead bodies, and Notre Dame in Paris, and the cafe in Greece with a roof made of leaves. And the log ride at Pleasurewood Hills Theme Park. And going up through clouds in the dark on the cable car to the Allmenalp. And landing on Orkney and finding the puppet workshop.' A mixed bag. I was content.

However, I also cherish the wise remark of a fellow journalist criticizing over-purposefulness on family holidays. It was important, she said, to remember that a vital part of holidays, for bigger children and adolescents, was lying upside down on a bunk bed while it rains outside, trying to follow the instructions in a dog-eared book of magic tricks. Don't try too hard . . .

Going on holiday with other families

This does not invalidate all the above family bonding; it can actually improve it, provided you are really friends and have roughly the same ideas about domestic squalor, money, bedtimes, discipline, and what constitutes bad language in the young. A modicum of family privacy for each set helps. So does a case or two of wine. However, two points: a) try it out on a weekend or two first, preferably under stressful conditions like a hire boat; b) make a firm pact that all parents are allowed to shout at all children, whether related or not, for any misbehaviour. Halfway down the case of wine, it becomes quite difficult to remember which of these children are yours anyway. If, that is, the holiday is going well.

Tribal gatherings

During the late years of the last Conservative government Britain was highly entertained by an enterprising reporter's group photograph of the Health Secretary, Virginia Bottomley, and forty-odd relations of all possible ages striding out across the Isle of Wight in chunky sweaters for their traditional Easter Monday all-weather tribal walk. They sang, if reports be accurate, Rolf Harris's 'Two Little Boys', then gathered around an old windmill while an uncle imparted heroism to a new generation – some of it still in baby buggies – by re-telling the stories of Captain Scott and the loss of the *Titanic*. These had, apparently, been told first at the time they were hot news, and ever since, each year, the Garnett clan assemble to tell them again. There was also some kind of ritual surrounding a fountain pen lost in 1918, but the family quite properly keeps the details to itself.

They got guyed for this excursion in certain public prints, with the words 'wholesome', 'clean', and 'Enid Blyton' being used in the authentic thin, sour tones of 1990s journalism as expressions of extreme disdain. But I think the clan Garnett/ Bottomley are on to something here. In an age when 'relationships' are more popular than relations, the rest of us might pick up a few useful post-modern tips from them. The event has been going on for nearly a century in the Garnett family, and is probably the best insurance the minister had of not turning into the kind of arrogant monster so many politicians make of themselves. Mrs Bottomley was the one accosted by the reporters, but their emphasis was clearly all wrong. Anyone who knows anything about large families will realize that it is most unlikely that she would have been the natural spokesman. Once sucked into a huge tribal gathering, she would revert to being someone's sister, someone's niece, just another listener in the respectful crowd round the uncle who for some mysterious family reason was top dog at the time and got to tell the stories. She was just another comparative junior, knowing her place.

One of the great merits of family gatherings is the way the pecking order imposed by the outside world (you Cabinet

Minister, me nonentity) counts for nothing once the family drawbridge is up. Cousins, still less siblings, are no respecters of persons. They know too much about your calf loves and acne. Taken in the right spirit, this is not only very good for the soul of the cabinet minister, film star or tycoon but provides reassurance for the rest of the family. There is nothing quite like an unimpressed auntie ('Rather a common skirt, dear, and you're looking pasty') to pull an international superstar down to size.

The second useful example set by the Garnett tribe is that they hold this event on a regular but unmomentous day. Big family gatherings get a bad name because most families only assemble en masse for funerals (sad, low-key, with the threat of a contentious will in the offing), weddings (where there is always a comparatively strange family present to inhibit everyone), or Christmas (where someone is fed up with cooking and the children are out of control). In our family we occasionally hold what is known as a Counting, after the Counting of the Family in Stella Gibbons' *Cold Comfort Farm*: 'We'm violent folk, we Starkadders. Some on us pushes others down wells. Others die o' drink or goes mad. Tes difficult to keep count on us, so once a year Grandmother she holds a gathering, and she counts us all to see how many on us 'as died in th' year.' My mother excels in the rôle of Aunt Ada Doom, and it is observable that these gatherings – ideally the four adult siblings, a cousin of our generation if available, partners and children and the odd terrified in-law or house guest – work best when they occur for no particular reason. They might be even better if built around an absurdity, like a wet picnic and a hunt for a 75-year-old fountain pen. The strain would be off.

But the main Garnett lesson was one of sheer scale. When people shrink away from the idea of a family gathering, they are not really thinking of great festivals like this. The really hellish family gatherings are the small claustrophobic ones, the kind where parents fuss over adult children through an endless Easter weekend, where social differences arise with new daughters-in-law, or one distant, depressing relation comes on a duty visit to a tight and nervy nuclear family. Avoid

335

these by all means, but foster instead the huge, momentous tribal rally. Every child has a right to have an Aunt Ada Doom smelling of mothballs and cursing in black; to hear antique feuds creaking back into life and being suppressed; to be told the terrible tale of Uncle Walter and to discover how strangely like him (or her) his cousins look. Multi-generation gatherings are the best history lesson that school can never provide. Never mind if they are not pure pleasure. Remember Amos in *Cold Comfort Farm*: 'He liked to have his kith about him. Although of course, he never said so, or cheered up when they were.' There are, however, one or two pointers for families which find themselves (usually by owning the largest room) the hosts of family gatherings:

Never compete It does not matter that your mother, or mother-in-law, always has four courses at Christmas dinner, homemade nibbles and everyone in their best dress. Do it your way, the way that you can cope with. Feed people what is reasonably easy, or what someone else in the family can help with. And smile, and lubricate everyone with drinks and jokes. I find paper streamers and cardboard balancing butterflies hurled all over a table distract people wonderfully from the non-matching cutlery and plates. A prevailing scrappiness of cooking and presentation can be driven right out of everyone's mind by the simple expedient of concluding the pudding course with those dreadful indoor fireworks, a succession of tipsily lit coloured mini-volcanoes culminating in the Giant Serpent which shoots out of its black tablet in the most obscene fashion. Britain seems to have banned these now, so we have to search abroad; but the reek of gunpowder will forever be associated in the various cousins' minds with Auntie Libby going a bit manic again.

Never apologize The point of coming together as an extended family is to see one another, and reminisce, and get a good look at how big the cousins have grown. If, for uncontrollable reasons, the barbecue food is a bit burnt or the plaster has come down from the ceiling two days before and made everything white, it does not matter. My mother, whose youth was colourfully well-travelled, always helpfully says, 'Imagine you are all in the ruins of Warsaw. This would be luxury.' So have low standards. Frankly, if any of the cousins are under seven, they will lower them anyway before you know where you are.

Be a UN peacekeeping force if you have to. Only don't be afraid to show the warring factions your heavy artillery. If someone threatens to ruin the gathering by dredging up some dreary family quarrel over religion, inheritance, or who stole whose toy train in 1952, raise your voice commandingly and say, 'I will not have ill-feeling over my table at Christmas/Easter/a family party. It is a bad example to the children. Peace and goodwill to all men. Thank you.' The trick is to take precisely the same tone with everyone, whether it is Great-Granny or the new toddler or your spouse or child. It works surprisingly well, provided you don't burst into tears.

Grow up Someone has to. The trouble with tribal gatherings is that siblings, when they meet thirty years later, always revert to the age of about six for a while. Big brothers start teasing, little sisters taking offence, mothers boss their grown daughters and fuss over sons who are forty-three, for heaven's sake. This is not a Freudian therapy session or a rebirthing process, it is a party. Unresolved family conflicts can damn well stay unresolved – unless you are prepared to whirl round and confront them with fearless openness, one-to-one in a corner of the kitchen, as in, 'Look, Nigel, I know I let your white mice die while you were away at boarding school but they would be dead now anyway, and you are a bishop now, so I think you ought to forgive me.'

The family year

The family year needs milestones, something on the calendar to look forward to. You can justify them by saying they represent cultural heritage, or religious faith, or you can just take them as a bit of fun, especially at the duller times of year. We have celebrated, in our time, not only all four birthdays and Christmas but New Year, Epiphany, Pancake Day, Easter, Harvest Supper, Hallowe'en, Guy Fawkes, May Day, St Nicholas's Day, and Pudding Thursday (a bit obscure that, but all you need do is eat Yorkshire pudding). Give me time and I shall devise ways of marking Shakespeare's birthday, Michaelmas, Midsummer's Eve, St Andrew's Day, St Patrick's Day (for the Scottish and Irish connection) and if any Americans should drop in I will include Thanksgiving and Groundhog Day with pleasure. On discovering that 14 April used to be celebrated as First Cuckoo Day, I seriously considered a Cuckoo cake, a Cuckoo race, a Cuckoo-imitating competition . . . anything. One Comic Relief charity day we organized a sponsored Filth-a-thon (get as filthy as you can in five minutes, mud and paint and flour provided, Polaroids taken) and to my slight horror I then found it considered to be an annual event. 'At next year's, we could have jam to smear on our hair as well . . .'

Celebrating does not have to be expensive: a paper flag or two to paint, a meal around the table, a game if you can. Some families make beautiful things, blow their own Easter eggs and paint gorgeous scenes on them, build their own flower garlands, crystallize violets and cook marvellous traditional dishes. Others, more like us, go for the broad sweep, and merely haul out the candlesticks, the paper butterflies and the fancy napkins, wind up the collection of tinplate toys to give a festive air, and haul in a couple of other families to have an egg hunt, or an Epiphany cake with a bean in it and paper crown for the beanfinder. Family and neighbourhood celebrations should be relaxed, and if you are so cack-fisted that relaxed equals shoddy (blown eggs cracked and mended with Sellotape), so what? Colour and celebration matter more than arts and crafts in this context. If you devise a family year that everyone likes, early on, you may find to your infinite, touched, sentimental joy that even huge hulking teenagers with safety pins in their noses and luminous hair will suddenly say, 'Hey, where's the wax Easter lamb? We always have it out!' Aaaah.

House guests and sleepovers

Oh, I do love a houseful. It is a marvellous excuse to let standards slip even further than usual. My happiest weekends at home have been spent with visiting families of six all laid out like sardines, head to tail in sleeping bags on a heap of cushions. It must be admitted that my husband does not feel quite the same about this matter, but if sufficiently lubricated, he gets by. Children loved it too. Lots and lots of people to play cricket with! Visiting babies to show off to! One or two suggestions, though, from bitter experience:

Respect children's territory In some households, it is customary for one child at least to be regularly ousted from their bedroom when visitors come, thus enabling the visitor to sleep in a choo-choo train bed, under posters of Jason Donovan and with a plentiful reading supply of *Star Trek* annuals by the bed. Fine. But if you happen to have the kind of child who feels passionately about territory, forget it. It is not worth risking the fuming atmosphere. To put the guest on a camp bed in the sitting room would be much, much better all round. Or move out of your own room, if you like. Sometimes, of course, children can be persuaded by various means to give up their rooms, but you run the risk of them glaring at the guest halfway through the weekend with, 'My Mummy had to pay me three pounds to let you have my bed.'

Sharing with visiting children or cousins they do not know is equally fraught. Whereas most children of all ages adore having their own friends share their room, alien children – perhaps with funny habits, like folding their clothes – can be worrying. They might snore. You could try persuading your reluctant sharer, but a better way is massive bribery of an imaginative nature. As in, 'It'll be like a party. When you wake up in the morning, if you creep downstairs together you'll find a special breakfast. But you'll have to look for it. There are rhyming clues all over the ground floor of the house.' Then you, and the visiting parents, get quietly pie-eyed and make up the

339

rhyming clues late at night. You can offer further inducements if the children are quiet enough not to wake you up.

Spoiling is OK It is a special occasion . . . One night, a visiting nine-year-old without parents present got so upset and wailing that I decided on extreme bribery. After trying repeatedly to calm him down, with the help of his big brother, I went in, switched on the light and said, 'Right. We can do two things. Either I can get dressed and drive you home to your mother, which is boring. Or you can shut up, not make another sound, and when you wake up in the morning there will be a mystery present on your pillow and everyone else's pillow' (one always has a stock of mystery presents, does one not? Surely!). Within ten minutes everyone was asleep, including me. What the child was upset about, or pretending to be upset about, we never found out, really.

Keep hospitality simple It is tempting to plunge into the world of homemade croissants and designer food, especially if long-lost friends or distant family have come on a rare visit. Don't. Unless your teenagers are old enough to make a lot of it. As the Bible almost says, better a dinner of herbs where love is than a stalled ox and a lot of histrionics about the gravy therewith.

Give single people space Friends with children, especially small children, are usually so grateful to have their entire family absorbed into your household for the weekend that they fall in happily with anything you are doing. Even going down to someone else's supermarket instead of your own is a pleasant holiday. But childless guests, it is easy to forget, can be over-whelmed by family life.

In a family, you become so accustomed to constant company of whatever age that you hardly notice it any more. What to you might seem a pleasant, good-tempered susurration of youthful chat could sound like a bloody awful racket to an ageing great-uncle or nervy career girl trying to brood about her latest man. As I am always pointing out how wonderful single friends are for families to have, how liberating and amusing and generally nice to know, it is worth putting some thought into not driving them crazy when they do come round. How you do it depends on your own habits, house and family timetable. But think about it.

Don't try to show off your perfect family This will only annoy everybody, those with families of their own and those without. Do not make children of any age perform unless they want to, whether their forte is the cello or tap-dancing. Do not mention the latest scintillating exam results, rosettes, cups or certificates. And however hard it is to be natural under the scrutiny of outsiders, try to act the way you normally would. Particularly with younger children, be yourself: shout where you would shout, cajole and cuddle where you would cajole and cuddle. Otherwise a strange, false, tense atmosphere will build up. Of course older children and teenagers have to learn the idea of 'company manners' and making outsiders feel comfortable. But even they should not be expected to change every single aspect of their behaviour for visitors. If it is that bad, perhaps they should be changing it full-time . . .

Money Matters

I wish I were Chancellor of the Exchequer. It would be so nice to have people listen respectfully to your budget speech:

'The past fiscal year has been a mixed one for the economy. On the one hand, considerable savings have been made in the area of Scalextric by this government's firm initiative in buying only the basic set.' *(Cries of 'Shame! Yah!')* 'On the other hand, the consumption of chocolate biscuits has risen out of control and requires firm fiscal management.' *(Catcalls, booing.)*

'On the clothing front, a blow was sustained by the simultaneous outgrowing of no fewer than five almost new pairs of trainers and football boots owing to rapid foot inflation. But in fairness, this additional burden has been partly offset by younger members' willingness – nay, determination – to spend every weekend in the same tracksuit bottoms which end two inches above the ankle and are full of rips.' *(Cries of 'Eeyah, eeyah, yah!')* 'The cat food situation is also under review *(miaow!)* following the calculation that two years' worth of the present brand would buy a week in the Seychelles. We have resolved on downgrading from Luxury Kittentreat to Bargain Gristlechunks.' *(Uproar in the House. Cries of 'Poor Tibbins!' 'It's made of dead shark, Mummy!!' and 'She'll get BSE!')* 'Furthermore, owing to severe losses, the supply of replacement Cub woggles and karate belts is to be privatized, and borne from pocket money rather than central funds. Pocket money itself is frozen' *(Cries of 'Shame! Resign!' Uproar, breaking of crockery)* 'and we are demanding co-operation from all members regarding excessive electricity consumption on landing lights. Moreover, a ceiling has been put on Scotch, gin, and other beverages of 1.4 litres per fortnight . . .'

And so on, until I sit down amid thunderous applause at five o'clock, having once more saved the domestic economy from ruin. All a lovely dream, of course. Like most families not in immediate trouble, we shall continue to muddle along, buying on impulse, saving the odd 2p on a special offer and immediately squandering £4.99 on the strength of it. Reason has little to do with family spending. If we have had a tough week at work we feel entitled to spoil ourselves or our children (it comes to almost the same thing when you are in a good family mood). If we sustain a rush of affection for our spouse, out comes the plastic card to prove it. When a tax bill comes in, we economize in a fit of panic and then cheer ourselves up with a meal out.

But a decent approach to family finance is, alas, vital to a decent family life. If you have a lot of money it is easier than if you are skint, but even the wealthiest families often fall out over money. It has an unfortunate way of becoming a symbol of other things which you don't talk about. Like sex. Or a particular child going through a crucifyingly annoying phase. Or grandparental interference in your life.

Who runs the money?

Whether you deal in large sums or small, high living or survival, whatever money there is has to be managed. And a family being a merged, corporate entity, it has to be managed quite differently from a carefree single's private loot. A London market researcher once remarked that whenever you do marketing surveys of couples and ask the question, 'Who handles the family finances?' the men will reply unhesitatingly, 'I do.' When the researcher asks the wife, in a separate room, the identical question, she too replies, 'Oh, I do.'

You could hardly get a better cautionary introduction to the whole minefield of financial aggravation, misunderstanding and plain comedy that lies ahead of every pair of idealistic newlyweds. Possibly the two partners mean something different by 'handle the finances'. Perhaps the man means that he fills out the annual tax return and that he was the one who originally made the appointment with the building society about the mortgage. Whereas the wife means that she gets landed with regularly checking, paying, and filing the bills. Or perhaps the husband is the one who fiddles around at the desk for hours, putting bills on spikes and calling his overdraft a 'cash flow shortfall', but the wife considers she 'handles the family finances' because she is the one who juggles the housekeeping from day to day and makes crucial executive decisions as to whether the children can have new trainers before the old ones are actually gaping at the toes.

Or perhaps the husband is right, and the family is run on old-fashioned lines whereby the wife never sees a bill or a bank statement, but is ceremonially handed the Housekeeping Money every week and applies humbly to him for more. Even such traditional men, however, can be the type to be attracted to large-scale finance and prefer to leave penny-pinching to the women. One wonderful story concerned a wife who said that her husband had spent three hours reassessing their finances on his new computer, surrounded by rapidly emptying cans of beer as he created spreadsheet after spreadsheet, pie-chart after pie chart, finally to emerge triumphantly at bedtime to announce that he had balanced the books and 'identified the areas of pressure', so that all that was needed was a 'downward readjustment' of 9.27 per cent on household spending and children's clothes. 'He seemed so genuinely pleased and proud of this idea,' she said sadly, 'that I hadn't the heart to hit him with the poker.' The father was clearly a victim of the disease which grips so many governments: the touching belief that if it looks right on paper, it is right.

But some accommodation between temperaments has to be reached. The days of the pretty little featherhead who doesn't trouble her head about money are over. Wives are educated, and equal, and have to take a partnership role even if they aren't earning significantly themselves. Practicality and pride, independence and co-operation have to live together. The phrases 'Mean swine!' and 'Extravagant cow!' have no place in harmonious family life. Organization is the key.

Early in marriage, it pays to decide very firmly how you are going to arrange your bank accounts and bills. No billing and cooing, no sentimentality, none of that stuff about endowing each other with worldly goods. These things do not go with

344

banking. Wise newlyweds compose themselves to gravity, stop making vague promises about giving each other the earth, and soberly consider the pitfalls of each system.

They might decide on the system where both pay their earnings into a joint account, and draw it as necessary. It sounds wonderful but in practice the word 'necessary' needs a bit of expanding upon. And besides, it immediately makes it impossible for either lovebird to give the other one a present without the bank statement unromantically revealing the price to both partners. It doesn't feel like a present anyway, if you have paid half of it yourself.

For another thing, it can get very depressing for the wife when she stops working to look after the children, either for a short time or a long one. A lot of women who stay at home end up feeling very guilty about every penny they take out of 'his' money for themselves. Despite an unremitting eighteen-hour day with toddlers, they hardly feel justified in buying a lipstick or a Mars bar because they aren't formally putting anything in. It is depressed feelings like this which led to the 1960's 'Wages for Housework' campaign. In a society which measures people by their earning power, having no salary can be lowering.

Curiously, there is evidence that when women are the only earners in the household, after a while they start developing traditional male patterns of meanness. One wrote in the *Guardian* that she had turned into an old-fashioned, mean and domineering 'husband' of the worst sort since her man had been out of work. She grudged him his large appetite, his extravagance with toilet paper and even (I love this bit) his political opinions – because she had paid for the newspaper which enabled him to have opinions at all.

Sometimes partners get round the danger of feeling this way by reverting to the old system of 'housekeeping money', generous enough for a proportion of it to be tacitly accepted as the non-earner's mad money out of which she can guiltlessly buy herself treats, and him presents. Direct debits and standing orders help, because the physical handing over of money depresses a previously independent spirit.

Then, of course, there is the other traditional, more working-class system in which the wage-earner gets home and hands over the whole lot to his wife (or, I suppose, her husband, though I know of no such cases. Women, I fear, are suspicious souls who stick to their own cash as long as they can). In this system, the wife then hands the breadwinner back some beer money, and manages the rest herself.

This can be a surprisingly cheerful arrangement. One man – a doctor, in fact, and quite a senior one – once told me that he was so disastrously bad with money that when his second child was born he gave up completely, and had his whole salary paid straight into his wife's bank account. She then handed him some pocket money every morning, and everything worked perfectly. He saved out of his pocket money to buy her presents, just as the children did. They kept one credit card of his, locked away in his wife's drawer, so that if he was travelling to a conference or on holiday he would not be embarrassed. The children, both being girls, find it exquisitely funny that they often have more cash than Daddy. My only worry about Daddy is that if he is ever widowed or divorced, he will be in exactly the same position as those dear little featherhead wives who have never seen a bill: middle-aged yet as clueless as a teenager.

If both partners are earning, and both keep their own bank accounts, you have to decide who pays what. Does he pay the mortgage, rates, and fuel while she pays food and holidays? Who gets the car serviced, the cat neutered? And is it fair to ask one partner to see all his salary dribble away on deeply boring bills, while the wife gets the satisfaction of signing cheques for fun and games and smart new sofas? One wife said to me that her money was to 'put jam on the bread' and that it nearly killed her to write a £200 cheque for new guttering once. 'Who could enjoy paying for a gutter?'

But haven't men a right to such delicate feelings too? Remember poor old Rumpole, in *Rumpole of the Bailey*, seeing his hard-won court fees 'recklessly expended on pan-scourers and Vim'? True equality means women getting used to paying for roofing felt and car insurance. Of course, you could choose to split every single bill down the middle, like fiercely independent cohabiting couples; but that way you end up with complicated and deeply unromantic sessions late at night working out whether the gas bill and the TV licence add up to roughly the same as the telephone bill and the bulk consignment of vacuum cleaner bags. Life is too short for such self-inflicted miseries.

On the whole, I favour the increasingly common system of a joint account which is fed, in varying proportions, by two private ones. The joint account pays the house bills and standing orders; the private accounts, however small, remain strictly private. Psychologically, the best thing about this system is that once you have paid your standing order into the joint account, it doesn't feel like your own money any more – it is gone, and that is that. So in a mysterious way all the household bills become 'free'.

In a rather less mysterious way, of course, the joint account invariably becomes overdrawn. But every scheme has its snags and it is not only governments who deal in imaginary money. But even if the joint account system is problematical, the advantage here is that each one's private account can mount up or run down, for richer for poorer, according to its owner's temperament; £12.72 of your very own to squander is worth a hundred in the joint account any day. Everyone needs a holiday from pinching pennies.

Pester power

Whatever your income, someone is after it. And one of their favourite weapons is your children. Marketeers and advertisers are now aiming campaigns directly and deliberately to harness 'pester power'. Not just for toys; for household commodities, foods, even pet foods.

You have to be aware of this, and make a decision about how far you are going to allow children to make such choices. My own view is that if you are going to do it, make them work for it. Make them cost out the different cereals, work out the difference, decide whether the extra 70p for Oat 'n' Honey is worth it, how much difference it would make over the year,

347

and what else you might do with that £44. Go to the cinema and have a burger? Put it towards a new bike? Take taxis instead of the bus when the shopping is heavy?

As for nonsense like fancy pet food, make them write to the manufacturer to ask more about what makes it different. Or buy one can, and try it out in a blind test on the dog. Whatever you do bring intelligence into play: where intelligence flowers the power of advertising withers. Expose rackets: show them pictures in the business section of the wealthy men and pretentious designers who are raking in your hard-earned money and spending it on persuading you to spend even more.

This applies even more when the pestering is for something the child itself wants. Even four-year-olds have been known to pester for the right designer labels; it is nothing unusual for parents to spend £80 on a pair of trainers for a child whose feet are still growing two sizes a year. Parents in a recent survey admitted to running up debts to buy these things, pleading the 'guilt' of being a working mother, or a single parent. I bite my tongue. It would be unhelpful to remark that anyone who is that much of a wimp has no business taking responsibility for a child at all. Perish the thought.

But here is a great truth: you do not *have* to let your children turn into mindless, grasping, boring little consumers. A baby is not born with the word 'Reebok' stamped on its heart. It wants colour and movement and interest, not labels. The things which turn children into grasping beasts are a) television and b) peer pressure. The cure for a) is to stop television becoming the centre of their lives. Encourage them to criticize it, analyse the commercials and why they are appealing, make up their own advertisements and take the mickey out of them. Offer alternatives: read books with them, travel, talk, dig a hole in the garden, build a card house. The only reason adolescent children get addicted to television is that their lives are so narrow otherwise. And any parent who can afford £170 for a designer jacket can afford books, theatres, a trip up a mountain or on a canal. The credit card is the lazy way out.

As for b), peer pressure is indeed painful, but children who suffer from it most are those who feel insecure anyway, either through home troubles or through being nagged too much. They can't buy friends anyway, poor little rats. The popular child in a class is very, very rarely the one with the newest tracksuit or most expensive fancy pen. It is the most alert, happy and confident one.

Be honest about the family budget; show it to them as they get older. Give teenagers – even bright eleven-year-olds – a clothes allowance to cover non-essentials like fancy T-shirts, and make them stick to it. As they get older, encourage paper rounds and babysitting; offer to give up having a cleaner and pay the children instead for the same standard of work. Bring children gently into the real world of financial decisions.

Supporting the family

Dealing with adult feelings about money is a lot trickier. If one partner is single-handedly supporting the family, or merely earning much more, it should be made clear – out loud and as often as necessary – that they are happy, indeed honoured, to be doing so. Also that neither of you values the other, as the world does, according to bank balance; and that everyone understands that there are other kinds of contribution to the world's wellbeing than the kinds which attract a salary.

It is easier to think this way once you have children, because a baby has no bank balance at all and yet is the most precious person in the house. Children, fond though they get of money at certain phases, still instinctively value people for themselves, not their wealth or success. Call it a sentimental truism, but that attitude is the only thing which is going to get you through if – heaven forbid – you come to the crunch.

The crunch

With the recession of the early nineties, that Victorian spectre, Ruin, returned to haunt the modern First World, and has not gone away yet. Probably, in the new age of short contracts, downsizing and freelance distance working, it never really will.

349

How families cope with financial disaster is a subject we could all usefully study. It could be you, or me.

There was a time when children's books were wonderful on the subject of financial ruin. Remember those bright, brave E. Nesbit mothers, like the one in *The Railway Children*? 'Now, my chickabiddies, we're going to have to play at being poor!' Remember how she gently broke the news that from now on it is 'Butter or jam, not both', while Daddy languished in prison over an obscure business injustice? Or think of *The Wouldbegoods*, the five Bastable children with their adventurous ploys for restoring their ruined father's fortunes. Or Sara Crewe in Frances Hodgson Burnett's *A Little Princess*, starving in her attic bedroom when her father's diamond mines went bust. Oh yes, those late Victorian children's authors knew how to twist the financial knife all right. But their characters were always troupers, and bankruptcy was just another big family adventure, the ultimate challenge to industry and optimism.

Yet money troubles probably break up as many families as sexual difficulties. The crisis is made worse in a property-owning, mortgage-owing society because the physical symbol of your family, the home itself, is so immediately at risk when the crunch comes; and a change of home may mean a change of school and neighbourhood, a loss of friends, and a stressful isolation of the beleaguered family.

So how is it, when families face the Crunch? How do relationships adjust to it? Do marriages break down? The evidence of the last recession suggests that they do; although often only into those curious armed truces in which couples stay under the same roof because they can't sell. But marriages which break down under financial disaster are in a way the least interesting. What has long fascinated me is the way in which they manage to survive, and even flourish, in the ways which ultimately matter.

A familiar pattern is that the man, previously the breadwinner, collapses temporarily with guilt and horror while the wife takes over leadership and eases the immediate cashflow situation by doing part-time, humble jobs. But this in turn, adds to the man's humiliation and rage. The stress redoubles while he is out of work unless he has the flexibility and good humour to take over the domestic and parenting side of family life, and the sense to see how valuable his new role is.

One of the keys to handing the situation seems to be to avoid any form of retrospective reproach. Be willing to start from where you are. Another is to have a network of friends who remain steadfast. Another is not to have depended previously on your income for your whole family identity. One woman who lost everything said to me, 'You must not ever, ever, put too high a value on what you are losing. I cried over my big garden and the friends I couldn't afford to live near any more. But I could always see the wood for the trees. You have to think of money as rain: sometimes it showers down on you, sometimes it doesn't. It's nothing personal. You are the same person, it is the same marriage. I always knew that in the end we'd still be a family.'

Another principle seems to be that the younger the children, the less they actually mind. One pair said to their parents as soon as they heard the house was to go, 'Are you going to divorce?' They had enough friends, at six and eight, to know that these things happened. The moment they were assured that the family would stay together, even if it was in a tent, they were happy and co-operative and creative about it. But another apparently united family, with teenagers, found that a sudden drop in income hit their family life harder than they had expected.

'They were thirteen and fifteen,' says their mother. 'Still dependent financially, but wanting to feel independent. I never realized how much of their self-respect was paid for with money, and I deeply regret having let that happen. Emma had a horse, you see, and won cups at the Pony Club. John had a racing dinghy. The most painful scenes were about those things because, although we financed them, they did belong to the children. They represented their greatest talents and greatest joys, and their common interests with their friends.'

Horse and boat both had to go when the family moved to a small flat. Erica told the children that they could sell them and keep the money: 'But that rankled with me. I was keeping us all

351

on fifty-two pounds a week and taking in typing, and they suddenly got these windfalls of over one thousand pounds each. I resented it. The kids were so wrapped up in their own misfortunes they never suggested helping me at all.' Her mistake, she now says, was never having noticed that their interests were entirely dependent on expensive equipment. 'You just don't realize how much of modern social life and happiness hangs on money. A car, a boat, a caravan . . . all toys, but without them we snap.'

Perhaps that is the moral. You can cope with a financial crunch provided you have not let money too far into your life in the first place. And provided that one of you has not valued him or herself entirely in terms of what money they bring in. Several of the families I talked to, the Nouveau Ruined, were remarkably happy, giggly and full of jokes about their plight. It would seem that there are temperaments and relationships which will always float above crisis, and perhaps we should all be working on developing that elusive, airy, bubble quality. As the saying goes, sit loose to comfort, and the fall hurts less.

Dual Careers

This is a new world. Women have advanced in rights and confidence until there is virtually no job we cannot be considered for. Like it or not, the old notion of a male breadwinner and a supportive woman at home is all but gone. Every now and then journalists excitedly announce that it is back, and that the New Housewife is the vogue for the future, but they are whistling in the dark. Except in cases of exceptional affluence and security, the modern uncertainty of work makes it downright imprudent for a family to think it can rely on just one job until the children leave home. Dual career families are here to stay.

But the first flush of women's professional triumphalism really has passed away. The truly ridiculous stress under which many families place themselves is plainly as great an evil as female subservience ever was, and does even more harm to children. Both men and women need to accept that paid work is to be considered as part of the family picture. Once you have children, it is folly to think that you can both go on dedicating yourself wholly to your careers, and just let the family dangle off you any old how. Where there are two ambitious individuals and a set of dependent ones, something is going to have to give. It is not fair to expect the children to make all the sacrifices.

Of course you need money. Home life has got to be paid for, somehow, so unless you have no choice but to live on ever more meagre state benefits, at least one of you is going to need to work. For some of the time, both of you are. Our generation has painted itself into a corner with absurd housing costs, consumer goods seen as essentials and a spiral of personal credit, so that for a great many families there is no option but for both parents to earn, if they can.

And besides, work is satisfying. It links you to the outside world, gives you a place beyond the family circle and a useful wider perspective. You can return to a cross, fed-up child who temporarily hates school with more real understanding if you have spent your own day getting fed up with your colleagues and boss. And working parents are a constant reminder to a child or teenager that the virtues of punctuality, conscientious-ness, and turning up to work even when you don't feel like it are not tiresome abstract disciplines or futile things urged on schoolchildren to torment them. They are the way adult human beings get to earn their daily bread, and put jam on it.

Working mothers still tend to take the brunt of the guilt and ambiguity of the situation. The guilt is pointless – if you feel that guilty, don't work. If you have no choice but to work, then why feel guilty? Come home smiling, and as early as humanly possible. Make the weekends and evenings really good for everyone, even if it means skimping the housework and cook-ing (and it does, it does). And don't patronize or criticize your sisters who don't work outside the home for being 'house-wives'; different systems suit different people, and all children are different in their susceptibilities and how happy they can be with nurseries or nannies. There are happy families in both camps, and bloody miserable ones too.

But one word of warning: it is absolutely essential to talk out any conflict between fathers and mothers about dual careers. A working mother can be undermined, fatally, by the spoken or unspoken criticism of her husband. So can a stay-at-home mother. Good humour, kindness, and mutual support are essential in both cases. If you really can't agree, then debate it properly and openly, preferably over a café table and without the children present.

In the early years, oddly enough, two-career families are easier to maintain. Babies who cannot speak cannot complain, and toddlers do not have enough experience of the world to know that there is an alternative to the way things are with their childminder or au pair. As children get older, the problem changes. They make their own breakfast, may pack their own sandwiches; they are at school until quite late, they can travel

354

home alone and come in with their own keys, and they have decided views of their own about what to do in the holidays. But they still need you, and in some ways it is harder to fit in their needs. The older a child gets, the more unpredictable are the moments when he or she wants to talk things over. Sometimes the mothers who behave most callously in their children's teens are those who stayed home when their children were tiny. Having always felt a bit uneasy about leaving the children, working mothers continue to come home from the office wanting to work on their relationship, well into the teen years. I have met several mothers who stayed at home faithfully until their children were eight or nine, and then took up a career again with an ambitious passion which almost wiped out their family life. The subtext here was, 'Look, I gave you a decade of my life. Now push off and leave me alone.' The children didn't think much of that.

The great challenge for a woman – and also for a man, though fewer realize it – is to balance that ambitious working passion with the emotional needs of family life. It is not an impossible balance to find, but it is a tricky one. There has been a post-feminist backlash recently against that monster of myth, the hard-eyed, shoulder-padded 'Career Mum'. Dewy-eyed novels have appeared, starring women who decide to leave the bitter, combative boardroom world to stay at home with their babies. They usually set up cosy little Aga-centred businesses at home which threaten to become huge and drag them back into the stock market.

What irritates me about all this is the posing, the all-or-nothing approach which suggests that a woman is either a hard bitch in smart suits with a briefcase, or a lovely Mummy in soft heathery cardigans who arranges dried flowers. There is never any suggestion that it is possible to make both corporate decisions and apple pies; no space for women who run businesses but have crooked hems, or dare to own both Agas and briefcases.

Doing justice to children and a career is not easy; but then, nor is it easy to mix a job with a passion for local politics, or ocean-racing, as men have done for ages. Adult mothers apply the same intelligence to their life as to their job. Any fool can see that small children will not thrive if they never know when they will see their mother again; any fool can see the drawbacks of trying to combine parenthood with jobs without boundaries, the kind which suck you in, hype you up, and render you unfit for any but colleagues' company. One of the most nauseating complaints of the age is that the high-flying career woman is somehow 'a victim'. She does not have to be. Trapped, under-paid workers must suffer silently as they struggle home by public transport to the childminder; executive women, and men, ought to use their money and clout to reorganize the schedule and hurry home.

And they do, in real life. A BBC news producer tells the story of meeting Harriet Harman, MP, on the train away from the Labour conference at Brighton the day before the big speeches. It turned out that both women were dashing home – Ms Harman for a school function, the producer to treat her three children with headlouse shampoo. They were both back in politics by dawn. Another woman, a senior manager in a large company, celebrated her pregnancy by going to the MD with the information that she had done an analysis of the depart-ment's work, and that he had three-quarters of a job vacancy, just below her level. She offered to swap her full-time job for it, three and a half days a week. He agreed. The undramatic truth is that women who value their family life often make the decision to give up time, money, and status; but not necessarily all of it.

All we need now is for more men to recognize the same truths and make the same compromises.

Ways off the treadmill

Working at home When employers are inflexible, some parents go ingeniously independent. During the peak years of the Thatcher government, cocktail guests at No. 10 Downing Street were often fed by a small, determined catering firm consisting of two women from Suffolk with seven children under ten between them. In the cartoon universe of female stereotypes, this would have blown up into a million-pound business, with its directors wearing power blouses and neglecting their children and husbands. As it is, they continued to turn up at the school gates looking faintly dishevelled, but triumphant, even after their biggest functions.

A lot of us take the option of working at home. Or, as we like to say, *'from* home'. Sales reps can do this (a good few men do, successfully, and mind their children for part-time working wives as well). Journalists can do it, so can teleworkers, illustrators, copy-editors, dressmakers, knitters, craftspeople and caterers.

It can be terrific. Instead of travelling to work you shamble into the spare bedroom, or the kitchen, possibly still in your dressing gown, and there you are. At work. If children are home sick from school, you can let them read, or lie around in your work room, grumbling softly and being chucked the occasional sandwich. Even the smallest children can be trained not to pick up the telephone when it rings, and not to interrupt you while you are on it. Even the most inconsiderate teenager can be persuaded that if he steals all your paper and envelopes, your wrath will be so great it isn't worth it.

You soon learn such basic skills as conducting a professional conversation while a sharp-clawed kitten climbs up your trousers, ignoring the mound of washing-up until evening, putting up shelves which don't crash down on your computer, and recognizing the distinctive footsteps of a Jehovah's Witness or a time-wasting neighbour on the front path in time to dive under the desk. Your full-time housewife friends and assorted relations also get into the habit of asking whether it is a good moment to ring/call/deliver the parish newsletter/flop at your kitchen table with the gory details of their operation. Working at home saves money and fossil fuel, and is generally a green and sensible way to operate.

But beware. I have been a homeworker for eighteen years, with odd days in various offices, and many is the morning when I would give anything to go to a chummy office instead of a chilly, messy, lonely little room. I yearn for a cup of canteen coffee and an update on the temp's love life, but what I get is a

357

blank screen and a telephone. In primary school days I looked forward keenly to ten minutes' company at the school gates every afternoon, and the worst day of my life was when we got our own fax machine. I used to go to the post office and have a little chat and it was the highlight of my day. Now I can fax off the screen and don't even get to go downstairs.

Down the ages, writers have complained about the loneliness of their craft; telecommuting will extend that isolation to other workers. Nobody prone to loneliness, no newly separated woman with her children growing independent, should attempt it. There are times when we need an office the way that debs need dances. The absence of a visible, fussing boss may seem like a bonus (and indeed, on a sunny spring morning it is a great privilege to go for a bike ride or a swim, knowing you can make up the time). But a homeworker needs to be her or his own fussy boss: you require iron discipline, what with the biscuits and the coffee and the children's computer games so close at hand. Many people frankly fall apart. They straighten paperclips, they make tea, they read the old newspapers in the cat-litter tray and decide to turn out the kitchen drawers.

If both partners start to work at home, they may discover that their marriage actually thrived on separations and reunions and gossip from the outside world. Young mothers can go weepy and depressed when they look out of the study window and see an *au pair* playing in the sun with their baby while they are trying to revise the sales figures. And some of us are fatally untidy. My study, without the discipline of a fierce secretary or ruthless office cleaner, is a nightmare of torn-up paper, scribbled notes, tottering bookshelves, unanswered letters and obsolete tangles of cable. I dress like a tramp. If I were a factory, the council would close me down. Consider your strengths and weaknesses before you take the plunge.

Part-time work and jobshares Logistically these are the ideal solution for working mothers. But ambitious, talented women ought to consider, however briefly, the emotional implications. In many professions, part-time work attracts little respect. Nor do jobshares. If you really are a high-flyer, undamped by maternal hormones, a little work can feel worse than none. You have perforce to take instructions from people who are less talented, but lack your home responsibilities. You can get frustrated and morose.

At worst, you might take it out on the children, and even if this only happens in your secret thoughts it is a very depressing thing to do. I used to have a colleague who would smash up breadsticks savagely in Fleet Street restaurants and tell anyone who would listen that 'if it hadn't been for the blasted, blasted children I would have been an editor by now . . .'

This is not constructive. If you are going to compromise because your family is of high value to you, and at a phase when they need you, then recognize that you are doing it. Weigh the demands of duty against those of personal fulfilment. Get it all out in the open. And be prepared to modify your decision, in either direction, if it clearly isn't working.

Balancing two careers

If a married couple both work, and intend to go on living together, there has to be some kind of agreement on whose career matters most at any given moment. The crunch point may be a big one, like relocation to the other side of Europe, or it may be a small one, like who is going to be late for work in order to go home and fetch the cello your son forgot to take in on orchestra day. Women are better at subordinating the importance of their careers (though they sometimes grow bitter, later on). Most men find it very painful and embarrassing to play second fiddle to a wife.

That does not mean that they should never do so; but the wife concerned should exercise tact and chivalry about the matter. It is astonishing how obtuse women can be about this; perhaps it is a hangover from those centuries of being sidelined, but they sometimes say the most astonishingly dismissive and contemptuous things about husbands who fly lower than they do. It should go without saying that if a wife's high-flying career has disrupted the family and called for sacrifices of time and convenience from her husband, she automatically forfeits all right to suggest – ever – that he is not pulling his financial weight. Family men are rarely allowed, these days, to be autocratic because they are breadwinners. Women shouldn't try it on either.

Work colleagues

One of the great advantages of women having invaded the workplace in greater numbers is that, at last, our sex is getting to understand the joys of relationships with colleagues. This should ideally make us less mean and suspicious about our husbands' working friendships. There are real loves, hates, tendernesses and comradeships in office life – and real betrayals, too. People do not stop being human just because they are at work. You can't shut them away from nine to five and expect them not to have emotions during that time. So even the most cool and professional people will develop friendships at work even if they don't see those people outside.

What both adult partners in a family have to understand is that this does not necessarily mean an affair. A man who gets home and begins every sentence with 'Lucinda says', and a woman who becomes devoted to a male ally at work are not necessarily on the point of wrecking their homes. I knew a pair of friends once who worked in a broadcast news department. Whenever they were on the same shift, an electric current flowed. They loved one another's minds, shared flair and ideas, and fought internal battles side by side. At the office party, a no-spouses function by long tradition, they danced like dervishes and hugged like children. Her husband didn't like it one bit, and nor did his girlfriend. There was no affair, but almost as much trouble as if there had been.

How do you handle this? If you are both out in the unisex working world, these intense extra-marital friendships are bound to happen. Probably the best cure is to seize the bull by the horns and move the friendship into the family where it is less threatening. Have Sunday lunches all together. Mix partner and colleague socially. Make both sides accept the other relationship. You don't have to let your friendships with the rest

360

of the human race be limited just because you have a family; but nor is it worth risking a good marriage for a racy infatuation. Don't live in two worlds; one will suffer, and it will probably be the one where your children live.

Success, excuses, cop-outs

One of the rarely discussed aspects of family life is how useful it is as an excuse. Anyone who has had children would probably confess to having used them as a cop-out. 'We'd love to come barn-dancing, but we can't get a babysitter . . . Of course, we'd love to help, but with three children . . . Well, we don't see enough of the dear old lady, but of course, you see, Justin gets car sick . . .' Sometimes the excuses are genuine, sometimes they are not. We take children's names in vain because we do not want to do things anyway. Mine stand round jeering in the kitchen when they hear me say soupily to some editor, 'Oh goodness. I'd love to do a feature about a lesbian folk-dancing group in Newcastle, but I'm a bit tied up, you see, with the children . . .'

This is all quite harmless, and using children as excuses serves to reinforce the perfectly healthy world view that personal relationships are more important than notches on one's Filofax. But the child-as-excuse becomes more insidious when we begin to say, 'Look, I'm a working mother, I don't have time to dress up like a supermodel.' (Translation: I don't fit into the clothes any more.) Or 'Since the children, I simply can't keep up with the newspapers.' (Translation: I only read the features pages because thinking about the Euro gives me a headache.)

So far so good; but this can lead on to another refinement. We all know women who would have been the world's greatest brain surgeon if it hadn't been for their noble dedication to 'the children'. In the late sixties there was a rash of novels about a figure known as the Captive Graduate Wife. This was inevitably a brilliant girl with so little sense that she married young, started breeding, and only then twigged that someone was going to have to look after these children. This can end in real bitterness, as witness the number of thin-lipped, railing middle-aged women genuinely convinced that they have wrecked their lives for their ungrateful offspring.

It will not do. Most human beings are not straightforward creatures who see what they want and go for it. Most of us are a walking web of indecision, held back by laziness, self-doubt and fear of failing. If there is a handy way to convince ourselves that we are actually being held back by saintliness, it feels much better. But intense family dependence is – though precious – fairly brief. If you really were going to be a world-class novelist, you would be writing that novel now. On the kitchen table. If you don't want to – fine, but don't blame the children. Or husband. Or wife. Men don't do it so much; I have yet to read a failed politician's memoirs in which he blamed his lack of lustre and power on the fact that his daughter was doing O-levels and the baby kept him awake at night.

Confidence

Women who leave the workplace when their children are young and try to return later have a notoriously hard time, and much of it is because of their own feelings. Jill Freud, wife of the MP and boss of her own theatre company, once told me that when she first tried to plunge back into the professional theatre in her forties after five children, the worst bit was to face auditions and realize that for the first time in years you were not particularly important to anyone in the room. After being the heart of the family, the indispensable Mum, it is hard to go back into the ranks.

The same effect can hit younger women, too. I am constantly amazed by the shiny, brittle, snappy confidence of professional young women I know without children. Although I have stayed a semi-detached part of the working world, I still have far more lapses of professional confidence as a mother than I ever did as a childless woman. It has something to do with the great vulnerability of mothers. You know, from the first time your baby stirs, that you have given a hostage to fortune. You know that one disaster – losing that child – could devastate you. You imagine it, all through babyhood, childhood, early

362

independence. There is a pit at your feet always, which the shiny singletons do not see. Your emotions are more widely diffused across the world: you cry in news bulletins for the sadness of the world's children. Sometimes that sense of a pit can extend itself into your working life, so that you feel uneasy, hesitant, unable to 'go for it' in the gung-ho way you might have done before.

But you pull yourself together, grit your teeth, and do it all the same. You hope that on balance you have gained more from motherhood than you have lost: the ability to sing some new notes, to understand a little more of the marvellous strangeness of life, to love the human race a little more. And, with luck, to carry that gentler vision out into the working world, and change some of its ways.

Home

Back in the 1950s when I was growing up, every women's magazine had a story about a happy housewife. It was probably reaction against the war years, when many women had to work in factories or in the services, and live in barracks or land-girl huts wondering whether their men would ever come home again. The stories were a deliberate titillation of the nesting instinct, a pornography of homemaking: 'Laura sang happily as she whisked around her gay, neat little kitchen, enjoying the sunlight on the cheerful red curtains, and lovingly arranging her spick and span new plates on the dresser she and Ronnie had chosen together . . .'

Laura was perfectly happy at home, like Mrs Tittlemouse, although to give the story a bit of drama she would have a problem – worrying about Ronnie seeming a bit distant, or whether she had spent too much on loose covers. This was always resolved, not by going out for a walk together or on holiday, but firmly within the wee bower itself. An embrace concluded the story, with a bit more stuff about the 'bright modern wallpaper' framing Ronnie's manly head, or the cheerful brass fender winking merrily at their happiness.

The result of being raised on this stuff was, for me, an abiding sense of guilt at not feeling quite as keen as Laura on my little nest. I can do the bit with the bright curtains and winking brass for a little while, but the shine goes off it if I think I can't get out. Straw-polling amongst friends of all ages reveals a remarkable number of women, career as well as homebodies, who find the domestic interior less than totally thrilling. At one stage I used to spend the odd summer night sleeping in a shed on wheels in the garden, an old shepherd's lambing hut. It was a kind of very short camping holiday, with a bare bunk and a candlestick. I would wake in the morning to a different world, with birds twittering instead of the boiler humming, and pad barefoot across the wet grass to the kitchen with considerable reluctance.

Indeed, sometimes there is nothing more claustrophobic than one's own family home. Wherever you look there is something to be done. Curtains to hem. Letters to answer. Odd socks to rescue. Niffy trainers lying around. Phone messages to respond to. Complicated forms from the school. Cats to feed. People's precious stamp collections being chewed up by an escaped hamster behind the sofa. The sink-tidy overflowing with old teabags. Pictures you meant to hang eighteen months ago. There is barely any room in the house which does not carry its quota of accusing clutter, and on those summer mornings it took iron self-control not to turn 180 degrees and flee back to the nice bare little hut. You can see why people get so keen on youth hostelling.

Clutter

Clutter is a terrible domestic enemy. If you hate waste, and are always thinking things will come in handy, you will have kitchen drawers full of half-finished glue, ping-pong balls, cardboard photograph frames, clever machines for piercing the ends of eggs, boxes of clothes that you mean to take to the jumble, outgrown single shoes it would be a crime to throw away, pottery badges of villainous design, etc. If you are sentimental you will never throw away any artefact the children bring home from nursery school, and some of these are large, awkwardly shaped and, after five years or so, really rather pointless. The eggbox duck on the fridge is acceptable; the shoebox made into a combine harvester with rather sucked-looking straws sticking out of it is, after a while, rubbish. Familiar and beloved rubbish, but nonetheless junk.

If you are maternal, you will keep all your old baby clothes just in case. If you are family-minded, you will keep horrid great bin bags full of toddler clothes until your sister-in-law's baby gets big enough to have them forced on to its mother, willing or not. I know one woman who bombarded her sister-

in-law with so many foul old clothes that in the end the victim
took desperate action and stuffed a pouffe with them. One day
that pouffe will explode at the seams during a family gathering,
acrylic dungarees will spill everywhere, and there will be a
very, very painful scene. Finally, if you are one of those women
who is always changing size, like me, then you will have
dreadful hampers and cupboards full of outmoded clothes
which might a) fit you again one day and b) come back into
fashion. The year that I lose two stone and psychedelic loon
pants come back into fashion, I shall be ready.

Some clutter is just a symptom of healthy, varied, relaxed
family life. Nothing is more chilling than an utterly tidy house
when you know that children live in it. They are generally TV
addicts (a few parents positively encourage computer games
because they make no mess. Creepy, I call it). But clutter can
become a menace and an oppression, and the bigger your
house is, the worse this clutter problem will be. Inhabitants
of small houses do, in the end, find that common sense prevails
over sentiment and miserliness, and get on the phone to a skip
hire firm. But a big house swallows everything until like all
indiscriminate gluttons it starts to feel unhealthy, blemished
and depressing.

There are two ways that whichever parent is Head of Tidiness can approach the problem. Either she (he) enlists the full
help and co-operation of every single family member in select-
ing what will be thrown out; or she (he) does it all in deadly
secret while they are away. If you take the latter, ruthless
course, you have to steel yourself to ignore all agonized cries
of 'Where's my broken bit of toy tractor I use to prop up the
corner of my fort?' and 'My old camouflage jacket! I love that
jacket! It must have been stolen!'

You must be consistent. Nothing brings out accusations of
favouritism like throwing away one child's sacred cardboard
box while sparing the other's collection of dead starfish, or
tearing up a ten-year-old's beloved tracksuit trousers (worn
well above the anklebone after two years) when you haven't
the nerve to do the same to his teenage brother's repulsive
tattered Verve T-shirt. And if Father's golf clubs are allowed to

366

live in the lobby, and Mummy's exercise bike blocks the landing, why must Jimmy's equally cherished cricket bat be hurled
into the toy cupboard?

Clutter, like layers of fond memory and photo albums, is part
of healthy family life. But it can choke it, too, and stop you
thinking freely or accepting change in your children or your-
selves. So do the reasonable minimum, remembering that
affection, sympathy and a good joke take priority over tidiness
any day. A family is not a training exercise or a challenge in
time management; if the floors can be Hoovered, bicycles and
cricket bats are under cover at dusk, dirty clothes are in the
dirty-basket and clean ones claimed from the ironing board and
put away, that is enough to get on with. Once a year, or once
per holidays, you can give everyone a set of plastic boxes for
what they want to keep, and cardboard boxes for junk, and
refuse to let anybody go out until their area is clear.

Moving house

This is, next to a major fire, quite the best way to get rid of
clutter. Once we have seen it all in cardboard boxes out in the
merciless light of day, even the worst of us squirrels are happy
to abandon some of it for ever.

But moving house once you have a family is also a severe jolt.
Single, or as a bachelor couple without children, one seems able
to indulge a moment's sentimental retrospective and then
blithely move on, with little to fret about beyond rising damp,
builders, wall coverings and kitchen fittings. Parenthood
changes all that. If you don't believe me yet, just you wait
until you have to leave the house where you brought home
your first baby, stumbled through those sleepless nights, hung
up a bouncing carrycot, saw those fat legs make their first steps
and those big eyes fall on their first Christmas tree. Just you
wait until you find yourself thinking that selling this, marketing it, being persuasive with agents and buyers, is almost a
pornographic activity. It feels like putting your daughter on the
streets. You are pushing something from the very private side
of life out into the public, financial domain. The house agent's

brochure seems like lipstick on the whore; the contract of sale like a betrayal. Houses with children in become precious far more rapidly than houses with only adults.

And wait until you take the last walk round when the removal men have gone, and find a matted old rabbit lying abandoned behind a radiator. Sniff. Even hardened Daddies get maudlin at this point. Even when all of you have been longing to move, and the move is exciting, it hurts. If you are unwillingly downshifting, you will need all your resolution.

In the rush of moving, it is easy to forget that it probably bothers the children much more; whatever they say and however excited they are about the new place. They know they can take their things, and may even stay at the same school and have the same friends, but 'I can't take the fireplace, can I? We'll never sit by that fire again . . . and what about the beam in my bedroom that looks like a ship? Will my own curtain come, so the sun looks the same in the morning? Will the new bath have a mark like the old one?' If you are moving to somewhere bigger, or nicer, there is the adventure of the new house to hold out; if it is to the most inexperienced eye definitely a worse house, flat, or neighbourhood, they will need even more support.

I was much comforted in my most unwilling move – the one which bothered the children most – by watching a programme in the BBC *All Our Children* series, in which a little girl called Cristina was taken from a violent home in the slums of Brasilia and put in an orphanage. She took her blue stuffed rabbit and her two precious dolls and, in the clean bleakness of the Lor Betel home, she looked after her three younger brothers and their treasures with determination. She ranged her dolls on her bed each morning in exactly the same places. With these small duties and small icons Cristina created herself a new home, for a year. Then the cameras followed as she was moved seventy miles out of town to the orphanage's farm, where older children take a rapid and hardworking path to adulthood. Goodbye to the two smallest brothers, and to every remotely familiar urban vista. She packed the rabbit, the two dolls, a spare dress and a toothbrush, and that was it. She even sang on the bus. Six hours later she unpacked her few possessions and ranged them with superstitious care on her new bunk. In the same order as ever. And she took to the new life, and in time became contented.

The brave, distant little girl on the screen was a salutary reminder of the resilience of children in any change of home, provided that their own household gods – whether water pistols, china dogs or furry animals – are respected. Cristina made me more solicitous of my own children's possessions in the chaos of moving, more sympathetic to crazy theories about which way the bed should face and why the old curtains should be put up even though they did not fit. In the process, the removal men casually told me that one of the funniest aspects of house moves is that people always want the furniture arranging in the living room in the same way as in the old house even though it patently doesn't fit the new-shaped room. Since we have these half-superstitious feelings about home objects, we might as well indulge them and revel in them, and not allow anyone's tatty old chair or dog-eared pony poster to become a cause of friction. To move into a fresh, newly-painted home and allow your children to make their corner of it look as messy as the old one is not a sign of weakness or bad housekeeping. It is a sign of love.

And children are much nicer than we give them credit for. In one family undergoing a divorce, the eleven-year-old girl and her thirteen-year-old brother had to leave a large garden, a swing in a big mulberry tree, a wilderness of fruit bushes and a tree house for a town flat. They were not best pleased at the idea, although it had been very carefully sold to them as being close to school, close to friends, and highly suitable for the teenage lifestyles they were on the verge of. Still they sulked.

But two days before the move, their mother relates, the girl came to her with a request. She knew the buyers had younger children and she wanted to leave them a letter about the best parts of the house and garden, the dens and secret places she had grown up with. Her brother eventually decided to join in and together they produced a kind of will, leaving all the old pleasures to the next generation. It occupied all their time for

369

the last two days, and they brought an astonishing passion to the job. Their mother weepily photocopied it before she left the letter to the new family, so precious was the testament. Re-married now, with children at university and yet another different house, she has the document still.

And, although the divorce was not of her choosing and contained a degree of bitterness, after a brief struggle she sent a copy to her husband too, in memory of the times when family life had been happy under the mulberry tree. If the children could manage change with grace and generosity, so could she.

Territory

Every animal needs territory. Children who share bedrooms need a line across the floor, or private cupboards, or even a sacred box into which nobody else may go. Even bookshelves may have to be partitioned off, if that keeps the peace. Invasion of one another's territory – especially if it is not justified by a search for stolen property – is to be quite firmly discouraged.

Parents need territory too. Fathers tend to seize it more readily than mothers; most households seem to have a Dad's chair, but fewer have a Mum's chair. Men are adept at organizing themselves workshops, studies, sheds, corners of the garage where they potter about; women are modestly reluctant to take what Virginia Woolf identified as that great need, 'a room of one's own'. We stick to the kitchen, and the kitchen is always communal anyway, so we have nowhere.

We ought to try, though; certainly it does no harm for the smallest children (and largest husbands) to have it made perfectly clear to them that some cupboards, some surfaces like the dressing table, and even perhaps if you are lucky one room, is Mummy's Private Place. Sacred, vestal, feminine. Never to be filled with one-eyed rubber Boglins, or raided for face-painting sessions, fancy dress, or components to make a showjumping course for the kitten. Again, the more you respect other people's territory, the more they ought to respect yours.

When it comes to teenagers' bedrooms, opinions vary. Some

are in favour of ruthless, compulsory cleaning, either by the occupant or a parent. Others think that in order to ripen properly, teenagers should be left alone in their squalor, but not assisted to find things under the mess. The minimalist approach is to provide adequate shelving and storage (off to IKEA) and have a basic safety hygiene rule (no dirty underwear or socks, no cups and plates with mould on, no overloaded adaptors or trailing cables; any breach of this rule to be punished by a vicious, unprovoked clean-up which might include posters involving violent sexist slogans and immodest poses. So there). You can attempt to add a rule about having to draw the curtains open by day. I cannot report much success in this area.

What does *not* work is the tactic I tried all one summer holiday, of entering the room and promptly beginning to whimper like a beaten dog, 'Aaah . . . maaah . . . uhuh, uhuh,' while covering my eyes against the horror of it. He laughed cruelly and went on zapping aliens.

One other word on teenagers and their rooms. Don't get too worried if they hide in them for a while in the late teens. A reclusive thirteen-year-old is indeed a bit of a worry but older teenagers may simply be in the Chrysalis Phase. As my melodeon playing brother said in defence of his long purdah, 'You are not a lovely creature at that stage, spotty and uncouth. You are in a chrysalis, you don't want to see anybody.' He emerged quite happily after a year or two, formed folk bands, got out, met friends, courted, got married. Other teenagers are known to shut themselves away alone listening to music for unreasonable lengths of time, to read obsessively and hate all interruption, or to fiddle with motorbikes for hours. It seems that some adolescents are made to be outgoing and sociable, and others – sometimes the more interesting ones – need ages to grow up at their own pace.

Our job as parents is not to dragoon them or interfere with the décor of their rooms. It is to watch out for signs of drugs or drink – which do need swift intervention – and otherwise to let them be. Yes, it is irritating. Very. But a decent modicum of peace and privacy can be traded – if necessary by written

371

contract as some psychologists suggest – for reasonable behaviour at family gatherings and on holiday. Adolescents live in another country; as any international statesman will tell you, treaties work if you are patient and persistent. Invasion of territory and martial law very rarely do.

*   *   *   *

Index